591

THE PASTON LETTERS

Oxford University Press, Amen House, London E.C.4

GLASGOW   NEW YORK   TORONTO   MELBOURNE   WELLINGTON
BOMBAY   CALCUTTA   MADRAS   KARACHI   LAHORE   DACCA
CAPE TOWN   SALISBURY   NAIROBI   IBADAN   ACCRA
KUALA LUMPUR   HONG KONG

THE
PASTON LETTERS

A Selection in Modern Spelling

Edited with an
Introduction, Notes, and Glossary by
NORMAN DAVIS

LONDON
OXFORD UNIVERSITY PRESS
1963

PRINTED IN GREAT BRITAIN

CONTENTS

INTRODUCTION

THE Paston Letters, as they have been called since they first came to public notice in the eighteenth century, are unmatched in scope and variety of interest by any other medieval collection in English, though they are not quite the earliest. They begin about 1420 with William Paston, of Paston in Norfolk, who was born in 1378 and became a judge in 1429, and end approximately with the death in 1503 of his grandson Sir John Paston, of Caister, the third of that name and the second knight; but they are most numerous in the twenty years from 1460 to 1480. With various associated documents—indentures, inventories, draft petitions, wills—they number well over a thousand papers.

Only a small number of letters are preserved from the first William Paston's time. It was his son John who effectively founded the collection, and he did so for business reasons. The great concern of his life was property. He was often away from home on legal affairs connected with it, and left his estates in the charge of his wife Margaret and some of his employees. They reported to him what was going on, and he sent instructions— 'I pray you remember and read often my bill of errands and this letter till it be done' (no. 66); and these exchanges he filed, besides a good deal of other correspondence less directly useful. After he died his widow and their sons, who were often separated because the eldest, Sir John, was in London or Calais, continued to keep a great many of their letters to each other; but the third John, after his brother's death in 1479 and his mother's in 1484, seems to have lost the motive or interest to maintain the habit, and well before his death the surviving letters become sporadic and disconnected.

The collection remained in the possession of the family until the line became extinct with the death of William Paston, second Earl of Yarmouth, in 1732. When his estate was dispersed the letters were acquired by various antiquaries, and eventually by John Fenn of East Dereham, who published a selection in 1787 in two volumes, to which three others were later added. Many more of the letters were published by James Gairdner in a series of editions from 1875 to 1904. For those letters that Fenn had printed Gairdner relied mainly on his transcripts. (For the first two volumes he had no choice, because the manuscripts were in private hands, but for the rest the originals were in the British Museum well before his last edition was published.) Gairdner's text is therefore often unsatisfactory in detail, and some dates and attributions need correction.

The most immediately striking feature of the life reflected in the letters is the recurrence of violent usurpation of Paston lands—a lawlessness which matches the grim background of the conflict of the Roses, and yet is not paralleled in the records of other landed families of the time. Some of it is attributable, no doubt, to the uncertainty of John Paston's title. He suddenly rose to potentially great wealth on the death of Sir John Fastolf, a rich retired officer who was a connexion of his wife's and whose confidence he won so that he became the principal administrator and legatee of the estate when the old man died in 1459. His claim, however, was contested by other executors, who accused him of falsifying the will; and the dispute was still unsettled when he died, at the age of 45, in 1466—'Remember it was the destruction of your father', wrote Margaret Paston five years later (no. 100). Two of the Fastolf manors were seized from Paston by force: Hellesdon in his own lifetime in 1465 by the Duke of Suffolk (nos. 70, 71), Caister in his son's time in 1469 by the Duke of Norfolk after a full-scale siege (nos. 87–90), though Paston's title to it had by then been recognized. But even before he had anything to do with Fastolf's lands he had been subjected to violent dispossession, when the young Lord Moleyns attacked his manor of Gresham in 1448. He recovered it (as his son did Caister), but with no hope of redress because of his opponent's position (no. 15).

But these spectacular incidents, though they make the history of the Pastons uniquely eventful, by no means distract all attention from more ordinary affairs. Marriage prospects and negotiations, for instance, are conspicuous. They are often merely another approach to the acquisition of lands and money; yet oftener than might have been expected young people write of love, and with obvious sincerity: once provoking the shocked disapproval of a family horrified at an alliance between their daughter and sister and an employee (nos. 85, 86), once at least encouraging a match favoured on both sides—subject to the demands of property (nos. 120–4).

John Paston's wife Margaret is in some ways the central figure of the letters. We meet her about 1440, at her first encounter with her future husband (no. 2), and she is never far from the scene until her second son writes to her about her will over forty years later (no. 137). She managed her husband's estates conscientiously, and called herself 'captainess' of his men at Hellesdon (no. 57); she tried, without much success, to induce her eldest son to attend more vigorously to his interests, to spend less money, to relieve his brother besieged in Caister Castle, even to complete his father's gravestone; she did all she could to forward her second son's marriage, and to prevent her elder daughter's. But the rather authoritarian character that shows itself in much of this is pleasantly relieved by the earlier letters to her husband, which are full of naïve anxiety to please (nos. 4, 10), and her later relations with Sir John, whom she urged to come home and live with her in Norfolk (no. 113), or her concern for young Walter, from whom she hoped (in vain, for he died young) for more satisfaction than his elder brothers had given her (no. 108).

The first John Paston placed his two eldest sons (both also called John) in positions intended to promote their status in society: the first son in the King's household, the second in the Duke of Norfolk's. This did not prevent the Duke of Norfolk from seizing the manor of Caister in 1469, or the Paston brothers—perhaps in consequence of this—from fighting against the King in 1471. The eldest son, though he was knighted when he came of age in 1463, grievously disappointed his father by his failure to take advantage of his opportunities, and was even banished from home for a time (nos. 55, 56). His mother took his part then, but she too was often exasperated in later years by his ineffectiveness and extravagance (no. 99). Yet his lack of earnestness had its attractive side in the light-heartedness and enthusiasm that he often expressed (nos. 106, 109, 112), in refreshing contrast to his father's prevailing rigidity. The second son (who was also knighted, but not until 1487) was better fitted for the duties of land ownership than his brother. He too had a lively appreciation of courtly amenities (no. 79), and an easy humour (no. 105); but there was a dignity in his bearing after the loss of Caister (no. 90) and a sound appreciation of his family responsibilities (no. 137) which were appropriate to the task which faced him, when he succeeded to the estates, of consolidating the Paston fortunes after the upheavals of the previous twenty years.

These are only the leading characters in the story presented by the letters. Many of the less prominent figures effectively contribute a lively or pathetic part to it. What they write, however, is perhaps of smaller consequence than their ability to write it. The level of competence in writing, among so many people so early in the history of letter-writing in English, is very remarkable. Not only the men who had been educated at a university (as the first John and his brother William were at Cambridge, and Walter at Oxford), or an Inn of Court or Chancery (as the first John and both the Edmonds were), but their clerks and estate managers, and their wives and daughters, succeeded in expressing their thoughts and their characters clearly and vigorously. Usually the narrative is plain enough, but it often has unexpected force and even grace. The women for the most part did not write in their own hands, and they may have had some help from the clerks who wrote for them; but the consistency of style that runs through their letters shows that essentially the words were their own.

The unique value of such letters as these is that here, shortly before the introduction of printing made books more familiar than ever before, we see the English language used for a great volume of simple practical communication, almost without artifice and often close to speech. This is the first period in the history of the language of which this can be said. We see the unpolished material that lay to the hands of writers concerned for literary art, and can better judge how much of what they achieved was due to their own skill and how much they owed to the speech around them.

THIS EDITION

A selection in this space is necessarily extremely sketchy. The main object of this edition is to present an outline of as many of the principal concerns of the Paston family as can be made intelligible within its scope. This means that many of the letters selected for printing have had to be abridged, to exclude comparatively technical matters or passages requiring more annotation than these pages could accommodate. To save space the addresses of the letters have been omitted. In most cases the destination is obvious or unimportant; where it is not, it is given in a note.

The convenience of modern readers is the first concern of this edition, and accordingly the language of the manuscripts has been drastically, yet not completely, modernized. That is, it has not been simply transliterated into modern spelling by removing letters no longer used and regularizing such details as the use of *i* and *j*, *u* and *v*, and final *e*. This would have left too many merely technical obstructions to a reader unaccustomed to the variety of form characteristic of fifteenth-century English. For instance, in the manuscripts 'their' and 'them' are often *her(e)*, *hem*; 'give' is usually *yeue*; the past tense of 'see' is often *sey* or *sye*. Most of such archaic forms have been replaced by their modern equivalents. It does not, however, seem necessary to modernize familiar archaisms like *spake* or *saith*, or those verbal inflexions which do not impede understanding. Thus *-(e)n* has been retained in many occurrences of the infinitive (e.g. *buyen*, *writen*, *sayn*), the present plural (e.g. *arn*, *weeten*, *been*), and the past plural (e.g. *wern*, *hadden*); it has been omitted in many past participles (e.g. *be*, *do*, *know*); *-eth* has been kept in the few imperatives in which it occurs (e.g. *weeteth*, *cometh*), and an occasional present plural (e.g. *beth*); and the prefix *i-* has been kept in past participles (e.g. *ibound*, *ihad*, *iwriten*). The result is, of course, that the letters are given in a language that never existed at any time, for modern forms appear inconsistently together with medieval syntax; but this is true of any modernization, and this edition is not intended for readers interested in such details of language. (For them the original forms are preserved in

the edition in the Clarendon Medieval and Tudor Series
published in 1958.)

All editorial omissions, whatever their length, are shown
by. . . . Letters or words lost by damage to the manuscripts are supplied in ⟨ ⟩ when there is no reasonable
doubt about them. When reconstruction is uncertain, the
gap is shown by ⟨...⟩. Miswritten words are emended
without any notice if the error is judged to be obvious and
insignificant. If the change is of some substance, words or
letters omitted in the original but necessary to the sense
are printed in [ ]; letters substituted for others are
printed in ( ), but no note is given of the manuscript form
except when it is of special interest.

Grateful acknowledgement is made to the Trustees of
the British Museum and the Librarians of the Bodleian
and the Cambridge University libraries for permission to
print from manuscripts in their charge.

THE PASTONS

WILLIAM PASTON I. Born 1378, son of Clement Paston of Paston, Norfolk. Steward of the Duke of Norfolk 1415. J.P. Norfolk and elsewhere, and member of commissions, 1418 onwards. Married Agnes Berry 1420. Serjeant-at-law 1421. Justice of the Common Bench 1429. Trier of petitions in Parliament 1439, 1442. Died 13–14 Aug. 1444.

AGNES. Daughter and heiress of Sir Edmund Berry of Horwellbury near Royston, Herts. Lived mostly in Norwich, sometimes at Oxnead or Paston, until at least 1469; but before 1474 went to live in London with her son William. Died Aug. 1479.

Their children:

JOHN PASTON I. Born 1421. Educated at Trinity Hall and Peterhouse, Cambridge, and the Inner Temple. Married Margaret Mautby c. 1440. J.P. Norfolk 1447, 1456–7, 1460–6. Elected a knight of the shire 1455, but the election declared invalid by the Duke of Norfolk. An executor of Sir John Fastolf's will 1459. M.P. Norfolk 1460–1, 1461–2. Imprisoned in the Fleet 1461, 1464, 1465. Died in London 21 or 22 May 1466, buried in Bromholm Priory, Norfolk.

MARGARET. Daughter and heiress of John Mautby of Mautby. Lived mostly at Norwich, but from about 1474 at her old home at Mautby. Died 4 Nov. 1484.

EDMOND I. Born 1425. At Clifford's Inn 1445. Died in London 21 March 1449.

ELIZABETH. Born 1429. Married Robert Poynings 1458. He died 1461 and she married Sir George Browne probably 1471. Died 1 Feb. 1488.

WILLIAM II. Born 1436. At Cambridge 1449. J.P. Norfolk 1465–6, 1469–70, 1473–4. Married Lady Anne Beaufort, daughter of Edmund, Duke of Somerset, before 1470. M.P. 1472–5, 1478, 1491–2. Died in London 1496.

CLEMENT. Born 1442. In London under a tutor 1458. Died not later than 1487.

Children of John I and Margaret:

JOHN II. Born 1442. Joined Edward IV's court 1461. Knighted

1463. M.P. Norfolk 1467–8. In Princess Margaret's train for her marriage in Bruges 1468. J.P. Norfolk 1469–70. Took Lancastrian side 1470 and fought at Barnet under Warwick April 1471. Pardoned Dec. 1471. At Calais often 1473–7. M.P. Yarmouth 1478. Died in London 15 Nov. 1479.

JOHN III. Born 1444. Served under the Duke of Norfolk 1462–4. In Princess Margaret's train 1468. In command of Caister during siege by Norfolk 1469. Fought at Barnet 1471. Pardoned 1472. At Calais 1475. Married Margery Brews 1477. J.P. Norfolk 1480–2. Pardoned by Richard III 1484. M.P. Norwich and sheriff Norfolk and Suffolk 1485–6. Knighted at the battle of Stoke 1487. J.P. Norfolk 1494–7. Married Agnes, daughter of Nicholas Morley, after 1495. Died 1503.

MARGERY. Daughter of Sir Thomas Brews of Topcroft, Norfolk. Died *c.* 1495.

EDMOND II. At Staple Inn 1470. At Calais 1473. Indentured to the Duke of Gloucester for service with the King 1475. Married Catherine, widow of William Clippesby, 1480–1. Married Margaret, widow of William Lomnor and of Thomas Briggs, after 1491. Died not later than 1504.

WALTER. Born after 1455. Went to Oxford 1473. Took degree of B.A. June 1479. Died at Norwich about 19 Aug. 1479.

WILLIAM III. Born 1459. At Eton 1478–9. In the service of the Earl of Oxford 1488. Became insane after 1495.

MARGERY. Married Richard Calle 1469. Died not later than 1479.

ANNE. Married William Yelverton 1477. Died 1494–5.

Sons of John III and Margery:

CHRISTOPHER. Born 1478. Died before 1482.

WILLIAM IV. Born *c.* 1479. At Cambridge about 1495. Later knighted, married Bridget, daughter of Sir Henry Heydon of Baconsthorpe, Norfolk. Died 1554.

1. *William Paston I to the Vicar of the Abbot of Cluny*[1]

Probably 1430, April

My right worthy and worshipful lord, I recommend me to you. And forasmuch as I conceive verily that ye arn vicar general in England of the worthy prelate the Abbot of Cluny, and have his power in many great articles, and among other in profession of monks in England of the said order; and in my country, but a mile fro the place where I was born, is the poor house of Bromholm,[2] of the same order, in which arn divers virtuous young men, monks clad and unprofessed, that have abiden there ⟨without⟩ abbot nine or ten year, and by lenger delay of their profession many inconvenients arn like to fall; and also the prior[3] of ⟨the said house⟩ hath resigned into your worthy hands by certains notables and reasonables causes, as it appeareth by an instrument and a simple letter under the common seal of the said house of Bromholm, which the bearer of this hath ready to show you; whereupon I pray

[1] This letter is only a draft, mostly in the hand of a clerk but with corrections and conclusion in Paston's own hand. The sheet was later used for scribbling and bears various notes in Paston's hand, three of which mention dates in 1429–30. The Abbot of Cluny's vicar-general in England from 1419 to 1431 was Thomas Nelond, Prior of Lewes, the premier Cluniac monastery in England.

[2] Bromholm Priory, ruins of which still exist near Bacton, almost 2 miles from the present village of Paston (about 20 miles north-east of Norwich), was a Cluniac foundation. It was an important object of pilgrimage because it claimed to possess a piece of the True Cross, which is mentioned by both Chaucer and Langland.

[3] This prior was a certain John Wortes, who had been appointed by 1425 in opposition to a locally elected candidate supported by Paston. In the ensuing dispute in the papal court Paston lost his case and was fined and excommunicated.

you with all my heart, and as I ever may do you service, that it like to your grace to grant of your charity by your worthy letters to the prior of Thetford[1] in Norfolk, of the said order of Cluny, authority and power as your minister and deputy to profess in due form the said monks of Bromholm unprofessed. And that it like you overmore to accept and admit the said resignation by your said authority and power, with the favour of your good lordship, in comfort and consolation of your poor priests the monks of the said house of Bromholm;[2] and thereup to grant your worthy letters witnessing the same acceptation and admission of the said resignation, and all your said letters to deliver to my clerk, to whom I pray you to give faith and credence touchant this matter and to deliver him in all the haste reasonable. And I am your man and ever will be, by the grace of God, which ever have you in his keeping. Written at Norwich the   [3] of April.

                                Yours, WILLIAM PASTON

2. *Agnes Paston to William Paston I*

                                        Perhaps 1440, 20 April[4]

Dear husband, I recommend me to you, &c. Blessed be God, I send you good tidings of the coming and the bringing home of the gentlewoman[5] that ye weeten of fro

---

[1] Thetford was one of the four principal Cluniac houses in England and had the privilege of professing monks.

[2] The clerk's hand ends here.   [3] Left blank.

[4] John and Margaret Paston were married by 1441, so that this letter may well date from the previous year.

[5] Margaret, daughter of John Mautby, esq., of Mautby near Yarmouth, who died in 1434. Her mother, Margery, was the daughter of John Berney, esq., of Reedham, which is some 8 miles south-west of Mautby and 21 in a straight line from Paston. Margaret was born there. This John Berney died in 1440.

Reedham this same night, according to pointment that ye
made therefor yourself. And as for the first acquaintance
between John Paston and the said gentlewoman, she
made him gentle cheer in gentle wise, and said he was
verily your son. And so I hope there shall need no great
treaty betwixt them.

The parson of Stockton[1] told me if ye would buyen her
a gown, her mother would give thereto a goodly fur. The
gown needeth for to be had, and of colour it would be a
goodly blue or else a bright sanguine.

I pray you do buyen for me two pipes of gold. Your
stews do well.

The Holy Trinity have you in governance. Written at
Paston in haste the Wednesday next after *Deus qui erranti-
bus*,[2] for default of a good secretary,[3] &c.

Yours, AGNES PASTON

3. *Margaret Paston to John Paston I*

Probably 1441, 14 December[4]

Right reverend and worshipful husband, I recommend me
to you, desiring heartily to hear of your welfare, thanking
you for the token that ye sent me by Edmund Peres,
praying you to weet that my mother sent to my father[5]

---

[1] Five miles south of Reedham.

[2] The collect for the third Sunday after Easter: 'Almighty God,
who shewest to them that be in error the light of thy truth. . . .'
Easter Day in 1440 was 27 March.

[3] The point of these words is not clear, for the letter is written in a
neat, evidently practised hand, which seems to be that of the clerk who
wrote most of no. 1.

[4] The date appears to be during Margaret's first pregnancy. Her
eldest son was born before 15 April 1442.

[5] 'Mother' and 'father' here, and commonly, mean mother- and
father-in-law.

to London for a gown cloth of musterdevillers[1] to make
of a gown[2] for me; and he told my mother and me, when he
was come home, that he charged you to buy it after that
he were come out of London. I pray you, if it be not
bought, that ye will vouchsafe to buy it and send it home
as soon as ye may; for I have no gown to wear this winter
but my black and my green a lierre,[3] and that is so cum-
brous that I am weary to wear it.

As for the girdle that my father behested me, I spake
to him thereof a little before he yede to London last, and
he said to me that the fault was in you, that ye would not
think thereupon to do make it;[4] but I suppose that is not
so—he said it but for a scusation. I pray you, if ye dare
take it upon you, that ye will vouchsafe to do make it
against ye come home; for I had never more need thereof
than I have now, for I am wax so fetis[5] that I may not be
girt in no bar of no girdle that I have but of one.

Elizabeth Peverel[6] hath lay sick fifteen or sixteen weeks
of the sciatica, but she sent my mother word by Kate[7]
that she should come hither when God sent time, though
she should be crod in a barrow.

John of Damme[8] was here, and my mother discovered

[1] A grey woollen cloth named from the town of Mouster de Villers,
now Montivilliers, 8 miles north-east of Le Havre in Normandy.

[2] 'To make of a gown' was the normal idiom for 'to make a gown of'.

[3] Lierre is a town in Brabant, some 10 miles south-east of Antwerp,
which gave its name to certain kinds of black and green woollen cloth.

[4] 'to have it made'.

[5] This word meant 'neat, elegant', and is, of course, used ironically.

[6] Not mentioned elsewhere, but from the circumstances evidently
a midwife.

[7] A family servant, mentioned again in no. 10.

[8] Damme, who held the manor of Sustead about 9 miles north-
north-west of Oxnead where this letter was written, was a loyal friend
of the Paston family. He was one of the judge's executors, and helped
John I in his litigation. He was M.P. for Yarmouth in 1442 and for
Norwich in 1450, J.P. often, and was made recorder and a freeman of
Norwich in 1450. He died in 1462.

me to him; and he said by his troth that he was not gladder of nothing that he heard this twelvemonth than he was thereof. I may no lenger live by my craft, I am discovered of all men that see me. Of all other things that ye desired that I should send you word of, I have sent you word of in a letter that I did write[1] on our Lady's Day[2] last was.

The Holy Trinity have you in his keeping. Written at Oxnead[3] in right great haste on the Thursday next before Saint Thomas' Day.[4]

I pray you that ye will wear the ring with the image of Saint Margaret that I sent you for a remembrance till ye come home. Ye have left me such a remembrance that maketh me to think upon you both day and night when I would sleep.

Yours, M. P.

4. *Margaret Paston to John Paston I*

Probably 1443, 28 September[5]

Right worshipful husband, I recommend me to you, desiring heartily to hear of your welfare, thanking God of your amending of the great disease that ye have had; and I thank you for the letter that ye sent me, for by my troth my mother[6] and I were not in heart's ease fro the

---

1 'caused to be written'.
2 The Conception of the Blessed Virgin, 8 December.
3 This manor, 3 miles south-east of Aylsham, was bought by William Paston I in 1423 and settled on Agnes. In later generations it became the main residence of the family, and notable memorials to them are still to be seen in the church.
4 St. Thomas Apostle, 21 December.
5 The date is after the birth of John Paston II in 1442 and before the death of William Paston I in August 1444.
6 Agnes Paston, as in no. 3; but in the next paragraph 'my mother' is Margaret's own mother.

time that we wost of your sickness till we wost verily of
your amending. My mother behested another image of
wax of the weight of you to Our Lady of Walsingham,[1]
and she sent 4 nobles to the four orders of friars[2] at Norwich to pray for you; and I have behested to gon on pilgrimage to Walsingham and to Saint Leonard's[3] for you.
By my troth I had never so heavy a season as I had fro the
time that I wost of your sickness till I wost of your amending, and yet mine heart is in no great ease, ne not shall be
till I wot that ye been very whole.

Your father and mine was this day sevennight at
Beccles[4] for a matter of the Prior of Bromholm,[5] and he lay
at Geldeston[6] that night and was there till it was 9 of the
clock and the tother day. And I sent thither for a gown,
and my mother said that I should none have thence till
I had be there again; and so they could none get. My
father Garneys sent me word that he should be here the
next week, and mine eme also, and playn them here with
their hawks; and they should have me home with them.
And so God help me I shall excuse me of mine going
thither if I may, for I suppose that I shall readilier have

---

[1] The shrine of Our Lady of Walsingham was a celebrated place of
pilgrimage throughout the Middle Ages. It is about 20 miles north-
west of Oxnead.

[2] The four orders were the Dominicans, Franciscans, Augustinians,
and Carmelites.

[3] The Benedictine priory of St. Leonard, Norwich, a cell to the
Cathedral Priory.

[4] In Suffolk, on the south bank of the River Waveney which forms
the boundary with Norfolk.

[5] See p. 1, n. 2.

[6] The scribe spells this *Gerlyston*, but there is no doubt of its
identity. Geldeston lies on the north bank of the Waveney about
2 miles from Beccles. The manor was held by Ralph Garneys, who
married Margaret's mother after John Mautby's death. Margaret
wrote one of her extant letters from there in July 1444, and it is
likely that her second son was born there in that year; see no. 95.
Garneys died in 1446.

tidings from you here than I should have there. I shall send my mother a token that she took me, for I suppose the time is come that I should send it her if I keep the behest that I have made[1]—I suppose I have told you what it was.

I pray you heartily that [ye] will vouchsafe to send me a letter as hastily as ye may, if writing be none disease to you, and that ye willen vouchsafe to send me word how your sore doth. If I might have had my will I should a seen you ere this time. I would ye wern at home, if it were your ease and your sore might been as well looked to here as it is there ye been now, liefer than a new gown, though it were of scarlet.[2] I pray you, if your sore be whole and so that ye may endure to ride, when my father come to London that ye will asken leave and come home when the horse shall[3] be sent home again; for I hope[4] ye should be kept as tenderly here as ye been at London.

I may none leisure have to do writen half a quarter so much as I should sayn to you if I might speak with you. I shall send you another letter as hastily as I may. I thank you that ye would vouchsafe to remember my girdle, and that ye would write to me at this time, for I suppose the writing was none ease to you. Almight God have you in his keeping and send you health. Written at Oxnead in right great haste on Saint Michael's Even.[5]

Yours, M. PASTON

My mother greeteth you well, and sendeth you God's

---

[1] The 'token' probably signified a second pregnancy. The postscript shows that at this date there was only one son, and in July 1444 Margaret wrote of 'the children'.

[2] At this time a kind of rich cloth, not necessarily red.

[3] This is *xul* in the manuscript, a Norfolk spelling for *shul*, the old plural, showing that *horse* is an unchanged plural like *sheep*.

[4] 'think, believe', as often in medieval use.

[5] The eve of Michaelmas, 29 September.

blessing and her; and she prayeth you, and I pray you also, that ye be well dieted of meat and drink, for that is the greatest help that ye may have now to your health ward. Your son fareth well, blessed be God.[1]

5. *Agnes Paston to Edmond Paston I*

1445, 4 February[2]

To mine well beloved son. I greet you well, and advise you to think once of the day of your father's counsel to learn the law;[3] for he said many times that whosoever should dwell at Paston should have need to con defend himself.

The vicary of Paston and your father, in Lenten last was, were through and accorded, and doles set how broad the way should been;[4] and now he hath pulled up the doles and saith he will maken a ditch fro the corner of his wall right over the way to the new ditch of the great close. And there is a man in Trunch[5] hight Palmer,[6] that had of your father certain land in Trunch over seven year or eight year agone for corn, and truly hath paid all the years; and now he hath suffered the corn to been withset

---

[1] The postscript is written on the back in a different hand.

[2] The date is evidently in the year after William Paston I's death.

[3] The letter is addressed to Edmond at Clifford's Inn (off Fetter Lane), one of the ten Inns of Chancery, institutions for the study of law subordinate to the four Inns of Court.

[4] In 1443 William Paston was granted a licence to divert a public road in Paston and another in Oxnead. In Paston he was allowed to enclose $32\frac{1}{2}$ perches in length and 1 perch in width on the south side of his house, provided that he made another road of the same width on the north side.

[5] About 2 miles west of Paston.

[6] The manuscript has *to* here, followed by an incomplete letter. It should evidently have been cancelled.

for 8s. of rent to Gimingham,[1] which your father paid never. Geoffrey asked Palmer why the rent was not asked in mine husband's time; and Palmer said, for he was a great man, and a wise man of the law, and that was the cause men would not ask him the rent. . . .

I send you not this letter to make you weary of Paston, for I live in hope, and ye will learn that they shall be made weary of their work; for in good faith I dare well sayn it was your father's last will to have do right well to that place, and that can I show of good proof, though men would say nay.

God make you right a good man, and send God's blessing and mine. Written in haste at Norwich the Thursday after Candlemas Day.[2]

Weeteth of your brother John how many joists will serve the parlour and the chapel at Paston, and what length they must be and what brede and thickness they must be; for your father's will was, as I ween verily, that they should be 9 inches one way and 7 another way. And purveyeth therefor that they mow be squared there and sent hither, for here can none such be had in this country. And say to your brother John it were well done to think on Stanstead[3] church. And I pray you to send me tidings from beyond sea,[4] for here they arn afeared to tell such as be reported.

By your mother, AGNES PASTON

[1] A person of this name is mentioned in another letter; but here it may mean rather the manor of Gimingham Hall, a mile north of Trunch, of which William's father had held land.

[2] 2 February.

[3] About 10 miles north-west of Sudbury in Suffolk. Agnes Paston had inherited the manor.

[4] At this time William de la Pole, Marquis of Suffolk, was in France trying to negotiate a peace to extend the truce signed in May 1444. He had then arranged that Margaret of Anjou should marry Henry VI, and he stood proxy for the King at a marriage ceremony at Nancy in March 1445.

6. *Margaret Paston to John Paston I*

1448, 19 May

Right worshipful husband, I recommend me to you and pray you to weet that on Friday last past before noon, the parson of Oxnead being at mass in our parish church,[1] even at the levation of the sacring, James Gloys[2] had been in the town and came homeward by Wymondham's[3] gate. And Wymondham stood in his gate, and John Norwood his man stood by him, and Thomas Hawes his other man stood in the street by the cannel side. And James Gloys came with his hat on his head between both his men, as he was wont of custom to do. And when Gloys was against Wymondham, he said thus: 'Cover thy head!' And Gloys said again, 'So I shall for thee.' And when Gloys was further passed by the space of three or four stride, Wymondham drew out his dagger and said, 'Shalt thou so, knave?'[4] And therewith Gloys turned him, and drew out his dagger and defended him, fleeing into my mother's place; and Wymondham and his man Hawes

---

1 From what follows this is evidently in Norwich, and probably St. Mary Coslany, north of the Wensum, for both Wymondham and Margaret Paston left legacies to it.

2 The Paston family chaplain, and a very prominent figure in the letters, acting as a clerk and agent in many matters of business. He was a special confidant of Margaret, and twenty of her letters are written in his hand (e.g. no. 70). In later years bad feeling arose between him and her sons (see no. 103). He became Rector of Stokesby, not far from Mautby, in 1472 and died in 1473.

3 John Wymondham, or Wyndham, later of Felbrigg near Cromer, was associated with John Heydon and Sir Thomas Tuddenham, who instigated various acts of violence in Norfolk at this period; see p. 15, n. 2 and p. 91, n. 1. He was M.P. in 1439–40, 1459, and 1467–8, and died in 1475.

4 The ordinary form of address by this date, even between members of the same family, was *ye, you*. The use of *thou, thee* here was deliberately offensive.

cast stones and drove Gloys into my mother's place, and Hawes followed into my mother's place and cast a stone as much as a farthing loaf into the hall after Gloys, and then ran out of the place again. And Gloys followed out and stood without the gate, and then Wymondham called Gloys thief and said he should die, and Gloys said he lied and called him churl, and bade him come himself or ell the best man he had, and Gloys would answer him one for one. And then Hawes ran into Wymondham's place and fetched a spear and a sword, and took his master his sword. And with the noise of this assault and affray my mother and I came out of the church from the sacring, and I bade Gloys go into my mother's place again, and so he did. And then Wymondham called my mother and me strong whores, and said the Pastons and all their kin were ⟨. . .⟩[1] said he lied, knave and churl as he was. And he had much large language, as ye shall know hereafter by mouth.

After noon my mother and I yede to the Prior of Norwich[2] and told him all this case, and the Prior sent for Wymondham, and therewhile we yede home again, and Pagrave[3] came with us home. And while Wymondham was with the Prior, and we were at home in our places, Gloys stood in the street at my mother's gate, and Hawes espied him there as he stood on the Lady Hastings'[4] chamber. Anon he came down with a two-hand sword and assaulted again the said Gloys and Thomas my mother's man, and let fly a stroke at Thomas with the

---

[1] Perhaps ten letters lost at a hole in the paper.

[2] The Prior of the Cathedral Priory of the Holy Trinity, Norwich, from 1436 to 1453 was John Heverlond, who was succeeded by John Paston's friend John Mowth or Molet; see p. 161, n. 1.

[3] John Pagrave, esq., of Norwich, was a friend of the Paston family and one of William's trustees. His first wife was Margaret, daughter of William Yelverton (see p. 49, n. 5). He died in 1467.

[4] Wymondham had married Margery, widow of Sir Edward Hastings of Elsing, and she kept her former title.

sword and rippled his hand with his sword. And as for the latter assault, the parson of Oxnead saw it and will avow it. And much more thing was do, as Gloys can tell you by mouth.

And for the perils of that might hap by these premisses and the circumstances thereof to be eschewed,[1] by th' advice of my mother and other I send you Gloys to attend upon you for a season for ease of mine own heart, for in good faith I would not for £40 have such another trouble. . . .

The Lord Moleyns'[2] man gathereth up the rent at Gresham a great pace, and James Gresham[3] shall tell you more plainly thereof at his coming.

No more at this time, but Almighty God have you in his keeping. Written in haste on Trinity Sunday at even.

Yours, MARGARET PASTON

. . . When Wymondham said that James should die I said to him that I supposed that he should repent him if he slew him or did to him any bodily harm; and he said nay, he should never repent him nor have a farthing worth of harm though he killed you and him both. And I said yes, an he slew the least child that longeth to your

---

1 This piece of legal jargon is probably attributable to James Gresham; see n. 3 below.

4 Robert Hungerford, Lord Moleyns from 1445, became Lord Hungerford in 1459, was attainted in 1461, and executed in 1464. The manor of Gresham, 4 miles south-west of Cromer, had been bought by William Paston from Thomas Chaucer, but Moleyns claimed it and seized it by force. John Paston, petitioning the King in 1449 against this usurpation, dates the attack 17 February 1448; and this shows the date of the present letter.

3 James Gresham, 'gentleman', of Holt, appears often in the letters as a confidential servant and agent of the Pastons. He had been one of the judge's clerks, and took a prominent part in John I's legal affairs. The body of this letter is in his hand; the postscript is in that of another clerk not yet identified.

kitchen, an if he did, he were like, I suppose, to die for him. It is told me that he shall come to London in haste. I pray you beware how ye walken if he be there, for he is full cursed-hearted and lumish. I wot well he will not set upon you manly, but I believe he will start upon you or on some of your men like a thief. I pray you heartily that ye let not James come home again in none wise till ye come home, for mine heart's ease; for by my troth I would not that he were hurt, nor none man that longeth to you, in your absence for £20. And in good faith he is sore hated both of Wymondham and some of his men and of other that Wymondham telleth to his tale as him list, for there as Wymondham telleth his tale he maketh them believen that James is guilty and he nothing guilty. I pray you heartily hear mass and other service that ye arn bound to hear with a devout heart, and I hope verily that ye shall speed right well in all your matters by the grace of God. Trust verily in God and leve him and serve him, and he will not deceive you. Of all other matters I shall send you word in haste.

7. *Margaret Paston to John Paston I*

1448[1]

Right worshipful husband, I recommend me to you, and pray you to get some crossbows, and windases to bend them with, and quarrel; for your houses here been so low

---

[1] John Paston's petition to the King says that, after appeals to Moleyns, he took up residence again at Gresham on 6 October in a 'mansion within the said town', but that on 28 January his wife was forcibly driven out by 'a riotous people to the number of a thousand persons'. The present letter must have been written while Margaret was living in this 'mansion' and hoping to defend it against the kind of attack that was in fact made.

that there may none man shoot out with no long bow, though we had never so much need. I suppose ye should have such things of Sir John Fastolf[1] if ye would send to him. And also I would ye should get two or three short poleaxes to keep with doors, and as many jacks, an ye may.

Partridge[2] and his fellowship arn sore afeared that ye would entren again upon them, and they have made great ordinance within the house, as it is told me. They have made bars to bar the doors cross-ways, and they han made wickets on every quarter of the house to shoot out at, both with bows and with hand-guns; and tho holes that been made for hand-guns, they been scarce knee-high fro the plancher; and of such holes been made five. There can none man shoot out at them with no hand-bows. . . .

I pray you that ye will vouchsafe to don buy for me 1 lb. of almonds and 1 lb. of sugar, and that ye will do buyen some frieze to maken of your childer's gowns. Ye shall have best cheap and best choice of Hay's wife, as it is told me. And that ye would buy a yard of broadcloth of black for an hood for me, of 44*d.* or 4*s.* a yard, for ⟨there⟩ is neither good cloth nor good frieze in this town. As for the childer's gowns, an I have cloth I shall do them maken.

The Trinity have you in his keeping and send you good speed in all your matters.

---

1 A retired captain in the French wars, who profited greatly from his service, acquired immense estates, and built Caister Castle near Yarmouth, 1½ miles from Margaret's old home at Mautby. Born in 1380, he was serving in Ireland by 1401 and from 1412 to 1439 in France, where he held important commands and the governorship of Anjou and Maine. Margaret was evidently related to him, and John later won his confidence (see no. 24) and eventually became one of the executors of his will. From the inheritance that he left arose most of the disputes which occupy so much attention in the later Paston letters.

2 A servant of Moleyns left in charge of the manor of Gresham.

8. *John Damme*[1] *to John Paston I*

1448, 30 November

Please it your good mastership to know that my mistress your wife recommendeth her to you, and fareth well, blessed be God; and all your meinie faren well also and recommend them to you, &c. . . .

Partridge and his fellow bear great visage and keep great junkeries and dinners, and sayn that my Lord Moleyns hath written plainly to them that he is lord there, and will be, and shall be, and ye not to have it; but I trust to God's righteousness of better purveyance. Like it you to remember what Heydon[2] doth and may do by colour of justice of the peace, being of my lord's counsel and not your good friend nor well-willer, and to common with your sad counsel what ye must suffer by the law, and wherein ye may resist. On Sunday last past Gunnor[3] and Mariot and John Davy and other dined with Partridge, &c.; and after evensong Gunnor spake to my mistress that she should make her men to leave their wifles and their jacks. And she answered that they purposed to hurt no man of their own seeking, but for it was said that she should be plucked out of her house, she were loath to suffer that; and therefore she said they should go so till ye come home. And he said stately, but if they left their array it should be plucked from them. I trust he must have a better

[1] See p. 4, n. 8.

[2] John Heydon, gentleman, of Baconsthorpe (about 3 miles from Gresham) was a Norwich lawyer who encouraged Lord Moleyns in his attack on Gresham manor. He was J.P. 1441–50 and 1455–60, and M.P. 1445–6, 1459, and 1460–1, but was involved in many illegal and violent incidents. He died in 1479.

[3] Probably Simon Gunnor of East Beckham, just over a mile north-west of Gresham. He appears in other letters as an adversary of Paston, and is associated by Friar Brackley (see p. 33, n. 2) with Heydon and Sir Thomas Tuddenham (see p. 91, n. 1).

warrant than his stately language, or ell he shall not have it from them easily.

All this I remit to your good remembrance, with God's help, to whom I pray to guide your right to his worship and your heart's desire. Written at Sustead on Saint Andrew Day, &c.

Yours, J. DAMME

It were but well, as meseemeth, that ye might ordain now a fetis jack defensible for yourself, for there[1] con they do best, and best cheap, &c.

9. *Margaret Paston to John Paston I*

1449, 15 February[2]

Right worshipful husband, I recommend me to you, desiring heartily to hearen of your welfare. . . .

Barow and Hegon and all the Lord Moleyns' men that were at Gresham when ye departed hence been there still, save Bampton, and in his stead is come another; and I hear say they shall abyde here still till their lord come ⟨. . .⟩[3] to Barow as ye commanded me, to weeten what the cause was that they threat men. . . . I sent Katherine[4] on this foresaid message, for I could geten no man to do it, and sent with her James Halman and Harry Holt. And she desired of Barow to have an answer of her message, and if these foresaid men might liven in peace for them, and said there should ell been purveyed other remedy for them; and he made her great cheer, and them that were there

---

[1] Paston was in London.

[2] Margaret had been driven out of Gresham on 28 January, and John had evidently placed her in the care of John Damme's wife at Sustead, near by, while he and Damme went to London; see no. 10.

[3] Some words lost at a hole in the paper.

[4] This is presumably the servant called 'Kate' in no. 3.

with her, and said that he desired for to speaken with me, if it should been none displeasance to me. And Katherine said to him that she supposed that I desired not to speaken with him. And he said he should come forby this place on hunting after noon, and there should no more come with him but Hegon and one of his own men, and then he would bring such an answer as should please me. And after noon they came hither and sent in to me to weeten if they might speaken with me, and praying that they might speaken with me. And they abiden still without the gates, and I came out to them and spake with them without, and prayed them that they would hold me excused that I brought them not into the place. I said inasmuch as they were not well-willing to the goodman of the place I would not take it upon me to bring them in to the gentlewoman. They said I did the best; and then we welk forth and desired an answer of them for that I had sent to them for. They said to me they had brought me such an answer as they hoped should please me, and told me how they had commoned with all their fellowship of such matters as I had sent to them for, and that they durst undertake that there should no man been hurt of them that were re-hearsed, nor no man that longeth to you, neither for them nor none of their fellowship; and that they ensured me by their troths. Never less I trust not to their promise inasmuch as I find them untrue in other things.

I conceived well by them that they were weary of that they hadden done. Barow swore to me by his troth that he had liefer than 40*s*. and 40 that his lord had not com-manded him to come to Gresham, and he said he was right sorry hitherward inasmuch as he had knowledge of you before; he was right sorry of that that was done. I said to him that he should have compassion on you, and other that were disseised of their livelode, inasmuch as he had been disseised himself. And he said he was so, and told me that he had sued to my Lord of Suffolk[1] divers times, and would don till he may get his good again. I said to him that ye had sued to my Lord Moleyns divers times for the manor of Gresham sith ye were disseised, and ye could never get no reasonable answer of him, and therefore ye entered again as ye hoped that was for the best. And he said he should never blame my Lord of Suffolk for the entry in his livelode, for he said my said lord was set thereupon by the information of a false shrew; and I said to him in like wise is the matter betwixt the Lord Moleyns and you. I told him I wost well he set never thereupon by no title of right that he had to the manor of Gresham, but only by the information of a false shrew. I rehearsed no name, but methought by them that they wost who I meant.[2]

Much other language we had which should taken long leisure in writing. I rehearsed to them that it should[3] a be said that I should not long dwell so near them as I do, and they forswear it, as they do other things more, that it was never said; and much thing that I know verily was said.

I hear sayn that ye and John of Damme been sore threat alway, and sayn though ye been at London ye shall been met with there as well as though ye were here. And therefore I pray you heartily beware how ye walk there, and have a good fellowship with you when ye shall walk out. The Lord Moleyns hath a company of brothel with him

---

1 William de la Pole, fourth Earl of Suffolk 1415, Marquis 1444, Duke 1448. He was one of Henry VI's favourite ministers, but in February 1450 he was impeached on charges of treason in his conduct of the French war, and was exiled; but on his way to the Continent he was murdered at sea. See p. 9, n. 4, and nos. 14 and 62.

2 Doubtless John Heydon; see p. 15, n. 2.

3 This use of *should have* was common at this date to indicate that a reported statement about a past event is not vouched for by the writer.

that reck not what they don, and such are most for to dread. They that been at Gresham sayn that they have not done so much hurt to you as they were commanded to don. . . .

I would not John of Damme should come home till the country be stored otherwise than it is. I pray God grant that it mote soon been otherwise than it is. I pray you heartily that ye will send me word how ye don and how ye speed in your matters, for by my troth I cannot been well at ease in my heart, nor not shall been, till I hear tidings how ye don.

The most part of your stuff that was at Gresham is sold and given away. Barow and his fellow spake to me in the most pleasant wise, and meseemeth by them they would fain please me. They said they would do me service and pleasance if it lay in their powers to don aught for me, save only in that that longeth to their lord's right. I said to them, as for such service as they had do to you and to me I desire no more that they should do, neither to you nor to me. They said I might an had of them at Gresham what I had desired of them, and had as much as I desired. I said nay, if I might an had my desire I should neither a departed out of the place nor from the stuff that was therein. They said as for the stuff, it was but easy. I said ye would not a given the stuff that was in the place when they came in not for £100. They said the stuff that they saw there was scarce worth £20.

As for your mother and mine, she fareth well, blessed be God, and she had no tidings but good yet, blessed be God. The Blessed Trinity have you in his keeping, and send you health and good speed in all your matters. Written at Sustead on the Saturday next after Saint Valentine's Day. Here dare no man sayn a good word for you in this country, God amend it.

Yours, M. P.

10. *Margaret Paston to John Paston I*

1449, 28 February[1]

Right worshipful husband, I recommend me to you, desiring heartily to hearen of your welfare, beseeching you that
ye be not displeased though I be come fro that place that
ye left me in;[2] for by my troth there were brought me such
tidings by diverse persons which been your well-willers
and mine that I durst no lenger abide there, of which
persons I shall let you have weeting when ye come home.
It was done me to weet that divers of the Lord Moleyns'
men saiden if they might get me they should steal me and
keep me within the castle, and then they said they would
that ye should fetch me out; and they saiden it should
been but a little heart-burning to you. And after that I
heard these tidings I could no rest have in mine heart till
I was here, nor I durst not out of the place that I was in
till that I was ready to riden; nor there was none in the
place wist that I should come thence save the goodwife,
not an hour before that I came thence. And I told her that
I should come hither to don maken such gear as I would
have made for me and for the childer, and said I supposed
that I should be here a fortnight or three weeks. I pray
you that the cause of my coming away may been counsel
till I speak with you, for they that let me have warning
thereof would not for no good that it were discured.

I spake with your mother as I came hitherwards, and
she proffered me, if ye would, that I should abiden in this
town. She would with right a good will that we should
abide in her place, and deliveren me such gear as she
might forbear, to keepen with household till ye might

---

[1] This letter presents a development of the situation described in
no. 9.
[2] Sustead, where she had first taken refuge.

been purveyed of a place and stuff of your own to keep
with household. I pray you send me word by the bringer
of this how ye will that I be demeaned. I would been right
sorry to dwell so near Gresham as I did till the matter
were fully determined betwixt the Lord Moleyns and you.

Barow told me that there were no better evidence in
England than the Lord Moleyns hath of the manor of
Gresham. I told him I supposed that they were such
evidence as William Hasard said that your were—he said
the seals of them were not yet cold. I said I supposed his
lord's evidence were such. I said I wost well as for your
evidence, there might no man have none better than ye
have, and I said the seals of them were two hundred year
elder than he is. The said Barow said to me if he came to
London while ye were there he would drink with you;
for any anger that was betwixt you he said he did but as
a servant, and as he was commanded to don. Purry[1] shall
tell you what language was betwixt Barow and me when
I came fro Walsingham.

I pray you heartily, at the reverence of God, beware of
the Lord Moleyns and his men. Though they speak never
so fair to you, trust them not, ne eat not nor drink with
them, for they been so false it is not for to trust in them.
And also I pray you beware what ye eaten or drink with
any other fellowship, for the people is full untrusty.

I pray you heartily that ye will vouchsafe to send me
word how ye don and how ye speeden in your matters by
the bringer of this. I marvel much that ye send me no
more tidings than ye have sent. . . .

The Holy Trinity have you in his keeping. W⟨ritten
at⟩ Norwich on the Friday next after Pulver Wednesday.[2]

---

[1] Purry was one of the dependants of John Paston reported by
Margaret in no. 9 as having been threatened by Moleyns's men.

[2] Ash Wednesday—a term otherwise recorded only in Agnes
Paston's writings. It must have arisen from the words used during

11. *Agnes Paston to John Paston I*

Not after 1449[1]

Son, I greet you well with God's blessing and mine; and I let you weet that my cousin Clere[2] writted to me that she spake with Scrope[3] after that he had been with me at Norwich, and told her what cheer that I had made him, and he said to her he liked well by the cheer that I made him. He had such words to my cousin Clere that less than ye made him good cheer and gave him words of comfort at London he would no more speak of the matter. My cousin Clere thinketh that it were a folly to forsake him less than ye knew of another as good or better, and I have essayed your sister[4] and I found her never so willy to none as she is to him, if it be so that his land stand clear.

I sent you a letter by Braunton for silk and for this matter before my cousin Clere wrote to me, the which was written on the Wednesday next after Midsummer Day.[5] Sir Harry Inglose[6] is right busy about Scrope for one of his daughters.

the sprinkling of ashes on the heads of penitents in the Ash Wednesday service: 'Memento, homo, quia pulvis es, et in pulverem reverteris'—'Remember, man, that dust thou art, and unto dust shalt thou return' (cf. Gen. iii. 19).

1 Inglose (see n. 6) died in 1451, and the relation of the Wednesday and Saturday after Midsummer does not suit 1450.

2 Elisabeth Clere, widow of Robert Clere, esq., of Ormesby, who died in 1446. She lived until 1493 but never remarried. See no. 12.

3 Stephen Scrope, ward of Sir John Fastolf, the son of his wife Millicent by her former marriage to Sir Stephen Scrope, Deputy Lieutenant of Ireland. In 1466, in the record of examinations into Fastolf's will, he is described as 70 years old or about; he died in 1472. He translated Christine de Pisan's *Épître d'Othéa* and the *Dits moraulx des philosophes* (*The Dicts and Sayings of the Philosophers*).

4 Elizabeth Paston, at this time about 20.   5 24 June.

6 Sir Henry Inglose, of Dilham (about 6 miles east of Oxnead), is mentioned in Fastolf's will as 'of my consanguinity'.

I pray you forget not to bring me my money fro
Horwellbury[1] as ye come fro London, either all or a great
part. . . . I can no more, but Almighty God be our good
lord, who have you ever in keeping. Written at Oxnead in
great haste on the Satur[day] next after Midsummer.

By your mother, A. P.

12. *Elisabeth Clere to John Paston I*

Not after 1449, 29 June

Trusty and well beloved cousin,[2] I commend me to you,
desiring to hear of your welfare and good speed in your
matter, the which I pray God send you to his pleasance
and to your heart's ease.

Cousin, I let you weet that Scrope hath be in this country
to see my cousin your sister, and he hath spoken with my
cousin your mother. And she desireth of him that he
should show you the indentures made between the knight
that hath his daughter and him: whether that Scrope, if
he were married and fortuned to have children, if the
children should inherit his land or his daughter the which
is married.

Cousin, for this cause take good heed to his indentures,
for he is glad to show you them, or whom ye will assign
with you. And he saith to me he is the last in the tail of
his livelode, the which is 350 mark and better, as Watkin
Shipdham[3] saith, for he hath take account of his livelode
divers times. And Scrope saith to me if he be married and
have a son and heir, his daughter that is married shall

---

[1] Agnes was the daughter and heiress of Sir Edmund Berry of
Horwellbury, near Royston, Hertfordshire.

[2] 'Cousin' was used at this time much more loosely than it is today.

[3] Fastolf's receiver-general (collector of rents, &c.), who would
naturally know about his ward's property.

have of his livelode 50 mark and no more; and therefore, cousin, meseemeth he were good for my cousin your sister with[out] that ye might get her a better. And if ye can get a better, I would advise you to labour it in as short time as ye may goodly, for she was never in so great sorrow as she is nowadays; for she may not speak with no man, whosoever come, ne not may see ne speak with my man, ne with servants of her mother's, but that she beareth her on hand otherwise than she meaneth.[1] And she hath sin Eastern the most part be beaten once in the week or twice, and sometime twice on o day, and her head broken in two or three places.

Wherefore, cousin, she hath sent to me by Friar Newton in great counsel, and prayeth me that I would send to you a letter of her heaviness, and pray you to be her good brother, as her trust is in you. And she saith, if ye may see by his evidences that his children and her[2] may inheriten, and she to have reasonable jointure, she hath heard so much of his birth and his conditions that, an ye will, she will have him, whether that her mother will or will not, notwithstanding it is told her his person is simple; for she saith men shall have the more dainty of her if she rule her to him as she ought to do.

Cousin, it is told me there is a goodly man in your Inn[3] of the which the father died late; and if ye think that he were better for her than Scrope, it would be laboured. And give Scrope a goodly answer, that he be not put off till ye be sure of a better; for he said when he was with me but if he have some comfortable answer of you he will no more labour in this matter, because he might not see

---

[1] 'To bear on (*or* in) hand' meant 'to deceive'. So the sentence means that Elizabeth Paston could not see any visitor or servant unless she deceived her mother about her intentions.

[2] 'her' here is equivalent to modern 'hers'; cf. p. 8, l. 1, above.

[3] John Paston was a member of the Inner Temple.

my cousin your sister and he saith he might a see her an she had be better than she is, and that causeth him to deemen that her mother was not well-willing; and so have I sent my cousin your mother word. Wherefore, cousin, think on this matter, for sorrow oftentime causeth women to beset them otherwise than they should do; and if she were in that case I wot well ye would be sorry. Cousin, I pray you burn this letter, that your men ne none other man see it; for an my cousin your mother knew that I had sent you this letter she should never love me.

No more I write to you at this time, but Holy Ghost have you in keeping. Written in haste on Saint Peter's Day by candle-light.

> By your cousin, ELISABETH CLERE

13. *Margaret Paston to John Paston I*

1450, 12 March[1]

Right worshipful husband, I recommend me to you, desiring heartily to hear of your welfare, thanking [you] for the letter that ye sent to me. . . .

It is said in Gresham that Partridge sent home word that he should not come home till he come with his lord, and that he said should been within short time, and that he should been lodged at John Winter's place. And as for Capron, he dwelleth still in Gresham, and he saith, and other that been against you, though ye enter into the manor that ye shall never have it long in peaceable wise.

William Rutt, the which is with Sir John Heveningham,[2] came home from London yesterday, and he said

---

[1] The year is fixed by the reference to the Duke of Suffolk.

[2] Of Heveningham in Suffolk, but with land in Norfolk also. His sister Elizabeth married John Berney I of Reedham (see p. 2, n. 5), and he wrote to Margaret Paston as 'your own cousin'. He served on

plainly to his master and to many other folks that the Duke of Suffolk is pardoned and hath his men again waiting upon him, and is right well at ease and merry, and is in the King's good grace and in the good conceit of all the lords as well as ever he was.[1]

There been many enemies against Yarmouth and Cromer, and have done much harm and taken many Englishmen and put them in great distress and greatly ransomed them; and the said enemies been so bold that they come up to the land and playn them on Caister sands and in other places, as homely as they were Englishmen. Folks been right sore afeared that they will don much harm this summer but if there be made right great purveyance against them.

Other tidings know I none at this time. The Blissful Trinity have you in his keeping. Written at Norwich on Saint Gregory's Day.

Yours, M. P.

14. *William Lomnor[2] to John Paston I*

1450, 5 May

Right worshipful sir, I recommend me to you, and am right sorry of that I shall say, and have so wesh this little bill with sorrowful tears that uneaths ye shall read it.

---

many commissions, was often J.P. for Suffolk, and sheriff of Norfolk and Suffolk 1414–15 and 1437–8. He died in 1453; see no. 19.

[1] See p. 18, n. 1. The report of Suffolk's pardon was inaccurate. What happened was that after his impeachment, on 7 February 1450, he threw himself upon the King's mercy, and instead of being sent for trial by his peers he was exiled for five years.

[2] William Lomnor, gentleman, of Mannington (5 miles south-west of Gresham), was a trusted agent of the Pastons. He must have been related to them, for Margaret once referred to him as 'my brother' and both John II and John III called him 'my cousin'; and his widow

As on Monday next after May Day[1] there came tidings to London that on Thursday before the Duke of Suffolk came unto the coasts of Kent, full near Dover, with his two ships and a little spinner; the which spinner he sent with certain letters, by certain of his trusted men, unto Calais ward, to know how he should be received. And with him met a ship called *Nicholas of the Tower*, with other ships waiting on him, and by them that were in the spinner the master of the *Nicholas* had knowledge of the Duke's coming. And when he espied the Duke's ships he sent forth his boat to weet what they were, and the Duke himself spake to them and said he was by the King's commandment sent to Calais ward, &c. And they said he must speak with their master; and so he, with two or three of his men, went forth with them in their boat to the *Nicholas*. And when he came the master bade him 'Welcome, traitor', as men say; and further, the master desired to weet if the shipmen would hold with the Duke, and they sent word they would not in no wise; and so he was in the *Nicholas* till Saturday next following.

Some say he wrote much thing to be delivered to the King, but that is not verily know. He had his confessor with him, &c. And some say he was arraigned in the ship, on their manner, upon the apeachments, and found guilty, &c.

Also he asked the name of the ship, and when he knew it he remembered Stacy,[2] that said if he might escape the danger of the Tower he should be safe; and then his heart failed him, for he thought he was deceived. And in the

Margaret married Edmond Paston II. He was a Yorkist, for he was in a position to intercede for the Paston brothers after the battle of Barnet; see nos. 94 and 95. He was J.P. often between 1460 and 1474, and died in 1482.   [1] 4 May.

[2] Thomas Stacy was one of a large number of people, including the Duke of Somerset and the Duchess of Suffolk, against whom the Commons petitioned the King in 1451.

sight of all his men he was drawn out of the great ship into the boat, and there was an axe and a stock; and one of the lewdest of the ship bade him lay down his head, and he should be fair ferd with, and die on a sword; and took a rusty sword, and smote off his head within half a dozen strokes, and took away his gown of russet and his doublet of velvet mailed, and laid his body on the sands of Dover. And some say his head was set on a pole by it, and his men set on the land by great circumstance and prayer.[1] And the sheriff of Kent doth watch the body, and sent his undersheriff to the judges to weet what to do, and also to the King. What shall be do further I wot not, but thus far is it: if the process be erroneous, let his counsel reverse it, &c.

As for all your other matters, they sleep; and the friar also,[2] &c.

Sir Thomas Kyriell[3] is take prisoner, and all the leg harness, and about three thousand Englishmen slain. Matthew Gough[4] with fifteen hundred fled, and saved himself and them; and Piers Brusy[5] was chief captain, and had ten thousand Frenchmen and more, &c.

I pray you let my mistress your mother know these tidings, and God have you all in his keeping. I pray you this bill may recommend me to my mistresses your

[1] The precise meaning is not clear. Perhaps 'with assiduous attention and concern expressed for their welfare'.

[2] A certain Friar John Hauteyn had put forward a claim to Oxnead.

[3] Commander of troops sent to reinforce the Duke of Somerset in Normandy in March 1450. He was defeated at Formigny on 15 April.

[4] A distinguished commander in the French war. He was killed shortly afterwards, defending London Bridge against Cade's rebels in July 1450.

[5] Pierre de Brézé, seneschal of Normandy, who had helped to negotiate the marriage of Henry VI to Margaret of Anjou and remained closely attached to her interests; he commanded her expedition to the north of England in 1463. He was killed at the battle of Montlhéry in 1465.

mother and wife, &c. James Gresham hath written to
John of Damme, and recommendeth him, &c. Written in
great haste at London the 5 day of May, &c.

By your wife,[1] W. L.

15. *John Osbern[2] to John Paston I*

1451, 27 May[3]

Please it your mastership to weet that I have spoke with
the sheriff[4] at his place, moving to him, as for that that
was left with his undersheriff, it is your will he should
send a man of his for it; for though it were more ye would
gladly he should take it. He thanked you, and said his
undersheriff was at London, and himself had none deserved; and if he had he would a take it. And when I
departed from him I desired him again to send therefor,
and then he said it should abide till ye come home,
whereby I conceive he would have it, and be glad to take
it. Moreover I remembered him of his promises made
before to you at London, when he took his oath and
charge,[5] and that ye were with him when he took his
oath, and other divers times; . . . and then he said he
would do for you that he may, except for the acquittal of
the Lord Moleyns' men, insomuch as the King hath writ

[1] This extraordinary slip cannot be explained by the supposition
that Lomnor was accustomed to write Margaret's letters for her, for
none of her extant letters is in his hand. It looks rather as if he un-
consciously repeated the word 'wife' from the previous passage, which
in the manuscript is only one line above the signature.

[2] A yeoman, of Warham, who was in the service of John Paston I
and later conducted some matters of business for John II.

[3] The date appears from the sessions known to have been held at
Walsingham in May 1451.

[4] John Jermyn, esq., of Metfield, Suffolk.

[5] The oath on taking up the office of sheriff.

to him for to show favour to the Lord Moleyns and his men. And as he saith, the indictment longeth to the King and not to you, and the Lord Moleyns a great lord. Also, as he saith, now late the Lord Moleyns hath sent him a letter, and my Lord of Norfolk[1] another, for to show favour in these indictments. He dare not abide the jeopardy[2] of that that he should offend the King's commandment. He know not how the King may be informed of him and what shall be said to him.

And then I said as for any jeopardy that he should abide in anything that he doth for you or by your desire, ye have offered him, and will perform it, sufficient surety for to save him harmless, and therefore I supposed there would none reasonable man think but that he might do for you without any jeopardy. And then he said he might none surety take that passed £100; and the Lord Moleyns is a great lord, he might soon cause him to lose that and much mo. . . . As meseemeth it would do good an ye would get a commandment of the King to the sheriff for to show you favour, and to empanel gentlemen, and not for to favour none such riots, &c.; for he said that he sent you the letter that the King sent him, and ye said a man should get such one for a noble.

Item, I remembered him . . . that if he would make you very true promise ye would reward him as much as he would desire, or any other reasonable man for him, and as much and more than any adversary ye have would give him. Then he said he took never no money of none of them all. . . . And then he said if he might do for you, or if he do anything for you, then he will take your money with a good will; and other promise I could not have of

---

[1] John Mowbray, third duke (1432–61), one of the most powerful of the Yorkist lords. He died on 6 November 1461 leaving his son John a minor; see no. 69.

[2] 'run the risk'.

him but that he will do for you all that he may except for the indictments. I conceive verily he hath made promise to do his part that they shall be acquit; but I suppose he hath made none other promise against you for the livelode, but he looketh after a great bribe. But it is not for to trust him verily, without that he may not choose. I suppose he had no writing fro my Lord of Norfolk as he said. . . .

Written at Norwich the Thursday next after Saint Austin.[1]

By your servant, JOHN OSBERN

16. *Agnes Paston to John Paston I*

Perhaps 1451, 21 November[2]

I greet you well, and let you weet that on the Sunday before Saint Edmund,[3] after evensong, Agnes Ball came to me to my closet and bade me good even, and Clement Spicer with her. And I asked him what he would; and he asked me why I had stopped in the King's way. And I said to him I stopped no way but mine own, and asked him why he had sold my land to John Ball; and he swore he was never accorded with your father. And I told him if his father had do as he did, he would a be ashamed to a said as he said.

And all that time Warren Harman leaned over the parclose and listened what we said, and said that the change was a ruely change, for the town was undo thereby and is the worse by £100. And I told him it was no courtesy to meddle him in a matter but if he were called to counsel.

1 St. Augustine, apostle of the English, 26 May.
2 For an earlier stage in the dipute about the road in Paston see no. 5. From other letters it seems to have come to a head in 1451.
3 St. Edmund King and Martyr, 20 November.

And proudly going forth with me in the church, he said the stopping of the way should cost me 20 nobles, and yet it should down again. And I let him weet he that put it down should pay therefor. Also he said that it was well done that I set men to work to owl[1] money while I was here, but in the end I shall lose my cost. Then he asked me why I had away his hay at Walsham,[2] saying to me he would he had wist it when it was carried, and he should a letted it; and I told him it was mine own ground, and for mine own I would hold it; and he bade me take four acre and go no farther. And thus shortly he departed fro me in the churchyard. . . .

I received your letter by Robert Repps this day after this letter [was] written thus far. I have read it but I can give you none answer more than I have written, save the wife of Harman hath the name of Our Lady, whose blessing ye have and mine. Written at Paston on the day after Saint Edmund.

By your mother, AGNES PASTON

17. *Margaret Paston to John Paston I*

Perhaps 1453, 30 January[3]

Right worshipful husband, I recommend me to you, praying you to weet that I spake yesterday with my sister,[4] and she told me that she was sorry that she might not speak with you ere ye yede. And she desireth, if it pleased you,

---

[1] No suitable meaning of this word is recorded elsewhere; the sense seems to be 'acquire, collect'.

[2] North Walsham is less than 4 miles south-west of Paston.

[3] The date is doubtful. The handwriting of the scribe of this letter cannot be shown to appear later than 1454, and his particular style here is closest to that of a letter of July 1453.

[4] Elizabeth Paston; see nos. 11 and 12.

that ye should give the gentleman that ye know of such language as he might feel by you that ye will be well-willing to the matter that ye know of;[1] for she told me that he hath said before this time that he conceived that ye have set but little thereby. Wherefore she prayth you that ye will be her good brother, and that ye might have a full answer at this time whether it shall be yea or nay. For her mother hath said to her sith that ye riden hence that she hath no fantasy therein, but that it shall come to a jape, and saith to her that there is good craft in daubing; and hath such language to her that she thinketh right strange, and so that she is right weary thereof, wherefore she desireth the rather to have a full conclusion therein. She saith her full trust is in you, and as ye do therein she will agree her thereto.

Master Brackley[2] w(as) here yesterday to have spoke with you. I spake with him, but he would not tell me what his errand was.

It is said here that the sessions shall be at Thetford on Saturday next coming, and there shall be my Lord of Norfolk and other, with great people as it is said.

Other tidings have we none yet. The Blissful Trinity have you in his keeping. Written at Norwich on the Tuesday next before Candlemas. I pray you that ye will vouchsafe to remember to purvey a thing for my neck and to do make my girdle.

Yours, M. P.

---

[1] Surviving letters do not show which particular marriage negotiations were in mind. Besides those with Scrope (see nos. 11, 12, 22) there were also discussions with John Clopton of Long Melford, Suffolk, which went as far as a draft settlement, but came to nothing. Elizabeth did not marry until 1458, her thirtieth year; see no. 27.

[2] John Brackley, D.D., a Grey Friar of Norwich, who was for many years a confidant of John Paston. Many of his letters, written in a strange mixture of Latin and English, survive; see, for example, no. 28. He died early in 1466.

My cousin Crane[1] recommendeth her to you and prayeth you to remember her matter, &c., for she may not
sleep on nights for him.

18. *Margaret Paston to John Paston I*

Perhaps 1453, 20 April[2]

Right worshipful husband, I recommend me to you, praying you to weet that the man of Knapton[3] that oweth you
money sent me this week 39*s.* 8*d.*, and as for the remnant
of the money he hath promised to bring it at Whitsuntide.[4]
And as for the priest Howard's[5] son, he yede to Cambridge the last week and he shall no more come home till
it be midsummer, and therefore I might not do your
errand.

As for tidings, the Queen came into this town on Tuesday last past after noon, and abode here till it was Thursday 3 after noon. And she sent after my cousin Elisabeth

---

[1] Apparently Alice, daughter of John Crane of Woodnorton. A
letter is extant from her to Margaret, addressed 'To my cousin Margaret Paston'; it seems to date from about 1455.

[2] There is no record of a visit to Norwich by Queen Margaret at a
date suitable to this letter. But Norwich city archives record a visit by
the King's half-brothers apparently in 1453, and she may have gone
with them, or one of them.

[3] Less than a mile south-west of Paston.

[4] Whit Sunday in 1453 was 20 May.

[5] The name Howard without qualification is generally used in the
letters to mean John Howard of Stoke by Nayland, Suffolk, a cousin
through his mother of the Duke of Norfolk. He was knighted after
the battle of Towton in 1461 and was sheriff of Norfolk and Suffolk in
that year. He was treasurer of the King's Household from 1467 to
1474, and became Lord Howard in 1470. He was won over by Richard
of Gloucester by the promise of the dukedom of Norfolk, which was
granted to him on Richard's assumption of the crown in 1483. He was
killed at Bosworth in 1485.

Clere[1] by Shernborne[2] to come to her, and she durst not
disobey her commandment and came to her. And when
she came in the Queen's presence the Queen made right
much of her, and desired her to have an husband, the
which ye shall know of hereafter; but as for that, he is
none nearer than he was before. The Queen was right well
pleased with her answer and reporteth of her in the best
wise, and saith by her troth she saw no gentlewoman sin
she came into Norfolk that she liketh better than she
doth her.

Blake, the bailie of Swaffham,[3] was here with the King's
brother,[4] and he came to me weening that ye had be at
home, and said that the King's brother desired him that
he should pray you in his name to come to him, for he
would right fain that ye had come to him if ye had be at
home. And he told me that he wost well that he should
send for you when he came to London, both for Cossey[5]
and other things.

I pray you that ye will do your cost on me against
Whitsuntide, that I may have something for my neck.
When the Queen was here I borrowed my cousin Elisabeth
Clere's device, for I durst not for shame go with my beads

[1] See p. 22, n. 2, and no. 12.

[2] Thomas Shernborne, of Shernborne near Sandringham, was a
servant of Queen Margaret from 1451 until his death in 1459. He
was escheator (see p. 52, n. 5) of Norfolk and Suffolk in 1447–8,
sheriff in 1452–3, and M.P. for Norfolk 1449–50.

[3] This official appears in other letters as an opponent of John
Heydon and his associate Sir Thomas Tuddenham; see p. 15, n. 2.

[4] One or other of the King's half-brothers, Edmund Tudor, Earl
of Richmond, or Jasper, Earl of Pembroke (see p. 97, n. 1). They were
sons of Henry VI's mother Katherine of Valois, queen of Henry V,
by her later marriage to Owen Tudor.

[5] Costessey, about 4 miles north-west of Norwich. The manor was
held by the Duke of Suffolk. A good deal is heard of it in the letters
after Fastolf's death (1459), when John Paston occupied his neighbouring manors of Hellesdon and Drayton, which Suffolk claimed
(see no. 57, &c.); but the point of the present reference is obscure.

among so many fresh gentlewomen as here were at that time.

The Blessed Trinity have you in his keeping. Written at Norwich on the Friday next before Saint George.

By yours, M. PASTON

19. *Agnes Paston to John Paston I*

1453, 6 July[1]

Son, I greet you well and send you God's blessing and mine. . . . And as for tidings, Philip Berney[2] is passed to God on Monday last past with the greatest pain that ever I saw man. And on Tuesday Sir John Heveningham yede to his church and heard three masses, and came home again never merrier, and said to his wife that he would go say a little devotion in his garden and then he would dine; and forthwith he felt a fainting in his leg, and syed down. This was at 9 of the clock, and he was dead ere noon.

Mine cousin Clere prayth you that ye let no man see her letter, which is ensealed under my seal.

I pray you that ye will pay your brother William for four ounces and a half of silk as he paid, which he sent me by William Taverner, and bring with you a quarter of an ounce even like of the same that I send you closed in this letter. And say your brother William that his horse hath a farcin and great running sores in his legs.

God have you in keeping. Written at Norwich on Saint Thomas' Even in great haste.

By your mother, A. PASTON

[1] The date is fixed by the report of the death of Sir John Heveningham (see p. 25, n. 2), which occurred on 3 July 1453. 'Saint Thomas' Even' must therefore be the eve of the Translation of St. Thomas of Canterbury, 7 July.

[2] Brother of Margaret Paston's mother; see p. 2, n. 5.

20. *John Paston I to Lord Grey*[1]

1454, 15 July[2]

Right worshipful and my right good lord, I recommend me to your good lordship; and whereas it pleased your lordship to direct your letter to me for a marriage for my poor sister to a gentleman of your knowledge of 300 mark livelode, in case she were not married, wherefore I am greatly bound to do your lordship service, forsooth my lord she is not married ne ensured to no man. There is and hath be divers times and late communication of such marriages with divers gentlemen, not determined as yet; and whether the gentleman that your lordship meaneth of be one of them or nay, I doubt. And whereas your said letter specifieth that I should send you word whether I thought ye should labour farther in the matter or nay, in that, my lord, I dare not presume to write so to you without I knew the gentleman's name.

Notwithstanding, my lord, I shall take upon me, with the advice of other of her friends, that she shall neither be married nor ensured to no creature, ne further proceed in no such matter, before the feast of the Assumption of Our Lady[3] next coming; during which time your lordship may send me, if it please you, certain information of the said gentleman's name and of the place and country where his livelode lieth, and whether he hath any childer, and after I shall demean me in the matter as your lordship

---

[1] Edmund, Lord Grey of Ruthyn. At this time he was one of the Queen's party, but betrayed the Lancastrian cause at the battle of Northampton in 1460, and in 1465 was made Earl of Kent.

[2] The date depends on that of a letter from Grey to Paston which this answers. A note in Paston's hand on Grey's letter records its receipt on 14 July 1454. The present letter is a draft, in the hand of a clerk who wrote some twenty of Margaret Paston's letters (e.g. nos. 7, 9, 10), with corrections by Paston.

[3] 15 August.

shall be pleased. For in good faith, my lord, it were to me
great joy that my said poor sister were, according to her
poor degree, married by your advice, trusting then that
ye would be her good lord.

Right worshipful and my right good lord, I beseech
Almighty God to have you in his keeping. Writ at Norwich the 15 day of July.

21. *William Paston II to John Paston I*

1454, late July[1]

Right worshipful brother, I recommend [me] to you. And
as for tiding, mine Lord of York hath take mine Lord of
Exeter into his award. The Duke of Somerset is still in
prison, in worse case than he was.

Sir John Fastolf[2] recommend him to you, &c. He will
ride into Norfolk ward as on Thursday, and he will dwell
at Caister, and Scrope[3] with him. He saith ye are the
heartiest kinsman and friend that he knoweth. He would
have you at Mautby[4] dwelling.

I had great cheer of Billing[5] by the way, and he told me

---

[1] The date appears from the opening paragraph. In August 1453
Henry VI lost his reason. Richard, Duke of York (father of Edward IV),
gained control of the Council, which in December committed to the
Tower Henry's chief minister the Duke of Somerset (Edmund Beaufort, second duke, who was killed at St. Albans in 1455; William
Paston later married his daughter). In March 1454 York was made
'Protector and Defender of the Realm' and placed his own supporters
in positions of power. The Duke of Exeter (see p. 68, n. 6) joined the
Percies in organizing opposition to York in the north; but their plans
were forestalled, and on 24 July the Council instructed York to bring
him into custody at Pontefract.

[2] See p. 14, n. 1.   [3] See p. 22, n. 3.

[4] Margaret Paston's estate inherited from her father John Mautby.

[5] Thomas Billing, of Astwell, Northamptonshire, who was several

in counsel what he said to Ledham.[1] Ledham would a do his wise to a made a complaint to Pri[s]ot[2] in the shire house[3] of you; and Billing counselled him to leave, and told Ledham ye and he were no fellows, and said to Ledham, 'It is the guise of your countrymen to spend all the good they have on men and livery gowns and horse and harness, and so bear it out for a while, and at the last they arn but beggars; and so will ye do. I would ye should do well, because ye are a fellow in Gray's Inn, where I too was a fellow. As for Paston, he is a squire of worship, and of great livelode, and I wot he will not spend all his good as once,[4] but he spareth yearly 100 mark or £100. He may do his enemy a shrewd turn and never fare the worse in his household, nor the less men about him. Ye may not do so, but if it be for a season. I counsel you not to continue long as ye do. I will counsel you to seek rest with Paston.'

And I thanked Billing on your behalf. God have you in his keeping.

By your poor brother, WILLIAM PASTON

Much other thing I can tell an I had leisure. Recommend me to mine sister Marg[ar]et [and] mine cousin Elisabeth Clere I pray you.

times M.P., recorder of London 1450–4, and serjeant-at-law 1454. He was knighted about 1458, became a justice of King's Bench in 1464 and chief justice in 1469. He died in 1481.

[1] Robert Ledham, of Witton by Blofield, Norfolk. In 1453 a large number of 'knights and esquires' of Norfolk, including Sir John Heveningham, John Wymondham, John Berney, and John Paston, indicted him for various 'riots and offences', but he succeeded in obtaining a *supersedeas* to stop proceedings.

[2] Sir John Prisot, chief justice of the Court of Common Pleas 1449–61.   [3] The building in which the shire court sat.

[4] Perhaps *as* is merely miswritten for *at* (an easy error since *once* is spelt *onys*); but since *as* is often used idiomatically with adverbs, e.g. *as now*, *as here*, *as yet*, it may possibly have been intended here.

22. *William Paston II to John Paston I*

Right worshipful brother, I recommend me to you, desiring to hear of your welfare. Billing the serjeant[2] hath been in his country, and he came to London this week. He sent for me and asked me how I fared. I told him here is pestilence, and said I fared the better he was in good heal, for it was noised that he was dead. A[3] took me to him and asked how mine sister did, and I answered well, never better. He said he was with the Lord Grey,[4] and they talked of a gentleman which is ward to mine lord. I remember he said it was Harry Grey that they talked of; and mine lord said, 'I was busy within this few days to a married him to a gentlewoman in Norfolk that shall have 400 mark to her marriage; and now a will not by me, for 400 mark would do me ease and now he would have his marriage money himself; and therefore,' quoth he, 'he shall marry himself for me.'[5] This words had mine lord to Billing, as he told me. He understood that mine lord laboured for his own avail, and counselled to bid her be wise; and I thanked him for his good counsel.

I sent you an answer of your letter of Sir John Fastolf coming home as he told me himself.[6] Nevertheless he bode

---

[1] The date appears both from the reference to Fastolf, which connects this letter with no. 21, and from the report of the homage done by a new Archbishop of Canterbury. Thomas Bourchier, Bishop of Ely, was made Archbishop in April 1454; he lived until 1486.

[2] See p. 38, n. 5.

[3] An occasional colloquial form of *he*.

[4] See no. 20.

[5] That is, '. . . now he will not have my help in finding a bride. 400 marks would have been useful to me; but now he wants for himself the money set aside to endow his marriage, and so as far as I am concerned he must make his own arrangements'.

[6] No. 21.

lenger than he said himself he should a do. He told me he should make an end betwix Scrope and mine sister while he is in Norfolk. Many would it should not prove, for they say it is an unlikely marriage. In case Cressener[1] be talked of any more, he is counted a gentlemanly man and a worshipful—ye know he is most worshipful better than I. At the reverence of God, draw to some conclusion; it is time.

Mine Lord Chancellor[2] came not her sin I came to London, nor mine Lord of York. Mine Lord of Canterbury hath received his cross, and I was with him in the King's chamber when he made his homage. . . . .

Here is great pestilence. I purpose to flee into the country. Mine Lord of Oxford[3] is come again fro the sea, and he hath get him little thank in this country. Much more thing I would write to you, but I lack leisure. . . .

God have you in his blessed keeping. Written at London on the Friday before Our Lady's Day the Nativity[4] in great haste. I pray recommend me to mine sister and to mine cousin Clere.

By your brother, W. PASTON

23. *Edmund Clere[5] to John Paston I*

1455, 9 January

Right well-beloved cousin, I recommend me to you, letting you wit such tidings as we have.

[1] Alexander Cressener, esq., of Sudbury, Suffolk, who was sheriff of Norfolk and Suffolk in 1464–5 and 1480–1. He died in 1496.
[2] Richard Neville, Earl of Salisbury, York's brother-in-law, appointed chancellor by him in April 1454; see p. 38, n. 1.
[3] John de Vere, twelfth earl (1417–61). Together with six other peers and his brother Sir Robert de Vere he had undertaken to keep the sea for three years from 3 April 1454.   [4] 8 September.
[5] Son of Robert Clere of Stokesby, and cousin of Robert Clere of

Blessed be God, the King is well amended, and hath been sin Christmas Day; and on Saint John's Day[1] commanded his almoner to ride to Canterbury with his offering, and commanded the secretary to offer at Saint Edward.[2] And on the Monday after noon the Queen came to him, and brought my Lord Prince[3] with her. And then he asked what the Prince's name was, and the Queen told him Edward; and then he held up his hands and thanked God thereof. And he said he never knew him till that time, nor wist not what was said to him, nor wist not where he had be whiles he hath be sick till now. And he asked who was godfathers, and the Queen told him, and he was well apaid.

And she told him that the Cardinal[4] was dead, and he said he knew never thereof till that time; and he said one of the wisest lords in this land was dead.

And my Lord of Winchester[5] and my Lord of Saint John's[6] were with him on the morrow after Twelfth Day, and he spake to them as well as ever he did; and when they came out they wept for joy.

And he saith he is in charity with all the world, and so he would all the lords were. And now he saith matins of Our Lady and evensong, and heareth his mass devoutly; and Richard[7] shall tell you more tidings by mouth.

Ormesby (see p. 22, n. 2). He was born in 1417, was a member of the Royal Household from 1443 to 1460, M.P. 1447, and escheator of Norfolk and Suffolk 1464–5. He died in 1488.

[1] 27 December.

[2] No doubt the tomb of Edward the Confessor in Westminster Abbey.   [3] Born on St. Edward's Day (13 October) 1453.

[4] John Kemp, Cardinal Archbishop of Canterbury, died on 22 March 1454, after many years of high office in church and state.

[5] William Wainfleet, Bishop of Winchester 1447–86. He was chancellor from 1456 to 1460. See p. 209, n. 1.

[6] Robert Botill, Prior of the Order of St. John of Jerusalem, whose priory was at Clerkenwell in Middlesex.

[7] This, evidently the bearer of the letter, may well be Richard

I pray you recommend me to my Lady Morley,[1] and to Master Prior,[2] and to my Lady Felbrigg,[3] and to my Lady Heveningham,[4] and to my cousin your mother, and to my cousin your wife.

Written at Greenwich[5] on Thursday after Twelfth Day.

By your cousin, EDMUND CLERE

24. *Sir John Fastolf to John Paston I*

1455, 7 February

Right trusty and well-beloved cousin, I commend me to you. And please you to weet that I am advertised that at a dinner in Norwich, where as ye and other gentlemen were present, that[6] there were certain persons, gentlemen, which uttered scornful language of me, as in this wise, with more, saying, 'Ware thee, gossoon,[7] ware, and go we to dinner, go we! Where? To Sir John Fastolf's, and there we shall well pay therefor.' What their meaning was I know well to no good intent to me ward.

Calle, the most important of all the Paston estate servants from 1450 until at least 1475. See p. 61, n. 3.

[1] Isabel, widow of Thomas, Lord Morley, who died in 1435. She was a daughter of Michael de la Pole, second Earl of Suffolk.

[2] Presumably the Prior of Norwich, at this date John Mowth; see p. 11, n. 2.

[3] Catherine, widow of Sir Simon Felbrigg of Felbrigg, who died in 1443.

[4] Widow of Sir John; see no. 19.

[5] There had been a royal residence at Greenwich as early as 1300. Henry V granted the manor to Thomas Beaufort, Duke of Exeter; after him it passed to Humphrey, Duke of Gloucester, who named it 'Pleasaunce'. On Humphrey's death in 1447 it reverted to the Crown.

[6] Repeated in the manuscript.

[7] This, spelt *gosune* in the manuscript, must be a modification of earlier *garsoun* (OFr. *garçun*), used jocularly to mean 'lad'. The form is not otherwise recorded until the seventeenth century.

Wherefore, cousin, I pray you, as my trust is in you, that ye give me knowledge by writing what gentlemen they be that had this report, with more, and what mo gentlemen were present; as ye would I should, and were my duty to do for you in semblable wise. And I shall keep your information in this matter secret, and with God's grace so purvey for them as they shall not all be well pleased. At such a time a man may know his friends and his foes asunder, &c.

Jesu preserve and keep you. Written at Caister the 7 day of February, anno 33 H. VI.[1]

JOHN FASTOLF, Knight

25. *William Worcester*[2] *to John Paston I*

1456, 27 January[3]

Worshipful sir, after due recommendation please your good mastership to weet that whereas my master writeth to you so homely of so many matters to you of his, to be remembered unto his council learned by mean of you and

[1] 'in the 33rd year of the reign of King Henry VI', that is between 1 September 1454 and 31 August 1455.

[2] Servant and secretary to Fastolf from 1436. He was born in 1415 in Bristol, and educated at Oxford. He managed much of Fastolf's legal business, and wrote many of his letters. Fastolf made him one of his executors, and thinking that he had not had his just share in the estate he fell out with Paston and joined his fellow executor Sir William Yelverton (see p. 49, n. 5) in a suit in the Archbishop's court against him; yet in later years he worked for John Paston II and his brother. He was something of an author: he wrote a Latin *Itinerarium* based on his travels in England, compiled *The Book of Noblesse*, translated Cicero's *De Senectute* (printed by Caxton in 1481), and revised Scrope's translation of the *Dits moraulx* and other works (see p. 22, n. 3). He died in or soon after 1482.

[3] The date appears from other letters concerning Fastolf's administration of the Duke of Bedford's estate.

of his friends and servants there, I pray you and require
you not to wite it me that I am the causer of it that my
said master noyeth you with so many matters; for, by
God, himself remembereth the most part of them, albeit
the particular rehearsal of the matters be fresher in my
remembrance than in his. And, sir, in truth he boldeth
him to write to you for the great love and singular affec-
tion he hath in you before all other in his causes speeding,
and that ye will most tenderly of any other remember his
servants as well as others to whom belongeth to speed the
matters. He desireth my Lord Chancellor[1] should write
to him specially if he must needs come up, and a bill to
be made into Parliament for recovery of my Lord Bedford
goods.[2] . . .

In the end of this term[3] I suppose to be at London, and
into West Country.[4] My master writeth to you for a rent
of £8 of annuity charged of a township called Batham
Wylye,[5] that Master Scrope shall be benefited in the right
of it. Ye have need fare fair with him, for he is full dangerous when he will. . . . I pray you an ye see Master Ing at
a leisure to commend me to him, and trusting his good
mastership that he will be of my counsel against one
William Fowler of Buckingham, that keepeth from me a
little land. And if he will continue his good mastership to
me, ye may say him that I cast dwell in my country, and

---

[1] Thomas Bourchier, Archbishop of Canterbury (see p. 40, n. 1),
was chancellor from early 1455 until 11 October 1456.

[2] John, Duke of Bedford, brother of Henry V. He was Regent of
France from 1422 until his death in 1435. For all this time Fastolf
had been the chief steward of his household, and was made one of his
executors—the only one surviving by 1456.

[3] Hilary Term would end before the beginning of Lent, which in
1456 was on 10 February.

[4] The manor of Castle Combe in Wiltshire was one of Fastolf's
estates, and Worcester often visited it as surveyor. He also often
returned to his native town of Bristol.

[5] Now Bathampton, near Wylye in Wiltshire.

wait upon him to help get again a poor good of mine; for here I thrive not, but lose my time.

I pray Our Lord have you in his keeping. Writ hastily the 27 day of January.

Your own, W. WORCESTER

26. *Agnes Paston, Memorandum*

1458, 28 January

Endorsed: Errands to London of Agnes Paston the 28 day of January the year of King Harry the Sixth 36.

To pray Greenfield to send me faithfully word by writing how Clement Paston hath do his devoir in learning. And if he hath not do well, nor will not amend, pray him that he will truly belash him till he will amend; and so did the last master, and the best that ever he had, at Cambridge. And say Greenfield that if he will take upon him to bring him into good rule and learning, that I may verily know he doth his devoir, I will give him 10 mark for his labour; for I had liefer he were fair buried than lost for default.

Item, to see how many gowns Clement hath; and tho that be bare, let them be raised. He hath a short green gown, and a short musterdevillers gown, were never raised; and a short blue gown that was raised, and made of a side gown,[1] when I was last at London; and a side russet gown, furred with beaver, was made this time two year; and a side murrey gown was made this time twelvemonth.

Item, to do make me six spoons, of 8 ounce of troy weight, well fashioned and double gilt.

---

[1] That is, 'a "side gown" made of it'. A 'side gown' had its name not from the noun *side* but from an old adjective meaning 'ample, long', and was a long robe.

And say Elizabeth Paston that she must use herself to work readily, as other gentlewomen don, and somewhat to help herself therewith.

Item, to pay the Lady Pole[1]—26s. 8d. for her board.

And if Greenfield have do well his devoir to Clement, or will do his devoir, give him the noble.

27. *Elizabeth Poynings[2] to Agnes Paston*

1459, 3 January

Right worshipful and my most entirely beloved mother, in the most lowly manner I recommend me unto your good motherhood, beseeching you daily and nightly of your motherly blessing; evermore desiring to hear of your welfare and prosperity, the which I pray God to continue and increase to your heart's desire. And if it liked your motherhood to hear of me and how I do, at the making of this letter I was in good heal of body, thanked be Jesu.

[1] Perhaps the widow of either Sir Alexander or Sir John de la Pole, third and fourth sons of the second Earl of Suffolk (see p. 43, n. 1). Both died in France in 1429. Elizabeth Paston, after the various unsuccessful marriage negotiations, had evidently been boarded out with a titled family in London. In this same year she was married; see no. 27.

[2] Elizabeth Paston was married in 1458 to Robert Poynings of Maidstone, second son of Robert, fourth Lord Poynings. He had been on the rebel side in Jack Cade's rising in 1450. He was M.P. for Sussex 1450–1, but was imprisoned in 1451–2, then pardoned, but later again accused of treason and again pardoned. He was killed at the second battle of St. Albans in February 1461. Elizabeth in 1471 married Sir George Browne of Betchworth, Surrey, who was M.P. 1472–5, 1478, and 1483, often J.P., and sheriff of Kent 1480–1. He rebelled against Richard III and was executed in 1483. Elizabeth died in 1488.

And as for my master, my best-beloved that ye
call, and I must needs call him so now, for I find none
other cause, and as I trust to Jesu never shall; for he is
full kind unto me, and is as busy as he can to make me
sure of my jointure, whereto he is ibound in a bond of
£1000 to you, mother, and to my brother John, and to
my brother William, and to Edmund Clere,[1] the which
needed no such bond. Wherefore I beseech you, good
mother, as our most singular trust is in your good motherhood, that my master, my best-beloved, fail not of the
100 mark at the beginning of this term,[2] the which ye
promised him to his marriage, with the remnant of the
money of my father's will.[3] For I have promitted faithfully
to a gentleman called Bain, that was one of my best-
beloved sureties and was bound for him in £200, of which
he rehearseth for to receive at the beginning of this term
£120; and if he fail thereof at this time he will claim the
whole of us, the which were to us too great an hurt. And
he cannot make an end with none of his other sureties
without this said silver, and that can my brother John
tell you well enough an it lusteth him to do so.

And in all other things, as to my Lady Pole,[4] with
whom I sojourned, that ye will be my tender and good
mother that she may be paid for all the costs done to me
before my marriage; and to Christopher Hanson,[5] as ye
wrote unto my brother John that it should have been so.

---

[1] See p. 41, n. 5. Clere was one of William Paston I's executors.

[2] Hilary Term normally began on the octave of St. Hilary, 20
January.

[3] The judge's will provided that Elizabeth should have £200 on
her marriage if she married with the approval of her mother and her
father's executors.

[4] See p. 47, n. 1.

[5] Hanson had served in the French wars and as a 'collector' in
Fastolf's household, and was made searcher of ships at Great Yarmouth in 1458. He appears later as a financial agent of John Paston I
in London. He died in 1462.

And that it please your good motherhood to give credence to William Worcester.[1]

And Jesu for his great mercy save you. Written at London the Wednesday the 3 day of January.

By your humble daughter, ELIZABETH POYNINGS

28. *Friar John Brackley[2] to John Paston I*

1459, October–November[3]

Jesu mercy[4]

Right reverend master, &c., as soon as ye may goodly, cometh to Caister, and Yelverton[5] with you, an ye think it be to don; and sendeth home your men and horse till ye have do here, &c. And by grace of God, and your politic wisdom, ye shall conclude more effectually in great matters of substance, to my master's and your worship and profit.

It is high time. He draweth fast homeward, and is right low brought and sore weaked and feebled, &c. And ye must bring with you a form of a supplication made at

---

[1] See no. 25. Worcester was evidently to carry this letter.

[2] See p. 33, n. 2. The odd style of this letter, punctuated with '&c.' and composed partly in Latin, is typical of Brackley.

[3] Fastolf died on 5 November 1459.

[4] Some writers habitually began their letters with an invocation of this kind. Brackley used various formulas, some of them much more elaborate.

[5] William Yelverton, recorder of Norwich 1433–50, M.P. 1435 and 1437, serjeant-at-law from 1439, justice of the King's Bench 1443. He was knighted by Edward IV in 1461, and died probably in 1472. He was one of Fastolf's executors, and in 1464 began a suit in the Archbishop's court contesting the claim of John Paston and Thomas Howes (see p. 50, n. 7) to administer the estate. But probate was eventually granted to Paston and Howes on 26 August 1467.

London, in what manner wise Master R. Popy,[1] a cunning and a crafty[2] man, shall presenten and purposen to the King for the immortizing of Caister to Saint Benet,[3] &c., which he promitted up a certain money, &c., and undertook it, &c., and found that time no bones[4] in the matter, &c. And now he saith he will labour and ride and do his part, &c. And he would have me to help him, &c., quod non fiet,[5] &c., or ell a man of credence of my master's, &c., quod dubito fieri,[6] &c. God bring you soon hither, &c., for I am weary till ye come.

Sir Thomas[7] the parson, your own most true, &c., by mine troth, and I your bedeman and yours at your commandment in your letter, have no more touched of the matter, &c., to my master, &c. Every day this five days he saith, 'God send me soon my good cousin Paston, for I hold him a faithful man, and ever one man.' Cui ego,[8] 'That is sooth', &c. Et ille,[9] 'Show me not the meat, show

---

[1] Master Robert Popy, clerk, was nominated by Fastolf one of the supervisors of his will, together with the Archbishop of Canterbury, the Bishop of Norwich, and Hugh Fenn, a royal official. (Supervisors were usually men of some standing appointed to exercise a general control over the executors.)

[2] These words did not yet bear a derogatory sense. The meaning is 'learned and skilful'.

[3] The monastery of St. Benet (i.e. Benedict) of Holme, near the junction of the rivers Bure and Thurne in Norfolk.

[4] This is the first recorded occurrence of this expression.

[5] 'which will not be done'.

[6] 'which I doubt will be done'.

[7] Thomas Howes, parson of Castle Combe, Wiltshire (see p. 45, n. 4), and later of Blofield, Mautby, and Pulham in Norfolk. He lived mostly at Caister from 1450, and was one of Fastolf's most important agents in estate business. Fastolf appointed him and John Paston to be the two principal of his ten executors, charged with the active administration; but he fell out with Paston, asserting that he had falsified the will, and sided with Yelverton. He died in 1468-9.

The title *Sir* was commonly given to priests from the late fourteenth to the early seventeenth century.

[8] 'I [said] to him'.

[9] 'And he [replied]'.

me the man,' Hec verba replicat sepius cum magno stomacho, &c. . . .[1]

29. *William Paston II to John Paston I*

1459, 12 November[2]

Right well-beloved brother, I recommend me to you, certifying you that on Friday last was,[3] in the morning, Worcester and I were come to London by 8 of the clock. And we spake with mine Lord Chancellor,[4] and I found him well disposed in all thing, and ye shall find him right profitable to you, &c. And he desired me to write you a letter in his name, and put trust in you in gathering of the good together; and pray you to do so, and have all his good out of every place of his, his own place, wheresoever they were, and lay it secretly where as ye thought best at your assignment, &c., till that he speak with you himself; and he said ye should have all lawful favour. I purpose to ride to him this day for writs of *diem clausit extremum*,[5] and

---

[1] 'These words he often repeats very irritably.' The letter continues in Latin for several more sentences.

[2] This letter concerns the disposal of Fastolf's property immediately after his death.

[3] 9 November. The ride from Norwich to London usually took about three days. Since Fastolf died at Caister about 6 p.m. on 5 November William Paston and Worcester must have lost little time in setting out.

[4] Wainfleet; see p. 42, n. 5.

[5] 'He ended his last day.' This is the name of a writ announcing the death of a tenant in chief of the Crown and sent to the escheator (see p. 52, n. 5) of each county in which his estates were, directing an inquest (*inquisitio post mortem*) to be held to ascertain the date of death, annual value of the lands, and name and age of the heir. The writs for Fastolf for Norfolk and Suffolk, Surrey, Essex and Hertfordshire, Norwich, Yorkshire, Wiltshire, and Gloucestershire are entered on the Fine Roll under 10 November 1459, and some bear this date; but that for Norfolk and Suffolk was not issued until 13 May 1460.

I suppose ye shall have a letter sent from himself to you. As for the good of Paul's,[1] it is safe enough; and this day we have grant to have the good out of Bermondsey, without advice of any man saving Worcester, Plomer, and I mine self, and nobody shall know of it but we three.

Mine Lord Treasurer[2] speaketh fair, but yet many advise me to put no trust in him. There is laboured many means to entitle the King in his[3] good. Southwell[4] is escheator,[5] and he is right good and well disposed. Mine Lord of Exeter[6] claimeth title in mine master[7] place, with the appurtenants, in Southwark, and verily had purposed to have entered; and his council were with us, and spake with Worcester and me, and now afterward they have sent us word that they would move mine lord to sue by means of the law, &c. I have spoke with mine Lord of Canterbury[8] and Master John Stokes,[9] and I find them right well disposed both, &c.

Item, tomorrow or the next day ye shall have another

[1] St. Paul's in London.

[2] James Butler, Earl of Wiltshire and Ormond, treasurer 1455 and 1458–60. He was a particular friend of Queen Margaret, but had a reputation for misusing his office to enrich himself. He was executed by Edward IV in April 1461.

[3] That is, Fastolf's.

[4] Richard Southwell, esq., a retainer of the Duke of Norfolk and friendly to the Pastons; he wrote to John I as 'right trusty and well-beloved cousin'. He was M.P. for Yarmouth 1455–6, marshal of the Exchequer 1462–9, J.P. 1471–1504.

[5] A county official appointed annually by the treasurer to take account of the King's escheats—lands which fell to the King by the death of tenants in chief. His main duties were to hold inquests and to certify the state of deceased tenants' affairs to the Exchequer.

[6] See p. 38, n. 1. Exeter had been set free when Henry recovered his reason and York ceased to be Protector early in 1455.

[7] 'My master' here and elsewhere (e.g. no. 31) means Fastolf.

[8] Bourchier; see p. 40, n. 1.

[9] Master John Stokes, LL.D., of London, was protonotary of Chancery from 1444, and the Archbishop's testamentary judge. He was another of Fastolf's executors.

letter, for by that time we shall know more than we do now.

Mine Lord Chancellor would that mine master should be buried worshiply, and 100 mark alms done for him; but this day I shall wholly know his intent. Master John Stokes hath the same conceit and alms-giving. . . .

Item, we have get men of the spiritual law withholden with us, what case somever hap. We have Master Robert Kent.[1] But in any wise have all the good there together, and tarry for no letting, though ye should do it by day-a-light openly; for it is mine Lord Chancellor full intent that ye should do so.

As for William Worcester, he trusteth verily ye would do for him and for his avail, in reason; and I doubt not, an he may verily and faithfully understand you so disposed to him ward, ye shall find him faithful to you in like wise. I understand by him he will never have other master but his old master, and to mine conceit it were pity but if he should stand in such case by mine master that he should never need service, consi[de]ring how mine master trusted him, and the long years that he hath be with him in, and many shrewd journey for his sake, &c.

I write you no more, because ye shall [have] another letter written tomorrow. Written at London the 12 day of November in haste.

By WILLIAM PASTON

---

[1] Master Robert Kent, LL.B., of the dioceses of Canterbury, London, and Lincoln, appears in documents from 1440, serving as lieutenant of Henry, Duke of Exeter, when he was Admiral of England in 1452, and as proctor general of the Court of Canterbury in 1466.

30. *Margaret Paston to John Paston I*

1459, 24 December[1]

Right worshipful husband, I recommend me unto you. Please it you to weet that I sent your eldest son to my Lady Morley[2] to have knowledge what sports were used in her house in Christmas next following after the decease of my lord her husband. And she said that there were none disguisings nor harping nor luting nor singing, nor no loud disports, but playing at the tables[3] and chess and cards;[4] such disports she gave her folks leave to play, and none other.

Your son did his errand right well, as ye shall hear after this. I sent your younger son to the Lady Stapleton,[5] and she said according to my Lady Morley's saying in that, and as she had seen used in places of worship there as she hath been.

I pray you that ye will essay to get some man at Caister

[1] This letter must have been written in the year of Fastolf's death. There was ample time after he died on 5 November for Paston to have taken over Caister before Christmas.

[2] See p. 43, n. 1. The Morley estate was at Hingham, 15 miles south-west of Norwich, and when Lady Morley died in 1467 she was buried beside her husband in the church there. But she made her will in 1464 at her house in the parish of St. Peter's Mancroft, Norwich, and she was probably living there at this time.

[3] This was the ordinary name for backgammon until late in the seventeenth century.

[4] This is the earliest reference to card-playing in England.

[5] Catherine, second wife (1438) of Sir Miles Stapleton of Ingham (11 miles north-west of Caister), whom John Paston later called 'that knavish knight' (no. 37). He was escheator of Norfolk and Suffolk in 1437–8, sheriff 1439–40, J.P. for Suffolk 1438–42 and for Norfolk 1445–66, on many commissions, and several times M.P. He was knighted in 1444–5 and died in 1466. His wife was the daughter of Sir Thomas de la Pole (d. 1420), of Grafton, Northamptonshire, third son of Michael de la Pole, first Earl of Suffolk; and so she was Lady Morley's first cousin. See p. 247, n. 4.

to keep your buttery, for the man that ye left with me
will not take upon him to breve daily as ye commanded.
He saith he hath not used to give a reckoning neither of
bread nor ale till at the week's end, and he saith he wot
well that he should not con don it; and therefore I
suppose he shall not abide. And I trow ye shall be fain to
purvey another man for Simond, for ye are never the
nearer a wise man for him.

I am sorry that ye shall not at home be for Christmas.
I pray you that ye will come as soon as ye may; I shall
think myself half a widow because ye shall not be at home,
&c. God have you in his keeping. Written on Christmas
Eve.

By your M. P.

31. *William Paston II and Thomas Playter[1] to John Paston I*

1460, 28 January

After due recommendation had, please you to weet that
we came to London upon the Tuesday by noon next after
our departure fro Norwich, and sent our men to inquire
after my Lord Chancellor and Master John Stokes and
Malmesbury.[2] And as for my Lord Chancellor, he was

---

[1] Another employee of the Pastons, from about 1456 to 1475, who
was often sent to London on their business. He is described as 'esquire',
was escheator of Norfolk and Suffolk 1466–7, and on commissions in
1473 and 1478. His legal knowledge suggests that he was probably
the 'Thomas Playter of the Chancery' mentioned on the Close Roll
in 1448. This letter is written in his hand except for Paston's signature and the postscript, which are in Paston's.

[2] Described in one of Brackley's letters as 'a man of my Lord of
Canterbury'. For the other legal personalities see no. 29.

departed fro London and was ridden to the King[1] two days ere we were come to London; and as we understand he hasted him to the King because of my Lord Rivers'[2] taking at Sandwich, &c.

And as for Master John Stokes, he was at Mortlake, whither we yede and spake with him; and found by him by the beginning that he had been laboured against you, but by whom we could not knowen, for he would not tell; but he said he was spoken to by one which he could not remember that he should take good heed upon the probate of my master's will, how his lands should be guided, because there was a thing enseated as his will which was forged after my master's decease, &c. But ere we had thus much of his confession we were reasonably well in credence with him, but it was long ere we could find him faithfully disposed in our conceits. And when we had him reasonably after our intent we informed him of Yelverton needless wasting of my master's goods and the mistrust that he had in them whom my master most earthly trusted, and how his desire was singularly to have had the keeping of Caister and all stuff within it, and there to have lodged himself; and also how he did move my Lady Hevening-

---

[1] The King was at Leicester; see the postscript.

[2] Formerly Sir Richard Wydevill, steward to John, Duke of Bedford. After Bedford's death he married the Duchess, Jacquette of Luxembourg (see p. 133, n. 3), and Henry VI made him a peer in 1448. The incident mentioned here was an audacious stroke by the Earl of Warwick (Richard Neville, earl 1449–71, 'the king-maker'). After the Yorkist defeat at Ludford on 13 October 1459 Warwick, with his father the Earl of Salisbury and the young Edward, Earl of March, son of Richard, Duke of York (the future Edward IV), succeeded in escaping to Calais, the garrison of which supported him. The neighbouring garrison of Guines w accommanded by the Lancastrian Duke of Somerset (see p. 68, n. 5), and with the intention of reinforcing him the government sent Rivers to Sandwich to cross the Channel. But on 7 January 1460 Warwick sent a small raiding force to Sandwich, captured Rivers and his son Anthony, and carried them off to Calais with all their ships.

ham,[1] &c. Wherefore he adviseth you, for any writing or citation that cometh fro my Lord of Canterbury or fro him,[2] that ye yourself keep the goods still and let him alone for the purveyance of all such writings or citations. We asked him that, if Yelverton would not be reformed, whether for the discharge of all your conscience[3] a mean might be found to avoid him out of the testament;[4] and he said if he be false to the dead it is a cause reasonable, and perjury is another cause. And if ye will Master Stokes come to Norwich for the probate, &c., he will come himself, or make a commission to other persons as ye will assign; or ell as many as will take charge with you to make a proxy, be it to me or to some other, and send it him an ye will therewith, and it shall be proved by that mean. And all the favour that may be done for you shall be done. . . . And he giveth you leave with another executor or with your own clerk to minister and give alms at his peril; and if he should come hither he had liefer to come this Fastingong tide or after Eastern than in Lenten, but in Lenten he shall come if ye think it expedient; and therefore send us word as ye will we desire him in that point, if it like you.

Item, sir, William Worcester was come to London two days ere we were come, but we cannot espy openly that he maketh any labour, nor privily neither, by no manner of hearkening nor by no manner of talking, for I Playter have commoned with him and he saith right naught saving that he will be rewarded for his long true service of my master's good and like as my master promised him by his life. . . .

---

[1] Widow of Sir John; see no. 19.

[2] 'For' here has the sense 'notwithstanding' (as in *for all that*)— 'no matter what instructions may come . . .'.

[3] 'the consciences of all of you'.

[4] That is, to remove him from the body of executors of the will.

Item, sir, I Playter spake with Master Yelverton, and he taketh it greatly to displeasure that it was noised that he and William Wayte[1] should have laboured[2] to an indicted Master Thomas Howes;[3] for he saith for any anger he would not do so, and if he might weet that W. Wayte laboured it he should never do him service; and as touching to the provoking that my Lady Heveningham should sue forth for Caister, he saith he never thought it, but the sending to my said lady was by a man of his. . . . Howbeit I understand he will not be strange to fall in with you again, and also that he will not hurt you in your bargain if ye could be friendly disposed to him ward as ye have been, for without a friendlihood of your part him seemeth he should not greatly help you in your bargain, so I feel him. He liveth somewhat aloof, and not utterly malicious against you. The circumstance of our talking were too long to write, and therefore I express the substance as I conceive, &c. . . .

As for tidings, my Lord Rivers was brought to Calais and before the lords with eight score torches, and there my Lord of Salisbury reheted him, calling him knave's son that he should be so rude to call him and these other lords traitors,[4] for they shall be found the King's true liegemen when he should be found a traitor, &c. And my Lord of Warwick reheted him and said that his father was but a squire and brought up with King Harry the Fifth, and sithen himself made by marriage and also made lord, and that it was not his part to have such language of lords being of the King's blood. And my Lord of March reheted

---

[1] A clerk employed by Yelverton. Brackley writes of 'the judge and W. Wayte his mawment [puppet]'.

[2] See p. 18, n. 3.

[3] See p. 50, n. 7.

[4] York, March, Warwick, Salisbury, and many of their supporters had been attainted of treason at a parliament held at Coventry on 20 November 1459.

him in like wise,[1] and Sir Anthony[2] was reheted for his language of all three lords in like wise.

Item, the King cometh to London ward, and as it is said reareth the people as he come. But this is certain, there be commissions made into divers shires that every man be ready in his best array to come when the King send for them. . . .

No more, but we pray to Jesu have you in his most merciful keeping, amen. Written at London the Monday next after Saint Paul Day.[3]

Your brother, WILLIAM PASTON
THOMAS PLAYTER

Item, send us hither a letter betimes, that it may be he[re] by that time we come again, for tomorrow we ride toward mine Lord Chancellor. Let us have a letter by that we come again, and that will [be] five days for he is at Leicester. . . .

[1] The incident gains piquancy from the fact that only a few years later, in 1464, this same lord, by then Edward IV, married Elizabeth Wydevill, Rivers's daughter (widow of John Grey, Lord Ferrers of Groby). Rivers himself became a Yorkist soon after Edward's accession, and was made earl in 1466. He was executed by Warwick in 1469.

[2] Sir Anthony Wydevill was made Lord Scales by Edward in 1461 and became Earl Rivers in 1469. His greatest distinction was his interest in literature, especially of an edifying kind. 'He hath put him in devoir at all times', says Caxton, 'when he might have a leisure, which was but startmeal [by starts], to translate divers books out of French into English.' His version of *The Dictes or Sayengs of the Philosophres* was the first book printed by Caxton in England in 1477; a verse rendering of Christine de Pisan's *Moral Proverbs* appeared in 1478, and *Cordyal*, translated from a French work on the Four Last Things, in 1479. He was executed by Richard III in 1483.

[3] The Conversion of St. Paul, 25 January.

32. *Margaret Paston to John Paston I*

1460, 21 October[1]

R(ight) worshipful husband, I recommend me to you. . . . This day was hold a great day at Acle before the under-sheriff and the under-esch(eator for) the matter of Sir John Fastolf's lands, and there was my cousin Rookwood[2] and my cousin John Berney of (Reed)ham[3] and divers other gentlemen and thrifty men of the country; and the matter is well sped after your intent, blessed be God, as ye shall have knowledge of in haste.

I suppose Playter shall be with you on Sunday or on Monday next coming, if he may. Ye have many good prayers of the poor people that God should speed you at this parliament, for they live in hope that ye should help to set a way that they might live in better peace in this country than they have do before, and that wools should be purveyed for that they should not go out of this land as it hath be suffered to do before, and then shall the poor people mow live better than they have do by their occupation therein.

Thomas Bone[4] hath sold all your wool here for 20*d.* a stone, and good surety found to you therefor to be paid a Michaelmas next coming; and it is sold right well after that the wool was, for the most part was right feeble.

---

[1] The date is fixed by the report of the inquisition at Acle (11 miles east of Norwich) on Fastolf's lands, the record of which is dated the Tuesday after St. Luke, 39 Henry VI.

[2] William Rookwood, esq., of Warham. He served on various Norfolk commissions in 1449, 1450, and 1461, and died in 1474. His sister Margery married James Gresham; see p. 12, n. 3.

[3] This was the grandson of the first John (see p. 2, n. 5) and so Margaret Paston's first cousin. He died in 1473.

[4] Another of the Paston estate servants, whose name (sometimes spelt *Bonde*) occurs in the letters from 1459 to 1465; see no. 63.

Item, there be bought for you three horse at Saint Faith's fair,[1] and all be trotters—right fair horse, God save them, an they be well kept.

Item, your mills at Hellesdon[2] be let for 12 mark, and the miller to find the reparation; and Richard Calle[3] hath let all your lands at Caister; but as for Mautby lands, they be not let yet. . . .

There is great talking in this country of the desire of my Lord of York.[4] The people report full worshipfully of my Lord of Warwick. They have no fear here but that he and other should show too great favour to them that have be rulers of this country beforetime. . . .

The mayor[5] and the mayoress sent hither their dinners this day, and John Damme[6] came with them and they dined here. I am behold to them, for they have sent to me divers times sith ye yede hence. The mayor saith that there is no gentleman in Norfolk that he will do more for than he will for you, if it lay in his power to do for you. . . .

---

[1] St. Faith's Day is 6 October.

[2] Two miles north-west of Norwich, one of Fastolf's principal manors. The Pastons had already gone to live there, but the place was sacked by the Duke of Suffolk in 1465; see nos. 70 and 71.

[3] Calle was the head bailiff of the Paston estates from about 1450 for at least twenty-five years. He was evidently a native of Framlingham in Suffolk, the seat of the Duke of Norfolk—John Paston I in a petition to the Duke in 1462–3 wrote of Calle as 'servant to the said Paston put to him by my Lord's father'. In 1469, much against the will of the family, he married Margery Paston, daughter of John I (see nos. 84–86). He is later described as 'gentleman'.

[4] On 16 October 1460 Richard, Duke of York, in a statement to the lords in Parliament 'challenged and claimed the said realm and crown of England, purposing without any more delay to have been crowned on All Hallow Day then next following' (1 November).

[5] Thomas Ellis, merchant. He was sheriff in 1452, M.P. 1463–5, mayor again in 1465 and 1474. By the time of his second mayoralty he had strikingly changed his attitude to Paston and actively supported the Duke of Suffolk against him; see nos. 67 and 70.

[6] See p. 4, n. 8, and nos. 8 and 9.

And the Blessed Trinity have you in his keeping. Written in haste at Hellesdon the Tuesday next after Saint Luke.[1]

By yours, M. P.

33. *Clement Paston to John Paston I*

1461, 23 January[2]

Right reverend and worshipful brother, I recommend [me] to you, certifying you that your letter was delivered me the 23 day of January about noon season; and Richard Calle rode in the morning, and therefore I brake your letter, if there were any hasty matter; and I did Christopher Hanson[3] go to my Lord of Canterbury[4] to tell him as your letter rehearsed. And my lord said he had spoken with your man thereof the day before, and (i)f the Bishop of Norwich[5] would not do so much for him he is the less behold to him. . . .

And my Lord FitzWalter[6] is ridden northwards, and it is said in my Lord of Canterbury's house that he hath taken two hundred of Andrew Trollope's[7] men. And as

[1] 18 October.

[2] Queen Margaret's army heavily defeated the Yorkist forces near Wakefield on 30 December 1460. York and many of his leading followers were killed and the Lancastrian army marched southwards.

[3] See p. 48, n. 5.   [4] Archbishop Bourchier.

[5] Walter Lyhert, bishop 1446–72.

[6] James Radcliff, esq., of Attleborough, Norfolk, had married Elizabeth, daughter and heir of Walter, Lord FitzWalter, of Woodham Walter, Essex. They jointly had livery of the lands she inherited, and he was sometimes popularly known as 'Lord FitzWalter'. He was killed on the Yorkist side at Ferrybridge on 28 March 1461.

[7] Sir Andrew Trollope was an old soldier of fortune who had commanded troops at Calais under Warwick but, by deserting with them to the King's side, had brought about the rout of the Yorkists at Ludford (see p. 56, n. 2). He was killed on the Lancastrian side at Towton on 29 March 1461.

for Colt[1] and Sir James Strangways[2] and Sir Thomas
Pickering,[3] they be taken or else dead; the common voice
is that they be dead. Hopton[4] and Hastings[5] be with the
Earl of March[6] and were not at the field. What word that
ever he have fro my lords that be here,[7] it is well do and
best for you to see that the country be always ready to
come, both footmen and horsemen, when they be sent
for. For I have heard said the further lords will be here

[1] Thomas Colt, gentleman, of Netherhall in Roydon, Essex, had
been M.P. for Carlisle, Warwick, and Cumberland, and a member of
York's council since 1453. He was among those attainted after Ludford (see p. 58, n. 4). The 'common voice' was mistaken. He lived to
be a chamberlain of the Exchequer, chancellor of the earldom of
March, M.P. again, and a member of the King's council, until he
died in 1467 while taking part in peace negotiations at Rouen. He has
been called the "great commoner" of the Yorkist revolution'.

[2] Of Harlsey, Yorkshire. He was knighted in 1444-5, had been
J.P. and M.P. and on many commissions, and sheriff of Yorkshire
1445-6 and 1452-3. He also survived and prospered, being speaker in
the parliament of 1461-2, ambassador to Scotland in 1464, sheriff
again 1468-9, chief justice of Durham 1461-71. He died in 1480.

[3] This must be an error; there was evidently no Sir Thomas, but
there was a Sir James Pickering, of Ellerton, Yorkshire, who was one
of those attainted after Ludford. He was M.P. for Yorkshire, often
J.P., and on other commissions, and sheriff of Yorkshire 1449-50.
Of him rumour spoke truly: he was killed at Wakefield.

[4] Walter Hopton, esq., of Hopton, Salop, had been J.P. and commissioner in 1460, after being fined and pardoned for opposing the
King at Ludford. He died in 1461.

[5] William Hastings, esq., of Kirby, Leicestershire, and Burton
Hastings, Warwickshire. He was sheriff of Warwick and Leicester
1455-6, J.P. 1457-60, and was associated with Hopton in being
fined and pardoned after Ludford. He was knighted after the battle of
Towton, was soon afterwards made a baron and the King's chamberlain, and accompanied Edward IV into exile in 1470. He became
Lieutenant of Calais in 1471, and John Paston II served under him
there from 1473 to 1477. He was executed by Richard III in 1483.

[6] See p. 56, n. 2. March had gone to Shrewsbury to watch the
Lancastrians of Wales.

[7] Warwick himself was at the head of the Yorkist lords assembling
in London.

sooner tha(n) men ween, I have heard said ere three weeks to an end; and also that ye should come with more men and cleanlier arrayed than another man of your country should, for it lieth more upon your worship and toucheth you more near than other men of that country, and also ye be more had in favour with my lords here. In this country every man is well-willing to go with my lords here, and I hope God shall help them, for the people in the north rob and steal and been appointed to pill all this country and give away men's goods and livelodes in all the south country, and that will ask a mischief.[1] My lords that been here have as much as they may do to keep down all this country, more than four or five shires, for they would be upon the men in north, for it is for the well of all the south.

I pray you recommend me to my mother, and that I prayed her of her blessing. I pray you excuse me to her that I write her no letter, for this was enow ado. I dare not pray you to recommend me to my sister your wife, and the messenger I trow be so wise he cannot do it. Ye must pay him for his labour, for he tarried all night in this town for this letter. Written the 23 day of January in haste, when I was not well at ease. God have [you] in his keeping.

By CLEMENT PASTON, your brother

---

[1] This expression does not seem to be recorded elsewhere. From the context it appears to mean 'call for punishment', with *mischief* extended from its common meaning 'injury'.

34. *John Paston III perhaps to Thomas Playter*[1]

1461, March[2]

I recommend me to you, and let you weet that notwithstanding tidings come down, as ye know, that people should not come up till they were sent for but to be ready at all times, this notwithstanding much people out of this country have take wages, saying they will go up to London. But they have no captain nor ruler assigned by the commissioners[3] to await upon, and so they straggle about by themself and by likeliness arn not like to come at London, half of them. And men that come from London say there have not passed Thetford[4] not passing four hundred,

[1] This is a draft, written in the hand of William Lomnor (see p. 26, n. 2) without address or signature. It is only the contents of para. 2 that show it to be written on behalf of one of the sons of John Paston I. The brother whom John I thought of sending to London would surely be John II, who was at this time about 19, rather than John III who was two years younger. In fact by August of this year John II was in the King's household (see no. 39). Yet this letter can hardly have been composed by John III himself, for its style is much more mature than that of his earliest holograph letters (see, for example, no. 50). It may have been put together by Lomnor; but it seems to have been at least checked by John I, for the words 'my brother' in para. 2 are interlined, above a cancelled 'me', in a hand that is not Lomnor's, or either of the young men's, but looks like John I's. It appears therefore as if, perhaps for reasons of discretion, he meant to send this letter in John III's name (originally perhaps John II's, hence the cancelled 'me'). William Paston and Playter were acting for John I in London about this time, and the tone of the letter is appropriate to Playter, the family servant, rather than to William Paston, the nominal writer's uncle.

[2] Edward IV was proclaimed king and enthroned in Westminster Abbey on 4 March 1461. On 6 March he issued a proclamation calling on men between the ages of 16 and 60 to come to him prepared to fight, and the Duke of Norfolk was charged with the raising of men in Norfolk.

[3] Commissioners of array were charged with the mustering of troops.

[4] The normal route from Norwich to London went to Thetford,

and yet the towns and the country that have waged them shall think they be discharged.[1] And therefore if this lords above[2] wait after more people in this country, by likeliness it will not be easy to get without a new commission and warning; and yet it will be thought right strange of them that have waged people to wage any more, for every town hath waged and sent forth, and arn ready to send forth, as many as they did when the King sent for them before the field at Ludlow,[3] and tho that arn not go be in going in the same form.

Item, there was shrewd rule toward in this country, for there was a certain person forthwith after the journey at Wakefield[4] gathered fellowship to have murdered John Damme, as it is said; and also there is at the castle of Rising[5] and in other two places made great gathering of people and hiring of harness, and it is well understand they be not to the King ward, but rather the contrary and for to rob. Wherefore my father is in a doubt whether he shall send my brother up or not, for he would have his own men about him if need were here; but notwithstanding he will send up Daubeney,[6] his spear and bows with him, as Stapleton[7] and Calthorp[8] or other men of worship

and thence by the Icknield Way through Newmarket, Barkway, and Ware.

[1] That is, the towns that have recruited the men will assume that they have fulfilled their obligations and will not be asked to do more.

[2] 'Above' was probably meant to be 'above-mentioned', though none have in fact been named.

[3] The battle of Mortimer's Cross, 9 miles south-west of Ludlow, won by Edward on 3 February.

[4] See p. 62, n. 2.   [5] Four miles north of King's Lynn.

[6] John Daubeney, esq., was in the service of the Pastons at least from 1461, and wrote several of Margaret's letters (e.g. no. 51). He seems to have been entrusted especially with the defence of threatened property: he was killed at the siege of Caister Castle in 1469.

[7] See p. 54, n. 5.

[8] (Sir) William Calthorp, of Burnham Thorpe, J.P. and M.P.,

of this country agree to do. Wherefore demean you in doing of your errands thereafter, and if ye shall bring any message from the lords take writing, for Dancort's message is not verily believed because he brought no writing.

Item, this country would fain take these false shrews that arn in opinion contrary to the King and his council, if they had any authority from the King to do so.

Item, my brother is ridden to Yarmouth for to let bribers that would a robbed a ship under colour of my Lord of Warwick,[1] and long nothing to h(i)m[2] ward.

35. *William Paston II and Thomas Playter[3] to John Paston I*

1461, 4 April[4]

Please you to know and weet of such tidings as my Lady of York[5] hath by a letter of credence under the sign manual of our sovereign lord King Edward, which letter came unto our said lady this same day, Eastern Even, at 11 clock, and was seen and read by me, William Paston.

First, our sovereign lord hath won the field, and upon

sheriff of Norfolk and Suffolk four times between 1441 and 1476, knighted at Queen Elizabeth's coronation in 1465; died in 1494. John Paston II called him 'my cousin', and left the reversion of some manors to him in his will.

[1] Warwick, among his many offices, held the constableship of Dover Castle and the Cinque Ports.

[2] The manuscript has *hem* (= 'them'), which must be a slip.

[3] The letter is in Playter's hand, but Paston's subscription is autograph; cf. no. 31.

[4] This was obviously written just after the battle of Towton, fought on Palm Sunday, 29 March, 1461.

[5] Cecily, Duchess of York (daughter of Ralph Neville, first Earl of Westmorland), mother of Edward IV.

the Monday next after Palm Sunday he was received into York with great solemnity and processions. And the mayor and commons of the said city made their means to have grace by Lord Montagu[1] and Lord Berners,[2] which before the King's coming into the said city desired him of grace for the said city, which granted them grace. . . .[3]

Item, King Harry, the Queen, the Prince,[4] Duke of Somerset,[5] Duke of Exeter,[6] Lord Roos,[7] been fled into Scotland, and, and they been chased and followed, &c. We sent no ere unto you because we had none (certain

[1] John Neville, younger brother of the Earl of Warwick, noted especially for his quarrel with Sir Thomas Percy. He was among those attainted in November 1459 (see p. 58, n. 4), but was restored to his estates a year later and made chamberlain to Henry VI. He was created Lord Montagu in 1461, Earl of Northumberland in 1464, Marquis of Montagu in 1470 when the Northumberland earldom was given back to Henry Percy. He was killed at Barnet in 1471.

[2] Sir John Bourchier, created Lord Berners in 1455. He was a brother of Henry, Earl of Essex, and of Thomas, Archbishop of Canterbury (see p. 74, n. 3, and p. 40, n. 1), and was the Queen's chamberlain from 1465 to his death in 1474.

[3] There follows a list of men killed on either side, not entirely accurate.

[4] Edward, Prince of Wales, born in 1453 (see p. 42, n. 3). He was betrothed to Anne Neville, daughter of Warwick, in 1470, but was killed at Tewkesbury in 1471.

[5] Henry Beaufort, third duke, 1455–64. He commanded the victorious Lancastrian army at Wakefield. He was attainted in November 1461, but pardoned and restored in March 1463. Yet at the end of that year he deserted Edward IV (see p. 104), and his possessions were forfeited to Richard, Duke of Gloucester. He was defeated at Hexham and beheaded on 15 May 1464.

[6] Henry Holand, fourth duke, 1447–61. He was admiral of England and constable of the Tower 1447–60. He was a staunch Lancastrian, fighting at Blore Heath, Northampton, St. Albans, and Towton. He was attainted in November 1461 and forfeited all his honours. After exile in Flanders he returned to England with Henry VI in 1470, was in custody from 1471 to 1475, and was drowned in 1475.

[7] Thomas, ninth Lord Roos, 1430–64. He fought at both battles of St. Albans and at Wakefield, was attainted in 1461, and executed in 1464.

tidings)[1] till now, for unto this day London was as sorry
city as might. . . .

And Jesu speed you. We pray you that this tidings my
mother may know.

By your brother, W. PASTON
TH. PLAYTER

36. *Thomas Playter to John Paston I*

1461, June[2]

After my most special recommendation, please your
mastershi[p] weet the King because of the siege about
Carlisle changed his day of coronation to be upon the
Sunday next after Saint John Baptist,[3] to th'intent to
speed him northward in all haste. And howbeit, blessed
be God, that he hath now good tidings that Lord Montagu[4] hath broken the siege and slain of Scots six thousand,
and two knights whereof Lord Clifford[5] brother is one,
yet notwithstanding he will be crowned the said Sunday.
And John Jenney[6] informed me, and as I have verily
learned sithen, ye arn inbilled to be made knight at this

---

[1] Miswritten in the manuscript *certyngdys*.

[2] Queen Margaret, with the Prince of Wales, the Duke of Exeter,
and others, had led a Scottish army to Carlisle about the middle of
June.

[3] The Nativity of St. John Baptist is 24 June, and the Sunday after
it in 1461 was 28 June.

[4] See p. 68, n. 1.

[5] John, ninth Lord Clifford. He was sheriff of Westmorland,
governor of Penrith Castle, and commissary-general of the Scottish
Marches. He was one of the Lancastrian leaders at Wakefield, and was
killed at Ferrybridge on the eve of Towton.

[6] Of Intwood, Norfolk. He was a lawyer of Lincoln's Inn and
steward of the sheriff's court of Norwich. He was J.P. 1460–6 and
1473–5, and M.P. for Norwich 1478. He died in 1496.

coronation.[1] Whether ye have understanding beforehand
I wot not; but an it like you to take the worship upon you,
considering the comfortable tidings aforesaid, and for the
gladness and pleasure of all your well-willers and to the
pine and discomfort of all your ill-willers, it were time
your gear necessary on that behalf were purveyed for.
And also ye had need hight you to London, for as I conceive the knights shall be made upon the Saturday before
the coronation. And as much as may be purveyed for you
in secret wise withouten cost I shall bespeak for you if
need be, against your coming, in trust of the best. Nevertheless if ye be disposed ye had need send a man before in
all haste, that nothing be to seek. William Calthorp[2] is
inbilled; and Yelverton[3] is inbilled, which caused Markham,[4] because Yelverton looked to have been chief judge
and Markham thinketh to please him thus. . . .

No more, but I pray Almighty Jesu have you in his
keeping.

Your THOMAS PLAYTER

37. *John Paston I to Margaret Paston*

1461, 12 July[5]

I recommend me to you, letting you weet that the undersheriff doubteth him of John Berney;[6] wherefore I pray you

---

[1] Paston was in fact never knighted. In 1457 he had declined a
knighthood, and paid a fine in consequence.

[2] See p. 66, n. 8.   [3] See p. 49, n. 5.

[4] John Markham, serjeant-at-law from 1440, justice of King's
Bench 1444. He succeeded Sir John Fortescue as chief justice on
13 May 1461, and was knighted at this coronation. He was superseded in 1469 by Sir Thomas Billing (see p. 38, n. 5), and died in 1479.

[5] Relic Sunday was the third Sunday after Midsummer Day, on
which relics in the possession of a church were especially venerated.

[6] John Berney, esq., of Great Witchingham, a cousin of Margaret
Paston. He appears on Norfolk commissions from 1450, and he and

bring them together and set them accord if ye can, so
that the said undersheriff be sure that he shall not be hurt
by him nor of his countrymen. And if he will not, let him
verily understand that he shall be compelled to find him
surety of the peace[1] maugre in his head,[2] and that shall
neither be profitable nor worshipful. And let him weet
that there have be many complaints of him by that
knavish knight Sir Miles Stapleton,[3] as I sent you word
before; but he shall come to his excuse well enow, so he
have a man's heart, and the said Stapleton shall be understand as he is, a false shrew. And he and his wife and other
have blavered here of my kindred in hudder-mudder, but
by that time we have reckoned of old days and late days
mine shall be found more worshipful than his and his
wife's or else I will not for his gilt gipser.[4] Also tell the
said Berney that the sheriff[5] is in a doubt whether he shall
make a new election of knights of the shire because of him
and Grey,[6] wherein it were better for him to have the
sheriff's good will.

John Paston were elected knights of the shire in the summer of 1461.
He wrote to Paston and Rookwood (see p. 60, n. 2) on 10 July that
Stapleton and others were falsely accusing him and plotting to murder
him. He died in 1471; see no. 97.

[1] A bond guaranteeing to keep the peace.

[2] *Maugre* (French *malgré*) was often constructed with a genitive,
as *maugre his* 'in spite of him', and this was extended in various
fanciful ways, *maugre his teeth, cheeks, head,* &c. The *in* here is
abnormal. The meaning is 'in spite of himself, against his will'.

[3] See p. 54, n. 5.

[4] Some verb seems to have been omitted after *will not*, for the
meaning intended must be 'I will pay the value of his purse of gold'.
In the manuscript (which is in the hand of John Pamping (see no. 41),
with autograph signature) *all* is written after *for* but struck out.

[5] John Howard (see p. 34, n. 5) was sheriff from 6 March to
7 November 1461. He alleged that the election of Paston and Berney
had been irregular and declared it invalid, and a new one was held on
10 August.

[6] Presumably Henry Grey of Ketteringham, formerly in ward to

Item, methinketh for quiet of the country it were most worshipful that as well Berney as Grey should get a record of all such that might spend 40*s*. a year that were at the day of election, which of them that had fewest to give it up as reason would.

Written at London on Relic Sunday. . . .

JOHN PASTON

38. *Margaret Paston to John Paston I*

1461, 15 July

I recommend me to you. Please you to weet that I have sent to my cousin Berney according to your desire in the letter that ye did write[1] on Relic Sunday to me, whereupon he hath written a letter to you and another bill to me, the which I send you. He told the messenger that I sent to him that the undersheriff needeth not to fear him nor none of his, for he said after the election was do he spake with him at the Grey Friars and prayed him of his good mastership, and said to him that he feared no man of bodily harm but only Twyer[2] and his fellowship.

Lord Grey of Ruthyn; see no. 22. He was keeper of the armoury in the Tower, was knighted at the battle of Tewkesbury in 1471, and died in 1496.

[1] 'caused to be written'.

[2] John Twyer, esq., was J.P. for Norfolk and on many other commissions from 1461 to 1474, and was sheriff 1467–8. He died in 1481–2, in possession of manors at Heacham, Hunstanton, &c. On 15 September 1461 he was concerned in an unusual incident at Buckenham Castle, which he and others, headed by the Dukes of Norfolk and Suffolk, had been commissioned to take into the King's hands and remove John and William Knyvett, esqs. When he and two companions tried to enter they were prevented by Alice, wife of John Knyvett, who addressed him from a turret over the bridge in these words: 'Master Twyer, ye be a justice of the peace and I require you to keep the peace, for I will not leave the possession of this castle to

Item, Sir John Tattersall[1] and the bailie of Walsingham and the constable hath take the parson of Snoring[2] and four of his men and set them fast in the stocks on Monday at night, and as it is said they should be carried up to the King in haste. God defend it but they be chastised as the law will. Twyer and his fellowship beareth a great wite of Thomas Denys'[3] death in the country about Walsingham, and it is said there if John Osbern[4] had ought him as good will as he did before that he was acquainted with Twyer he should not a died, for he might [have] ruled all Walsingham as he had list, as it is said.

Item, Will Lynes, that was with Master Fastolf, and such other as he is with him go fast about in the country and bear men a hand, priests and other, they be Scots, and take bribes of them and let them go again. He took the last week the parson of Fritton,[5] and but for my cousin Jerningham[6] the younger they would a led h(i)m[7] forth with them. And he told them plainly if they made any such doings there, but they had the letter to show for them

die therefor; and if ye begin to break the peace or make any war to get the place of me I shall defend me, for liefer I had in such wise to die than to be slain when my husband cometh home, for he charged me to keep it.' So, says the report, they were unable to take the castle into the King's hands.

[1] Tattersall is mentioned only a few times in the letters, and does not seem to have held any post of authority in the county.

[2] Great Snoring is 1½ miles south-east of Little Walsingham.

[3] Denys had been coroner. In a letter written probably in June Margaret Paston reported that the parson of Snoring had seized Denys and accused him of hostility to Twyer and himself, and Denys was murdered on 4 July. John Paston and William Rookwood were his trustees.   [4] See no. 15.

[5] In Suffolk, 6 miles south-west of Yarmouth. The manor was part of Margaret's inheritance.

[6] John Jerningham, junior, esq., of Somerleyton, Suffolk. He came of a well-known family, but was never J.P. or M.P. He was a commissioner of array in 1484, and died in 1503.

[7] The manuscript has *hem* (= 'them') in error.

they should abuy on their bodies. It were well do that they were met with betimes. It is told me that the said Will reporteth of you as shamefully as he can in divers place.

Jesu have you in his keeping. Written in haste the Wednesday after Relic Sunday.

By your M. P.

If the undersheriff come home I will essay to do for him as ye desired me in your letter. As for money, I have sent about and I can get none but 13s. 4d. sin ye went out. I will do my part to get more as hastily as (I)[1] may.

39. *John Paston II to John Paston I*

1461, 23 August[2]

Most reverend and worshipful father, I recommend me heartily and submit me lowlily to your good fatherhood, beseeching you for charity of your daily blessing. I beseech you to hold me excused that I sent to you none erst no writing, for I could not speed to mine intent the matters that ye sent to me for.

I laboured daily my Lord of Essex,[3] Treasurer of England, to have moved the King, both of the manor [of] Dedham[4] and of the bill copy of the court roll,[5] every

---

[1] Manuscript *ye* in error.

[2] John Paston II is here seen in the King's household. Edward IV was in Sussex in late August 1461.

[3] Henry, Viscount Bourchier from 1446, brother of the Archbishop of Canterbury. He was treasurer in 1455–6, but deserted the Lancastrian side and was again treasurer 1460–2 and from 1471 until his death in 1483. He was made Earl of Essex by Edward IV in 1461, and was steward of the Household 1467–71.

[4] In Essex, one of Fastolf's manors, of which he was for a time dispossessed by the Duke of Suffolk.

[5] This appears to have been a formal copy of the record of an accusation made in the shire court.

morning ere he went to the King; and oftentimes inquired
of him an he had moved the King in these matters. He
answered me nay, saying it was no time, and said he
would it were as fain sped as I my self; so ofttimes delay-
ing me that in truth I thought to have sent you word that
I felt by him that he was not willing to move the King
therein. Nevertheless I laboured to him continually, and
prayed Baronners, his man, to remember him of it. I told
oftentimes to my said lord that I had a man tarrying in
town that I should a sent to you for other sundry matters,
and he tarried for nothing but that I might send you by
him an answer of the said matters; other times beseeching
him to speed me in those matters for this cause, that ye
should think no default in me for remembering in the said
matters.

And now of late I, remembering him of the same matter,
inquired if he had moved the King's Highness therein;
and he answered me that he had felt and moved the King
therein, rehearsing the King's answer therein: how that,
when he had moved the King in the said manor of Dedham, beseeching him to be your good lord therein, considering the service and true heart that ye have done and
ought to him, and in especial the right that ye have
thereto, he said he would be your good lord therein as he
would be to the poorest man in England. He would hold
with you in your right; and as for favour, he will not be
understand that he shall show favour more to one man
than to another, not to one in England.

And as for the bill copy of the court roll, when he moved
to him of it he smiled and said that such a bill there was,
saying that ye would an oppressed sundry of your countrymen of worshipful men, and the[re]fore he kept it still.
Nevertheless he said he should look it up in haste and ye
should have it. Baronners undertook to me twice or thrice
that he should so a remembered his lord and master that

I should an had it within two or three days. He is often-times absent, and therefore I have it not yet. When I can get it I shall send it you, and, of the King's mouth, his name that took it him.

I send you home Pecock[1] again; he is not for me. God send grace that he may do you good service, that by estimation is not likely. Ye shall have knowledge after-ward how he hath demeaned him here with me. I would, saving your displeasure, that ye were delivered of him, for he shall never do you profit nor worship.

I suppose ye understand that the money that I had of you at London may not endure with me till that the King go into Wales[2] and come again, for I understand it shall be long ere he come again. Wherefore I have sent to London to mine uncle Clement to get 100*s.* of Christopher Hanson,[3] your servant, and send it me by my said servant, and mine harness with it which I left at London to make clean. I beseech you not to be displeased with it, for I could make none other chevisance but I should a borrowed it of a strange man, some of my fellows, whi[ch] I suppose should not like you an ye heard of it another time.

I am in surety where as I shall have another man in the stead of Pecock.

My Lord of Essex saith he will do as much for you as for any esquire in England, and Baronners his man telleth me, saying, 'Your father is much beholden to my lord, for he loveth him well.' Baronners moved me once and said that ye must needs do somewhat for my lord and his, and I said I wost well that ye would do for him that lay in your power; and he said that there was a little money

---

[1] William Pecock, despite this complaint, remained in the Paston service until after John II's death, though in later years also he is sometimes unfavourably mentioned.

[2] Edward IV was at Ludlow from 18 to 26 September 1461, but did not himself go into Wales.

[3] See p. 48, n. 5.

betwixt you and a gentleman of Essex called Dyrward, saying that there is as much between my said lord and the said gentleman, of the which money he desireth your part.

It is talked here how that ye and Howard[1] should a striven[2] together on the shire day,[3] and one of Howard's me[n] should a stricken you twice with a dagger, and so ye should a been hurt but for a good doublet that ye had on at that time. Blessed be God that ye had it on.

No more I write to your good fatherhood at this time, but Almighty God have you in his keeping, and send you victory of your enemies and worship increasing to your life's ending. Written at Lewes on Saint Bartholomew's Eve.

By your servant and elder son, JOHN PASTON

40. *Clement Paston to John Paston I*

1461, 25 August

Right reverend and worshipful brother, I recommend me to your good brotherhood, desiring to hear of your welfare and good prosperity, the which I pray God increase to his pleasure and your heart's ease; certifying you that I have spoke with John Russe,[4] and Playter spake with him both, on Friday before Saint Bartholomew,[5] and he told us of

---

[1] See p. 34, n. 5.   [2] See p. 18, n. 3.

[3] Elections for knights of the shire were made at meetings of the shire court. John Paston and John Berney of Witchingham were elected for Norfolk in 1461, when Howard was sheriff; see p. 70, n. 6, and p. 71, n. 5.

[4] Russe had been a servant of Fastolf. In 1462 John Paston procured him an official post in the port of Yarmouth, and he acted as Paston's agent in various business. He was bailiff of Yarmouth often from 1466 to 1478, collector, deputy butler, and M.P. four times. He died in 1492.

[5] 24 August. It was a Monday in 1461.

Howard's guiding, which made us right sorry till we heard the conclusion that ye had none harm.

Also I understand by W. Pecock[1] that my nephew had knowledge thereof also upon Saturday next before Saint Bartholomew in the King's house. Notwithstanding upon the same day Playter and I writ letters unto him rehearsing all the matter, for cause if there were any questions moved to him thereof that he should tell the truth, in case that the questions were moved by any worshipful man, and named my Lord Bourchier,[2] for my Lord Bourchier was with the King at that time.

I feel by W. Pecock that my nephew is not yet verily acquainted in the King's house, nor with the officers of the King's house. He is not taken as none of that house, for the cooks be not charged to serve him nor the sewer[3] to give him no dish; for the sewer will not take no men no dishes till they be commanded by the comptroller. Also, he is not acquainted with nobody but with Wykes,[4] and Wykes had told him that he would bring him to the King, but he hath not yet do so. Wherefore it were best for him to take his leave, and come home till ye had spoke with somebody to help him forth, for he is not bold enow to put forth himself.

But then I considered that if he should now come home, the King would think that when he should do him any service somewhere that then ye would have him home,

---

1 See p. 76, n. 1.

2 He had now become Earl of Essex; see p. 74, n. 3.

3 'The Black Book of the Household of Edward IV', probably compiled about 1471–2, gives as one of the duties of the sewer: 'all that cometh to [the King's] board he setteth and directeth, except the office of pantry and buttery'.

4 John Wykes, esq., usher of the King's chamber, steward of Castle Rising 1461, squire of the King's body 1472. He was J.P. for Norfolk 1463–6 and 1469–70, and was still alive in 1484. One letter from him to John Paston survives, written at Lavenham, Suffolk, in 1462.

the which should cause him not to be had in favour; and also men would think that he were put out of service. Also, W. Pecock telleth me that his money is spent, and not riotously but wisely and discreetly, for the costs is greater in the King's house when he rideth than ye weened it had be, as William Pecock can tell you. And there we must get him 100*s.* at the least, as by William Pecock's saying, and yet that will be too little. And I wot well we cannot get 40*d.* of Christopher Hanson,[1] so I shall be fain to lend it him of mine own silver. If I knew verily your intent were that he should come home, I would send him none. There I will do as methinketh ye should be best pleased; and that methinketh is to send him the silver therefor, and pray you as hastily as ye may send me again 5 mark, and the remnant I trow I shall get upon Christopher Hanson and Luket.[2] I pray you send me it as hastily as ye may, for I shall leave myself right bare; and I pray you send me a letter how ye will that he shall be demeaned.

Written on Tuesday next after Saint Bartholomew, &c. *Christus vos observet.*[3]

By CLE⟨MENT PASTON⟩

---

[1] See p. 76.
[2] Luket Nantron, born in Paris, had been one of Fastolf's clerks.
[3] 'Christ protect you'.

41. *John Pamping*[1] *to John Paston I*

1461, 6 September[2]

Please your mastership to weet that I have be at Cotton[3] and spoke with Edward Dale, and he told me that Yelverton[4] and Jenney[5] were there on Friday, and took a distress of 26 or more bullocks of the said Edward's in the park, and drove them to a town thereby; and a neighbour there, understanding the beasts were Edward Dale's, and[6] bound him to pay the farm or else to bring in the beasts by a day. And when the said Edward understood the taking of the said beasts he went to Yelverton and Jenney and bound him in an obligation of £10 to pay them his farm at Michaelmas; which I told him was not well do, for I told him ye had be able to save him harmless. And because of

---

[1] John Pamping, gentleman, is first mentioned in the letters on 1 August 1461, but must have been in John Paston's service in the previous year because part of a draft petition apparently datable in October 1460 is in his hand. He later accompanied Paston on his legal business to London, and wrote many of his letters. He also served Paston's sons faithfully, and after the loss of Caister John III wrote of him and John Still as 'as good men's bodies as any live' (see no. 92); but John II disapproved of too close relations between Pamping and his sister Anne (see no. 110, end).

[2] The date appears from other letters about the Cotton dispute.

[3] The manor of Cotton Hempnall (so called to distinguish it from another manor in the village) had belonged to Fastolf, and remained an object of contention between Yelverton and the Pastons for years. Cotton lies 6 miles south-west of Eye in Suffolk.

[4] See p. 49, n. 5.

[5] William Jenney, of Theberton, Suffolk (rather more than 20 miles east of Cotton), elder brother of the John Jenney mentioned in no. 36 (see p. 69, n. 6). He had been several times M.P. and often J.P., and on other commissions. He became serjeant-at-law in 1463 and a justice of King's Bench in 1481. He was knighted by Richard III in 1483, and died the same year.

[6] Pamping has lost track of the construction, and this word is superfluous.

discharge of his neighbour he said he might none otherwise do. Nevertheless as for money, they get none of
him readily nor of the tenants neither, as he can think
yet.

The said Yelverton dined on Friday at Cotton, and
there charged the tenants they should pay no money but
to him, and hath flattered them and saith they shall be
restored again of such wrongs as they have had by Sir
Philip Wentworth[1] and other for Master Fastolf. And
because of such tales your tenants owe him the better will.
And I purposed to have gone to Cotton and spoke with
the tenants, and Edward Dale told me he supposed they
would be this day at Nacton;[2] and because[3] to speak with
them as ye commanded me I tarried not, but rode to
Ipswich to my bed. And there at the Sun was the said
Yelverton and Jenney and Thomas Fastolf;[4] and mine host
told me that the same afternoon they had be at Nacton,
but what they did there I cannot tell. And when I was

---

[1] Of Nettlestead, Suffolk. He had been King's serjeant 1446–50,
squire of the body 1449–52, King's carver 1452–60. Knighted in
1450–2, he was M.P. for Suffolk in four parliaments, J.P. and commissioner often up to 1461, sheriff 1447–8 and 1459–60. He was a
prominent Lancastrian. He carried the royal standard at the first
battle of St. Albans in 1455, but according to William Barker (one of
Fastolf's clerks; see p. 109, n. 5) he 'cast it down and fled—mine Lord
Norfolk saith he shall be hanged therefor, and so is he worthy; he is
in Suffolk now, he dare not come about the King'. But he was pardoned, and remained loyal to Henry VI. He fought at Towton and
escaped to Scotland, held Dunstanburgh for Queen Margaret in 1462,
was captured at Hexham on 15 May 1464 and beheaded four days
later. The reference here is to a claim he laid to the estate of John
Fastolf of Cowhaugh, Suffolk (also in Nacton), a 'poor kinsman' of
Sir John, which Sir John disputed.

[2] Five miles south-east of Ipswich. The manor of Burneviles here
had been Fastolf's; both it and Cotton Hempnall were released to
John Paston II in 1468.

[3] Some words such as 'I purposed' have evidently been left out.

[4] Of Cowhaugh, son and heir of the John Fastolf mentioned in
n. 1 above.

understand your man, Hogon, Jenney's man, asked surety
of peace[1] of me, and Jenney sent for an officer to have had
me to prison; and so mine host undertook for me that
night. And this day in the morning I went to St. Lawrence
church and there I spake to them, and told them ye
marvelled that they would take any distress or warn any
of your tenants that they should pay you no money. And
Yelverton said ye had take a distress falsely and untruly
of him that ought you no money, nor them neither; and
he said he was enfeoffed as well as ye.[2] And as for that,
I told him he wost other,[3] and though he were it was but
to your use; and so I told him that men were enfeoffed in
his land, and that he should be served the same within
few days. And he said he wost well ye were not enfeoffed
in his land, and if ye took upon you to make any trouble
in his land ye should repent it; and also he said that he
would do in like wise in all manors that were Sir John
Fastolf's in Norfolk as they have begun, and other language as I shall tell you.

And so I am with the jailer, with a clog upon mine heel
for surety of the peace; wherefore please your mastership
to send me your advice. . . .

Written at Ipswich the Sunday next before the Nativity
of Our Lady.[4]

Your servant, JOHN PAMPING

[1] See p. 71, n. 1.
[2] The executors of a will were jointly invested with the estate until
its disposition was settled; but Paston claimed that Fastolf had left
several manors to him personally. Pamping's rejoinder refers to the
common practice of placing land technically in the hands of trustees.
[3] 'he knew better'.
[4] 8 September.

42. *Clement Paston to John Paston I*[1]

1461, 11 October

Brother, I recommend me to you. After all due recommendations, &c. Sir, it was told me by right a worshipful man that loveth you right well, and ye him, and ye shall know his name hereafter, but put all things out of doubt he is such a man as will not lie: on the 11th day of October the King said, 'We have sent two privy seals[2] to Paston by two yeomen of our chamber, and he disobeyeth them; but we will send him another tomorrow, and by God's mercy an if he come not then he shall die for it. We will make all other men beware by him how they shall disobey our writing. A servant of our hath made a complaint of him. I cannot think that he hath informed us all truly, yet not for that we will not suffer him to disobey our writing; but sithen he disobeyeth our writing we may believe the better his guiding is as we be informed.' And therewith he made a great avow that if (y)e come not at the third commandment ye should die therefor.

This man that told me this is as well learned a man as any is in England; and the same 11th day of October he advised me to send a man to you in all the haste that might be to let you have knowledge, and that ye should not let for none excuse but that ye should make the man good cheer and come as hastily ye might to the King, for he understandeth so much that the King will keep his promise. Notwithstanding, by mine advice, if ye have [t]his letter ere the messenger come to you, come to the

---

[1] The original manuscript of this letter has been lost. It is printed from a transcript made in 1674 by Francis Sandford in his *Genealogy of the Paston Family*, now Cambridge University Library MS. Add. 6968.

[2] Summonses to the King's presence authenticated by the privy seal.

King wards ere ye meet with him, and when ye come ye must be sure of a great excuse. Also if ye do well come right strong, for Howard's wife[1] made her boast that if any of her husband's men might come to you there should go no penny for your life; and Howard hath with the King a great fellowship.

This letter was written the same day that the King said these words, and the same day that it was told me, and that day was the 11th day of October as abovesaid; and on the next morning sent I forth a man to you with this letter, and on the same day sent the King the third privy seal to you.

Also he that told me this said that it were better for you to come up than to be fot out of your house with strength, and to abide the King's judgement therein, for he will take your contumacy to great displeasure. Also, as I understand, the Duke of Norfolk[2] hath made a great complaint of you to the King, and my Lord of Suffolk[3] and Howard and Wingfield[4] help well to every day and call upon the King against you.

The King is at this day at Greenwich,[5] and there will be still till the parliament begin. Some say he will go to Walsingham,[6] but Master Soothill[7] said in the aula in the Temple that he heard no word of any such pilgrimage.

---

[1] Howard's first wife, who died in 1465, was Catherine, daughter of Sir William de Moleyns. [2] See p. 30, n. 1.

[3] John de la Pole, son of William who was murdered in 1450 (see no. 14). He married Edward IV's sister Elizabeth, and was confirmed in his title and lands on coming of age in 1463. He died in 1491. His enmity to Paston reached its height in 1465, when he attacked Hellesdon; see no. 70.

[4] Probably Sir John Wingfield, of Letheringham, Suffolk, who is mentioned four years later as a supporter of the Duke of Suffolk; see p. 147, n. 4.

[5] See p. 43, n. 5. [6] See p. 6, n. 1.

[7] Henry Soothill, appointed on 20 April 1461 attorney-general in all courts of record in England. He was J.P. for the West Riding of

No more, &c. Written the 11th day of October at midnight.

My nephew John told me also that he supposed there were out proclamations against you, &c., the same day.

By CLEMENT PASTON, your brother

43. *William Naunton[1] to John Paston I*

1461, October

Right worshipful sir, I recommend me to your good mastership. The cause why I write, I let yo(u) have knowledge of the men that be in Cotton Hall,[2] how they be strangely disposed against you; for as I hear say they make revel there. They melt lead and break down your bridge, and make that no man may go into [the] place but on a ladder, and make them as strong as they can against (you), by the supportation of Jenney[3] and Debenham and his son;[4] for they say there that Jenney hath sold the livelode unto Debenham, and that his son the knight shall dwell there. And therefore they have warned a court[5] against Monday, and now they are advised to keep it on Saturday before Monday. What they mean thereby I wot

Yorkshire from 1454 to 1473, and later for Leicester and Rutland until 1484. He was dead by 1486.   [1] See nos. 57, 58.

[2] See p. 80, n. 3.   [3] See p. 80, n. 5.

[4] Gilbert Debenham, esq., of Wenham, Suffolk, and his son Sir Gilbert. Both were retainers of the Duke of Norfolk. The father was M.P. for Suffolk often from 1427 to 1454, J.P. often to 1475, sheriff 1427–8; he died in 1481. The son was M.P. for Ipswich 1455–6, knighted probably in 1461, and took part in the siege of Caister in 1469 (see no. 87, &c.). He went into exile with Edward IV, and on his return in 1471 became King's carver, and was J.P. 1471–85. He was knight of the body to Richard III, was attainted in 1495, and died in 1500.

[5] The holding of a manor court was the symbol of effective ownership.

never, but as for the fellowship in the place that is there now, and have be here all this week, there is no man of substance, as we hear, and there have be but seven or eight all this week; but there will be a great fellowship this night or tomorrow upon Saturday, for then they will keep the court.

And as for Edward Dale,[1] he dare not abide well at home, they threat him so because he will send them no vitaly. And as for me self, Edward Dale dare not let me well be there for taking in suspicion.[2] And as for the tenants, they be well disposed except one or two, so that ye will support them in haste, for they may naught keep of their cattle off the ground long; and specially they desire to have your own presence, and they would be of great comfort.

No more I write to yo(u), but the Holy Ghost have yo(u) in keeping. Written on the Friday after my departing.

> By your servant, WILLIAM NAUNTON

44. *Margaret Paston to John Paston I*

1461, 2 November[3]

Right worshipful husband, I recommend me to you. Please it you to weet that I received your letter that ye sent me by John Holme on Wednesday last past, and also I received another letter on Friday at night that ye sent me by Nicholas Newman's man, of the which letters I thank you, for I should else a thought that it had be worse with you than it hath be, or shall be by the grace of Almighty God.

---

[1] See no. 41.   [2] 'in case he is suspected'.
[3] The date appears from a reference in the unprinted part to Sir William Chamberlain, who died in 1462.

And yet I could not be merry sithen I had the last letter
till this day that the mayor[1] sent to me and sent me word
that he had knowledge for very truth that ye were delivered out of the Fleet,[2] and that Howard was committed
to ward for divers great complaints that were made to the
King of him. It was talked in Norwich and in divers other
places in the country on Saturday last past that ye were
committed to Fleet, and in good faith, as I heard say, the
people was right sorry thereof, both of Norwich and in
the country. Ye are right much bound to thank God, and
all tho that love you,[3] that ye have so great love of the
people as ye have. Ye are much behold to the mayor and
to Gilbert[4] and to divers other of the aldermen, for faithfully they owe you good will to their powers.

I have spoke with Sir Thomas Howes[5] for such things
as ye wrote to me for, and he promised me that he should
labour it after your intent as fast as he could; and in good
faith, as my brother[6] and Playter[7] can tell you, as by his
saying to us he is and will be faithful to you. And as for
William Worcester, he hath be set so upon the hone, what
by the parson[8] and by other, as my brother and Playter
shall tell you, that they hope he will do well enow. The
parson said right well and plainly to him. . . .

I pray you that ye will send me word whether ye will

---

[1] William Norwich, who was sheriff of Norwich in 1455 and mayor
in 1461. He died in 1469–70, and his brass is still in the church of
St. George Colegate.

[2] The Fleet Prison, first mentioned in 1197, stood on a site in
what is now Farringdon Street. Paston's imprisonment may have
arisen from the circumstances lying behind no. 42. He was confined
in the Fleet not only on this occasion but also in 1464 and 1465

[3] 'and all tho', &c., is part of the subject, associated with 'Ye', not
of the object.

[4] John Gilbert, grocer, sheriff of Norwich in 1451, mayor in 1459
and 1464.   [5] See p. 50, n. 7.

[6] That is, brother-in-law, William Paston.

[7] See p. 55, n. 1.   [8] Howes.

that I shall remove from hence, for it beginneth to wax acold abiding here.[1]

Sir Thomas Howes and John Russe[2] shall make an end of all things after your intent as much as they can do therein this week, and he purposeth to come forward to you on the Monday next after Saint Leonard's Day.[3] My brother and Playter should a be with you ere this time but that they would abide till this day were past because of the shire.[4] I spake to my brother William as ye bade me, and he told me, so God him help, that he hired two horse two days before that ye ridden, that he might a rid forth with you; and because that ye spake not to him to ride with you he said that he weened ye would [not][5] have had him with you.

Thomas Fastolf's[6] mother was here on the next day after ye were ridden, to have spoke with you for her son. She prayeth you at the reverence of God that ye will be his good master, and to help him in his right that he may have his livelode out of their hands that have had it in his nonage.[7] She saith that they would make him a year younger than he is, but she saith that he is more than 21 and upon that she dare take an oath.

And the Blessed Trinity have you in his keeping and send you good speed in all your matters, and send the victory of all your enemies. Written in haste on Soulmas Day.[8]

By yours, M. P.

[1] Probably Hellesdon, where a later letter shows Margaret to have been at Christmas 1461. In a part of the present letter not printed here she writes of sending the parson of Hellesdon on an errand.

[2] See p. 77, n. 4.

[3] 6 November. The Monday following in 1461 was 9 November.

[4] That is, the shire court.

[5] 'not' is required by the sense but is not written.

[6] See p. 81, n. 4.

[7] In 1454 the wardship of Thomas Fastolf was granted to John Paston and Thomas Howes, but in 1455 to John Bocking (a clerk of Sir John Fastolf's) and William Worcester.   [8] All Souls' Day.

45. *Richard Calle*[1] *to John Paston I*

1461, 29 December

Right worshipful and my most reverend master, I recommend me unto your good mastership. Like you to wit that on Childermas Day[2] there were much people at Norwich at the shire, because it was noised in the shire that the undersheriff had a writ to make a new election; wherefore the people was grieved because they had laboured so often, saying to the sheriff[3] that he had the writ and plainly he should not away unto the time the writ were read. The sheriff answered and said that he had no writ, nor wist who had it. Hereupon the people peaced and stilled unto the time the shire was done, and after that done the people called upon him, 'Kill him, head him!'[4] And so John Damme, with help of other, gat him out of the shire house and with much labour brought him into Spurrier Row;[5] and there the people met against him, and so they avoided him into an house and kept fast the doors unto the time the mayor[6] was sent for, and the sheriff, to strength him and to convey them away, or ell he had be slain.

Wherefore divers of the t[h]rifty men came to me,

---

[1] See p. 61, n. 3.

[2] Innocents' Day, 28 December.

[3] Sir Thomas Montgomery, of Faulkbourn, Essex (knighted at Towton in March 1461), was appointed sheriff of Norfolk and Suffolk on 7 November 1461. He was a prominent courtier, being knight of the body 1461–83 and King's carver. He was sheriff again in 1466–7, accompanied Princess Margaret to Flanders in 1468 (see no. 79), and was often sent to negotiate abroad. He was still 'King's counsellor' under Richard III, and died in 1495. See nos. 93 and 112.

[4] The end of no. 46, and the mention of the sheriff below, show that 'him' refers to the under-sheriff, not the sheriff.

[5] According to Gairdner's information this is the street now called London Street, which joins the market-place at the north-eastern corner near the Guildhall.

[6] See p. 87, n. 1.

desiring that I should write unto your mastership to let
you have understanding of the guiding of the people, for
they be full sorry of this trouble; and that it please you to
send them your advice how they shall be guided and ruled,
for they were purposed to a gathered an hundred or two
hundred of the thriftiest men and to have come up to the
King to let the King have understanding of their mocking.
And also the people fear them sore of you and of Master
Berney[1] because ye come not home. . . .

My right worshipful and my most reverend master,
Almighty Jesu preserve you and send you the victory of
your enemies, as I trust to Almight Jesu ye shall. Written
at Norwich on Saint Thomas' Day after Christmas Day.

Your poor servant and bedeman, R. C A L L E

46. *Thomas Playter to John Paston I*

1461, end of December[2]

Like your mastership weet that at the last sessions Erping-
ham[3] hundred and other hundreds thereabout were not
warned, and the sheriff excused him because he could not
know who was officer there. Item, Yelverton[4] let the
people understand that the King would have his laws
kept, and that he was displeased with the manner of their
gathering, and that he would have it amended; for he
conceiveth that the whole body of the shire is well
disposed and that the ill-disposed people is but of a corner
of the whole shire, and yet that their misdoing groweth

---

[1] See p. 70, n. 6, and p. 71, n. 5.
[2] The report in the last paragraph is evidently of the same shire
court as that described in no. 45. There it had been held on the
previous day; this account sounds slightly later.
[3] Some 16 miles north of Norwich.
[4] See p. 49, n. 5.

not of their own disposition but of the abetment and stirring of some ill-disposed persons which is understand and know to the King's highness. Item, he let them weet that the King had commanded him to say if there were any man, poor or rich, that had cause to complain of any person, that he should put up his bill to the sheriff and him, and they should set a rule betwixt them; and if he would not abide their rule they should deliver the said bill of complaint to the King's highness, and he should set rule and such direction that the party complainant or defendant should be punished for his disobeisance of the said rule if the case required. And also, moreover, if there were any person that put up any such bill, and it might appear to them by their examination or otherwise false or untrue, or ell because of malice, that then such complainants should sharply be punished.

And then when he had said this, and much more, in discouraging to the people to put bills, as after my conceit, he reported him to the sheriff there present that the King thus commanded them thus to say, desiring the said sheriff if anything of the King's commanded were behind, unspoken by himself, that he would remember and help forth to tell it. And then the sheriff said, like as he rehearsed the King commanded, and moreover that the King named two men by name, Tuddenham[1] and Heydon, and if any man would put any bills against them he said in

---

[1] Sir Thomas Tuddenham, of Oxborough. He was knighted by 1431, sheriff of Norfolk and Suffolk 1432–3, M.P. six times, keeper of the Great Wardrobe 1446–50, treasurer of the King's Household 1458–60. He was often accused of instigating violence and injustice in Norfolk: in 1451 the town of Swaffham petitioned against his oppressions, and in 1452 the Duke of Norfolk accused him, together with Heydon, Stapleton (see p. 15, n. 2, and p. 54, n. 5), and Lord Scales of 'the greatest riots, horrible wrongs and offences'. In 1462 he was arrested as a rebel and adherent of Henry VI, and beheaded on 23 February.

faithful wise he would help them and further the matter
to the King's highness. And for his demeaning there every
man thought him right well disposed; but Yelverton had
forgotten to express the names of Tudd[en]ham and Heydon. . . .

Item, sir, at the last shire was much people, and ill
governed, for they would not be ruled by nobody. They
had almost a slain the undersheriff, for they told him writs
of election was sent down and he kept it aside to beguile
them and to make them labour again, and therefore he
that keepeth it is to blame, methinketh. . . .

Your THOMAS PLAYTER

47. *Margaret Paston to John Paston I*

1462, 7 January[1]

Right worshipful husband, I recommend me to you. Please
it you to weet that I sent you a letter by Berney's man of
Witchingham which was written on St. Thomas' Day in
Christmas; and I had no tidings nor letter of you sin the
week before Christmas, whereof I marvel sore. I fear me
it is not well with you because ye came not home or sent
ere this time. I hoped verily ye should have been at home
by Twelfth at the farthest. I pray you heartily that ye will
vouchsafe to send me word how ye do as hastely as ye
may, for my heart shall never be in ease till I have tidings
fro you.

People of this country beginneth to wax wild, and it is

---

[1] The fourth paragraph of this letter expresses the same fear as the
second paragraph of Calle's letter no. 45, which was written on the
same day as Margaret's previous letter mentioned in the opening passage here. (That letter is extant but is not printed here.)

said here that my Lord of Clarence[1] and the Duke of
Suffolk[2] and certain judges with them should come down
and sit on such people as be noised riotous in this country.
And also it is said here that there is returned a new rescue
upon that that was do at the last shire. I suppose such
talking cometh of false shrews that would make a rumour
in this country. The people saith here that they had liefer
go up whole to the King, and complain of such false
shrews as they have be wronged by afore, than they
should be complained of without cause and be hanged at
their own doors.

In good faith men fear sore here of a common rising but
if a better remedy may be had to pease the people in haste,
and that there be sent such down to take a rule as the
people hath a fantasy in, that will be indifferent. They
love not in no wise the Duke of Suffolk nor his mother.[3]
They say that all the traitors and extortioners of this
country be maintained by them, and by such as they get
to them with their goods to that intent to maintain such
extortion still as hath be do by such as hath had the rule
under them beforetime. Men ween an the Duke of Suffolk
come there shall be a shrewd rule but if there come other
that be better beloved than he is here.

The people feareth them much the more to be hurt
because that ye and my cousin Berney come not home.

---

[1] George, third surviving son of Richard, Duke of York, created
Duke of Clarence in June 1461, and at this date only 13 years of age.
He joined his father-in-law Warwick in rebelling against his brother
Edward IV in 1469, but soon changed sides—'false, fleeting, per-
jured Clarence'—and took part in Edward's victory at Barnet in 1471.
He was attainted of treason and executed in 1478.

[2] See p. 84, n. 3.

[3] She was Alice, daughter of Thomas Chaucer, son of the poet.
She married first Sir John Philip, killed in 1415, second Thomas
Montagu, ninth Earl of Salisbury, killed in 1428, and third, as his
second wife, William de la Pole (see p. 18, n. 1) in 1430. She lived until
1475.

They say they wot well it is not well with you, and if it be not well with you they say they wot well they that will do you wrong will soon do them wrong, and that maketh them almost mad. God for his holy mercy give grace that there may be set a good rule and a sad in this country in haste, for I heard never say of so much robbery and manslaught in this country as is now within a little time.

And as for gathering of money, I saw never a worse season, for Richard Calle saith he can get but little in substance of that is owing, neither of your livelode nor of Fastolf's.[1] And John Paston saith they that may pay best they pay worst; they fare as though they hoped to have a new world.

And the Blessed Trinity have you in his keeping and send us good tidings of you. Yelverton is a good thread-bare friend for you and for other in this country, as it is told me. Written in haste on the Thursday next after Twelfth.

By your MARGARET PASTON

48. *John Paston II to John Paston I*

1462, 13 March[2]

Right reverend and worshipful father, I recommend me unto you, beseeching you of your blessing and good fatherhood. Please it you to understand the great expense that I have daily travelling with the King as the bearer hereof can inform you, and how long that I am like to

[1] After this the manuscript has *they*, which apparently should have been cancelled; it was probably first meant to begin the next sentence, but superseded by the reference to John Paston II.

[2] Edward IV was at Stamford, on a progress to Lincoln and Leicester, in March 1462.

tarry here in this country ere I may speak with you again, and how I am charged to have mine horse and harness ready and in hasty wise; beseeching you to consider these causes and so to remember me that I may have such things as I may do my master service with and pleasure, trusting in God it shall be to your worship and to mine (a)vail in especial.[1] I beseech you that I may be sure where to have money somewhat before Eastern,[2] either of you or by mine uncle Clement when need is. Of other causes the bearer hereof can inform you.

No more to you at this time, but God have you in his keeping. Written at Stamford the 13 day of March.

By your son and servant, JOHN PASTON the older

49. *John Russe[3] to John Paston I*

1462, end of August[4]

Please your worshipful mastership to weet, here[5] is a ship of Hythe which saith that John Cole[6] came from the west coast on Wednesday last past; and he saith that the fleet of ships of this land met with sixty sail of Spaniards,

---

[1] This phrase might seem to belong to the following sentence, but the manuscript punctuates here.

[2] Easter Day in 1462 was 18 April.

[3] See p. 77, n. 4.

[4] The threat to Calais mentioned in the second paragraph was in August 1462. The fair mentioned in the third paragraph was presumably Bartholomew Fair, the greatest of all London fairs; see p.200, n. 1. In 1462 the last day of the fair, 25 August, was a Wednesday, and it seems likely that this letter was written not later than the following Wednesday, 1 September, though the King did not in fact come to London (from Fotheringay) until 4 September.

[5] Presumably Yarmouth, where Russe was employed.

[6] A man of this name 'of Stoke' was accused by Sir John Fastolf in 1450 of having taken swans from Fastolf's estate at Dedham in Essex. Stoke is probably therefore Stoke-by-Nayland, Suffolk, which is only some 4 miles from Dedham.

Bretons, and Frenchmen, and there took of them fifty,
whereof twelve ships were as great as the *Grace de Dieu*.[1]
And there is slain on this part(y) the Lords Clinton[2] and
Dacre[3] and many gentlemen, Ince[4] and other, the number
of four thousand. And the said Spaniards were purposed
with merchandise into Flanders. My Lord's of Warwick's[5]
ship, the *Mary Grace* and the *Trinity*,[6] had the greatest
hurt, for they were foremost. God send grace this be true.
On Thursday last past at London was no tidings in certain
where the fleet was nor what they had done, and therefore I fear the tidings the more.

Item, sir, as for tidings at London, there were arrested
by the Treasurer[7] forty sails lying in Thames, whereof
many small ships; and it is said it is to carry men to Calais
in all haste for fear of the King of France for a siege, and it
was told me secretly there were two hundred in Calais
sworn contrary to the King's will for default of their

[1] The largest English-built ship of the time, often mentioned in
commissions, &c. She could carry 500 men.

[2] John, fifth Lord Clinton. He had joined the Yorkists in 1459,
and been attainted at Coventry (see p. 58, n. 4), but he was restored
to his title and estates by Edward in 1461. This report was false—he
did not die until 1464.

[3] Lord Dacre 'of the South', Sir Richard Fiennes of Herstmon-
ceux, Sussex, who had married Joan, Baroness Dacre. His daughter
Elizabeth married Lord Clinton. The report of his death was as false
as that of Clinton's: he became one of the Queen's chamberlains, and
lived until 1483.

[4] Perhaps Thomas Ince, sheriff of Essex and Hertfordshire 1461.

[5] It is not certain that the ''s' ending is intended in both words. It is
represented in the manuscript by a mark which is normally an abbrevia-
tion but which Russe occasionally uses as a mere flourish.

[6] The *Mary of Grace* of 240 tons and the *Trinity* of 350 tons
appear in a list of eight ships belonging to Warwick in 1464.

[7] John Tiptoft, fourth Earl of Worcester (1449–70), constable of
England 1462–7, had succeeded the Earl of Essex (see p. 74, n. 3) as
treasurer in April 1462 and held office until June 1463. He was steward
of the King's Household from then until 1467. See p. 195, n. 2.

wages, and that Queen Marg[ar]et was ready at Boulogne with much silver to pay the soldiers in case they would give her entress. Many men be greatly afeared of this matter, &c. The Treasurer hath much to do for this cause.

Item, sir, as for tidings out of Ireland, there were many men at London at the fair of the countries next them of Ireland, and they say this three weeks came there neither ship nor boat out of Ireland to bring no tidings; and so it seemeth there is much to do there by the Earl of Pembroke.[1] And it is said that the King should be at London as on Saturday or Sunday last past, and men deem that he would to Calais himself, for the soldiers are so wild there that they will not let in any man but the King or my Lord Warwick. . . .

No more unto you, my right honourable master, at this time, but Jesu send you your heart's desire and amend them that would the contrary.

Your bedeman and continual servant, JOHN RUSSE

50. *John Paston III to John Paston I*

1462, 1 November[2]

Right reverend and worshipful father, I recommend me unto you, beseeching you lowly of your blessing. Please

---

[1] Jasper Tudor, second son of Katherine, widow of Henry V, and Owen Tudor, whom Edward had executed after the battle of Mortimer's Cross in February 1461. Jasper had been created Earl of Pembroke probably in 1452. He escaped from Mortimer's Cross, was attainted, and eventually joined Margaret of Anjou in France. He was there, not in Ireland, when this letter was written. In October 1462 he landed with Margaret in Northumberland, was besieged in Bamburgh Castle, and surrendered in December. He took part in the restoration of Henry VI in 1470, and later fled again to Brittany. He was created Duke of Bedford by Henry VII (his nephew), and died in 1495.

[2] Margaret of Anjou, with about 800 men, landed in Northumber-

it you to have knowledge that my lord[1] is purposed to send for my lady, and is like to keep his Christmas here in Wales, for the King hath desired him to do the same. Wherefore I beseech you that [ye] will vouchsafe to send me some money by the bearer hereof, for in good faith as it is not unknow(n) to you that I had but 2 nobles in my purse, which that Richard Calle took me by your commandment when I departed from you out of Norwich. The bearer hereof should buy me a gown with part of the money, if it please you to deliver him as much money as he may buy it with; for I have but one gown at Framlingham[2] and another here, and that is my livery gown and we must wear them every day for the most part, and one gown without change will soon be done.

As for tidings, my Lord of Warwick yede forward into Scotland as on Saturday last past[3] with twenty thousand men, and Sir William Tunstall is take with the garrison of Bamburgh, and is like to be headed, by the means of Sir Richard Tunstall his own brother.[4] As soon as I hear any more tidings I shall send them you, by the grace of

land on 25 October 1462, and occupied Alnwick, Bamburgh, and Dunstanburgh castles.

[1] John Mowbray, fourth Duke of Norfolk, 1461–76. He was at this time only 18 years of age (see no. 69)—the same as John Paston III. He had married Elizabeth Talbot, daughter of the Earl of Shrewsbury.

[2] Framlingham Castle was the residence of the Duke of Norfolk; cf. p. 61, n. 3.   [3] 30 October.

[4] William Tunstall, of Northstead by Scarborough, was the younger brother of Sir Richard. He was evidently in command of Bamburgh and captured by the invading force. But he was not killed: he lived to be squire of the body to both Richard III and Henry VII, and died in 1501. Sir Richard was a noted Lancastrian for many years. He had been King's carver and squire of the body to Henry VI, fought at Wakefield and Towton, escaped to Scotland, and was attainted in 1461. He and Sir Philip Wentworth (see p. 81, n. 1) held Dunstanburgh in this campaign until 27 December, and after its surrender he escaped again, rejoined Henry and accompanied him into exile, and was

God who have you in his keeping. Written in haste at the
Castle of the Holt[1] upon Hallowmas Day.

Your son and lowly servant, J. PASTON, junior

51. *Margaret Paston to John Paston II*

1463, 15 November[2]

I greet you well, and send you God's blessing and mine,
letting you wit that I have received a letter from you the
which ye delivered to Master Roger at Lynn, whereby I
conceive that ye think ye did not well that ye departed
hence without my knowledge. Wherefore I let you wit
I was right evil paid with you. Your father thought, and
thinketh yet, that I was assented to your departing, and
that hath caused me to have great heaviness. I hope he
will be your good father hereafter, if ye demean you well
and do as ye owe to do to him; and I charge you upon my
blessing that in anything touching your father that should
be his worship, profit, or avail, that ye do your devoir and
diligent labour to the furtherance therein, as ye will have
my good will; and that shall cause your father to be better
father to you.

It was told me ye sent him a letter to London. What the
intent thereof was I wot not, but though he took it but
lightly, I would ye should not spare to write to him again

chamberlain of the Household during his restoration in 1470–1. In
spite of similar exploits later in the Lancastrian cause he was pardoned by Edward IV and his attainder was reversed, and he served
Edward and his successors in posts of some importance. He died in 1492.

[1] Holt Castle in Denbighshire, 5 miles north-east of Wrexham.
[2] This letter is addressed 'To my well-beloved son Sir John Paston'.
John II was knighted when he came of age in 1463. He had evidently
gone north to join the King, who was in Yorkshire in November of
that year.

as lowly as ye can, beseeching him to be your good father, and send him such tidings as beth in the country there ye beth in; and that ye beware of your expense better (than)[1] ye have be before this time, and be your own purse-bearer. I trow ye shall find it most profitable to you.

I would ye should send me word how ye do, and how ye have chevished for yourself sin ye departed hence, by some trusty man, and that your father have no knowledge thereof. I durst not let him know of the last letter that ye wrote to me, because he was so sore displeased with me at that time.

Item, I would ye should speak with Wykes[2] and know his disposition to Jane Walsham. She hath said, sin he departed hence, but she might have him she would never [be] married; her heart is sore set on him. She told me that he said to her that there was no woman in the world he loved so well. I would not he should jape her, for she meaneth good faith; and if he will not have her let me weet in haste, and I shall purvey for her in other wise.

As for your harness and gear that ye left here, it is in Daubeney's[3] keeping. It was never removed sin your departing, because that he had not the keys. I trow it shall apair but if it be take heed at[4] betimes. Your father knoweth not where it is. I sent your grey horse to Ruston[5] to the farrier, and he saith he shall never be naught to road, neither right good to plough nor to cart. He saith he was splayed, and his shoulder rent from the body. I wot not what to do with him.

Your grandam[6] would fain hear some tidings from you.

---

[1] Manuscript &.

[2] See p. 78, n. 4. He did not marry Jane Walsham, for his wife's name was Isabel.

[3] See p. 66, n. 6. This letter is in Daubeney's hand.

[4] 'unless it is attended to'.

[5] Presumably East Ruston, though it is about 15 miles north-west of Caister.   [6] Agnes Paston.

It were well do that ye sent a letter to her how ye do, as hastily as ye may. And God have you in his keeping, and make you a good man, and give you grace to do as well as I would ye should do. Written at Caister the Tuesday next before Saint Edmund the King.[1]

Your mother, M. PASTON

I would ye should make much of the parson [of] Filby,[2] the bearer hereof, and make him good cheer if ye may.

52. *John Paston II to John Paston I*

Probably 1464, 5 March

Right worshipful sir, in the most lowly wise I commend me to your good fatherhood, beseeching you of your blessing. Mote it please your fatherhood to remember and consider the pain and heaviness that it hath been to me sin your departing out of this country, here abiding till the time it please you to show me grace, and till the time that by report my demeaning be to your pleasing; beseeching you to consider that I may not, nor have no mean to, seek to you as I ought to do, saving under this form, which I beseech you be not take to no displeasure; nor am not of power to do anything in thi[s] country for worship or profit of you, nor ease of your tenants, which might and should be to your pleasing. Wherefore I beseech you of your fatherly pity to tender the more this simple writing, as I shall out of doubt hereafter do that shall please you to the uttermost of my power and labour. And if there be any service that I may do, if it please you to command me, or if I may understand it, I will be as glad to do it as anything earthly, if it were anything that might be to your pleasing.

---

[1] 20 November.   [2] Just over 2 miles west of Caister.

And no more, but Almighty God have you in keeping. Written the 5 day of March.

> By your older son, JOHN PASTON

53. *Margaret Paston to John Paston I*

1464, 6 May[1]

Right worshipful husband, I recommend me unto you. Please it you to weet that, on Thursday last was,[2] there were brought unto this town many privy seals, and one of them was endorsed to you and to Hastings[3] and to five or six other gentlemen, and another was sent unto your son and endorsed to himself alone, and assigned within with the King's own hand; and so were but few that were sent, as it was told me, and also there were more special terms in his than wern in others'.

I saw a copy of tho that were sent unto other gentlemen. The intent of the writing was that they should be with the King at Leicester the 10 day of May, with as many persons defensibly arrayed as they might, according to their degree; and that they should bring with them for their expenses for two months. As for the letter that was endorsed to you and to other, it was delivered to William Yelverton, for there appeared no more of the remnant. Hastings is forth into Yorkshire.

---

[1] This letter must date from Edward IV's reign, for only he would have used 'more special terms' to John Paston II. Edward spent ten days at Leicester in May 1464, and commissions of array summoned men to join him. The object was an expedition against the Northumbrian castles which were again in Lancastrian hands.

[2] 3 May.

[3] John Hastings, esq., of Fenwick, Yorkshire, and Elsing, Norfolk. He was constable of Norwich Castle from 1441, J.P. and on other commissions in Yorkshire from 1448 and in Norfolk from 1470, sheriff of Norfolk and Suffolk 1474-5. He died in 1477.

I pray you that ye vouchsafe to send word in haste how ye will that your son be demeaned herein. Men think here that been your well-willers that ye may no less do than to send him forth. As for his demeaning sin ye departed, in good faith it hath been right good and lowly, and diligent in oversight of your servants and other things, the which I hope ye would a be pleased with an ye had be at home. I hope he will be well demeaned to please you hereafterward. He desired Arblaster[1] to be mean to you for him, and was right heavy of his demeaning to you. I sent you word also by Arblaster how I did to him after that ye were go, and I beseech you heartily that ye vouchsafe to be his good father, for I hope he is chastised and will be the warer hereafter.

As for all other things at home, I hope that I and other shall do our part therein as well as we may. But as for money, it cometh but slowly in. God have you in his keeping and send you good speed in all your matters. Written in haste at Norwich on the Sunday next before the Ascension Day.[2] Sir, I would be right glad to he[ar] some good tidings fro you.

By yours, M. P.

54. *John Paston III to John Paston I*

1464, 1 March

Right reverend and worshipful father, I recommend me unto you, beseeching you lowly of your blessing, desiring

---

[1] James Arblaster, esq., of Fishley near Acle, is often mentioned as an agent and adviser of the Pastons from 1450 to at least 1477. He was a dependant of the Earl of Oxford, and the Countess asked John Paston I to be 'good friend' to him. He was J.P. 1466, 1469–70, and died in 1492.

[2] 10 May.

to hear of your welfare and prosperity, the which I pray
God preserve unto his pleasance and to your heart's
desire; beseeching you to have me excused that ye had
no writing fro me sith that I departed from you, for so
God me help I sent you a letter to London anon after
Candlemas[1] by a man ⟨of⟩ my lord's, and he forgat to
deliver it to you and so he brought to me the letter again,
and sith that time I could get no messenger till now.

As for tidings, such as we have here I send you. My
lord and my lady[2] are in good heal, blessed be God, and
my lord hath great labour and cost here in Wales for to
take divers gentlemen here which were consenting and
helping unto the Duke of Somerset's going.[3] And they
were appealed of other certain points of treason and this
matter, and because the King sent my lord word to keep
this country is cause that my lord tarrieth here thus long.
And now the King hath give my lord power whether he
will do execution upon these gentlemen or pardon them,
whether that him list; and as farforth as I can understand
yet they shall have grace. And as soon as these men be
come in my lord is purposed to come to London, which
I suppose shall be within this fortnight. . . .

The commons in Lancashire and Cheshire were up to
the number of a ten thousand or more, but now they be
down again; and one or two of them was headed in
Chester as on Saturday last past.[4]. . .

---

[1] 2 February.

[2] The Duke and Duchess of Norfolk; see no. 50.

[3] See p. 68, n. 5. Henry VI had been established in Bamburgh
and Alnwick since the autumn of 1463, and Somerset joined his
garrison at Alnwick in December. This led to Lancastrian risings
in various places including Wales, where the Earl of Pembroke (see
p. 97, n. 1) took the leading part. The last stand of the Lancastrians
was at Hexham on 15 May 1464, after which Somerset and many
other leaders were executed.

[4] 25 February.

I suppose verily that it shall be so nigh Eastern[1] ere ever my lord come to London that I shall not mow come home to you before Eastern. Wherefore I beseech you that ye will vouchsafe that one of your men may send a bill to mine uncle Clement, or to some other man, who that ye will, in your name, that they may deliver me the money that I am behind of this quarter sin Christmas and for the next quarter in part of that sum that it pleased you to grant me by year; for by my troth the fellowship have not so much money as we weened to have had, by right much, for my lord hath had great cost sin he came hither. Wherefore I beseech you that I may have this money at Eastern, for I have borrowed money that I must pay again (at)[2] Eastern.

And I pray to Almighty God have you in keeping. Written in the Castle of the Holt in Wales the first day of March.

Your son and lowly servant,

JOHN PASTON the youngest

55. *John Paston I to Margaret Paston, John Daubeney, and Richard Calle*

1465, 15 January[3]

I pray you see to the good governance of my household and guiding of other things touching my profit, and that ye, with Daubeney and Richard Calle, and with other such of my friends and servants as can advise you after

[1] Easter Day was 1 April.
[2] Manuscript *ast*.
[3] The date is fixed by a reference in the part not printed here to Edmund Clere as escheator, which he was from November 1464 to November 1465; see p. 41, n. 5.

the matter requireth, weekly take a sad communication
of such things as be for to do, or oftener an need be; taking
advice of the master[1] and of the vicar[2] and Sir James[3] in
that is for to say, as well for provision of stuff for mine
household as for the gathering of the revenues of my livelode or grains, or for setting a work of my servants, and
for the more politic mean of selling and carrying of my
malt, and for all other things necessary for to be do; so
that when I come home I have not an excuse, saying that
ye spoke to my servants and that Daubeney and Calle
excuse them that they were so busy they might not
attend; for I will have my matter so guided that if one
man may not attend another shall be commanded to do
it, and if my servants fail I had liefer wage some other man
for a journey or a season than my matter should be unsped.

As for my livelode, I left with Daubeney a bill of many
of my debts, whereby ye all might have be induced
whether ye should have sent for silver.

It liketh me evil to hear that my priests and poor men
be unpaid, and that no money sent to me more than
10 mark by Berney[4] of all this season. And yet thereof tell
Richard Calle he sent me 8 nobles in gold for 5 mark, and
that as long as gold was better payment than silver I had
never so much gold of him at once; and tell him that I will
not that he shall keep that use, for I trow my tenants have
but little gold to pay.

---

[1] Fastolf's will required Paston to found 'within the great mansion
at Caister' a college of seven monks or priests and seven poor folk, one
of the monks or priests to be master.

[2] Presumably the Vicar of Caister, Robert Cutler, who was also
presented to Mautby by Paston in 1465.

[3] Gloys; see p. 10, n. 2.

[4] Probably Osbern Berney, son of the third John Berney of Reedham (d. 1473), who was grandson of the first John (see p. 2, n. 5)
and so Margaret Paston's cousin. He helped John Paston III in the
defence of Caister in 1469; see p. 184, n. 1.

Also remember you in any household, fellowship, or company that will be of good rule, purveyance must be had that every person of it be helping and furthering after his discretion and power, and he that will not do so, without he be kept of alms, should be put out of the household or fellowship.

Item, where ye desire me that I should take your son to grace, I will for your sake do the better, and will ye know that he shall not be so out of my favour that I will suffer him to mischief without by eftsoons his own default. And howbeit that, in his presumptuous and undiscreet demeaning, he gave both me and you cause of displeasure, and to other of my servants ill example, and that also guided him to all men's understanding that he was weary of biding in mine house, and he not ensured of help in any other place, yet that grieveth not me so evil as doth that I never could feel nor understand him politic nor diligent in helping himself, but as a drone amongst bees which labour for gathering honey in the fields, and the drone doth naught but taketh his part of it. And if this might make him to know the better himself, and put him in remembrance what time he hath lost and how he hath lived in idleness, and that he could for this eschew to do so hereafter, it might fortune for his best. But I hear yet never, from no place that he hath be in, of any politic demeaning or occupation of him; and in the King's house he could not put himself forth to be in favour or trust with any men of substance that might further him. Nevertheless, as for your house and mine, I purpose not he shall come there, nor by my will none other, but if he can do more than look forth and make a face and countenance. . . .

Item, remember you, ere ever I had ado with Fastolf's livelode, while I took heed to my livelode myself it both served mine expenses at home and at London and all other charges, and ye laid up money in my coffers every year, as ye know. And I wot well that the payment of my priests, and other charges that I have for Fastolf's livelode, is not so great as the livelode is, though part thereof be in trouble. And then consider that I had naught of my live-lode for mine expenses at London this twelvemonth day. Ye may verily understand that it is not guided wittily nor discreetly, and therefore I pray you heartily put all your wits together and see for the reformation of it. And ye may remember by this how ye should do if this were yours alone, and so do now.

And that ye will remember I have sent you all many letters touching many matters, and also a bill now last, by Pecock, of errands, desiring you to see them all together and send me an answer articularly; and such as ye cannot speed at this time, let them be sped as soon as ye may; that ye see over my said letters ofttimes till they be sped.

Item, I remember that mine hay at Hellesdon the last year was spent and wasted full recklessly, and coloured under[1] my sheep. I pray you see that I be not served so this year. . . .

Item, if one man may not attend to gather silver, send another, and send me word what hath be received and spent.

Item, that I have an answer of all my letters, and of every article in them.

Item, but if ye make such purveyance that my priests be paid, and poor men, beside other charges, and purvey money for me beside, either ye gather shrewdly or else ye spend lewdly. . . .

Item, Calle sendeth me word that Sir Thomas Howes[2] is sick and not like to escape it, and Berney telleth me the contrary; wherefore I pray you take heed thereat and let me have knowledge, for though I be not behold to him I would not he were dead for more than he is worth. . . .

---

[1] 'falsely blamed on'.   [2] See p. 50, n. 7.

Item, remember well to take heed at your gates on nights and days for thieves, for they ride in divers countries with great fellowship like lords, and ride out of one shire into another.

Written at London the Tuesday next after Saint Hilary.[1] . . .

56. *Margaret Paston to John Paston I*

1465, 8 April[2]

Right worshipful husband, I recommend me to you. Please you to wit that I send you a copy of a deed that John Edmonds of Taverham[3] sent to me by the means of Dorlet. He told Dorlet that he had such a deed as he supposed that would don ease in proving of the title that the Duke of Suffolk claimeth in Drayton.[4] For the same deed that he sent me, the seal of arms is like unto the copy that I send you, and nothing like to the Duke of Suffolk's ancestors'.

Item, the said Edmond[s] saith if he may find any other thing that may do you ease in that matter he will do his part therein.

Item, John Russe sent me word that Barker[5] and Harry Porter told him in counsel that the Duke of Suffolk hath

---

[1] 13 January.

[2] The year is fixed by the Duke of Suffolk's claim to Hellesdon (see p. 61, n. 2).

[3] Some 3 miles north-west of Hellesdon.

[4] Two miles north-west of Hellesdon, another Fastolf manor taken over by Paston.

[5] William Barker, one of Fastolf's clerks, who in a much later document describes himself as 'late household servant by the space of 21 year with Sir John Fastolf'. After Fastolf's death he entered the service of the Pastons.

bought one Brytyeff[1] right, the which maketh a claim
unto Hellesdon; and the said Duke is proposed to enter
within short time after Eastern;[2] for insomuch the said
Russe fel(t) by the said Barker and Porter that all the
feoffees will make a release unto the Duke, and help him
that they can into their power, for to have his good lordship. . . .

Item, there be divers of your tenantries at Mautby that
had great need for to be repaired, a(nd) the tenants be so
poor that they are not a power to repair them; wherefore
if [it] like you I would that the marsh that Bridge had
might be kept in your own hand this year, that the
tenants might have rushes to repair with their houses.
And also there is windfall wood at the manor that is of no
great value that might help them with toward the reparation, if it like you to let them have it that hath most need
thereof. I have spoke with Burgess that he should hain
the price of the marsh, or else I told him that he should
no longer have it, for ye might [get] other farmers thereto
that would give therefore as it was let before; and if he
would give therefore as much as another man would, ye
would that he should have it before any other man. And
he said he should give me answer by a fortnight after
Eastern. I can get none other farmer thereto yet.

Item, I understand by John Pamping[3] that ye will not
that your son be take into your house, nor holp by you,
till such time of year as he was put out thereof, the which
shall be about Saint Thomas' Mass.[4] For God's sake, sir,

---

[1] This is the manuscript spelling here. Elsewhere the same name
is written *Bryghtylhed*, and the correct form is uncertain.

[2] Easter Day was 14 April.   [3] See p. 80, n. 1.

[4] Since the letter is dated in April this must be the Translation of
St. Thomas of Canterbury, 7 July, rather than either of the feasts of
St. Thomas in December (cf. p. 122, n. 1). John II in fact came home
by May 1465 (see no. 57), though his father's disapproval continued
(see no. 59).

a pity on him, and remember you it hath be a long season sin he had aught of you to help him with, and he hath obeyed him to you, and will do at all times, and will do that he can or may to have your good fatherhood. And at the reverence of God, be ye his good father and have a fatherly heart to him; and I hope he shall ever know himself the better hereafter, and be the more ware to eschew such things as should displease you, and for to take heed at that should please you.

Pecock shall tell you by mouth of more things than I may write to you at this time. The Blessed Trinity have you in his keeping. Written at Caister in haste the Monday next after Palm Sunday.

Your M. P.

57. *Margaret Paston to John Paston I*

1465, 10 May

Right worshipful husband, I recommend me unto you. Please it you to wit that on Wednesday last past Daubeney,[1] Naunton,[2] Wykes,[3] and John Love[4] were at Drayton[5] for to speak with your tenants there, to put them in comfort and for to ask money of them also. And Piers Warren, otherwise called Piers at Sloth,[6] which is a flickering

[1] See p. 66, n. 6.

[2] See no. 43.

[3] John Wykes, in the Pastons' service from about 1463 to 1470. This letter is in his hand and so are several others of Margaret's and John II's in this and the next year. He is clearly distinct from the courtier of the same name mentioned in no. 40 (see p. 78, n. 4).

[4] Not mentioned elsewhere in the letters.

[5] See p. 109, n. 4.

[6] This nickname is based on the practice of identifying a man by some landmark near his home, which gave rise to several modern surnames such as Attlee, Atwell, Atwood. Cf. p. 251, n. 1.

fellow and a busy with Master Philip[1] and the bailie of Cossey,[2] he had a plough going in your land in Drayton; and there your said servants at that time took his plough-ware, that is to say two mares, and brought them to Hellesdon, and there they be yet. And on the next morning after, Master Philip and the bailie of Cossey came to Hellesdon with a great number of people, that is to say eight score men and more in harness, and there took from the parson's plough two horse, price 4 mark, and two horse of Thomas Stermyn's plough, price 40s., saying to them that there was taken a plaint against them in the hundred[3] by the said Piers for taking of the foresaid plough-ware at Drayton, and but they would be bound to come to Drayton on Tuesday next coming to answer to such matters as shall be said to them there, they should not have their beasts again; which they refused to do unto the time that they had an answer from you; and so they led the beasts forth to Drayton, and from Drayton forth to Cossey.

And the same afternoon following, the parson of Hellesdon sent his man to Drayton with Stermyn for to speak with Master Philip, to know a way if they should have again their cattle or not; and Master Philip answered them, if that they would bring home their distress again that was taken of Piers Warren, that then he would deliver them theirs, or else not. And he let them plainly wit that if ye or any of your servants took any distress in Drayton, that were but the value of an hen, they would come to Hellesdon and take there the value of an ox therefor, and if they cannot take the value thereof there, that then they

[1] Philip Lipyate, Rector of Sall (by presentation in 1460 of Thomas Brews (see p. 232, n. 3)), an agent of the Duke of Suffolk.

[2] About 1½ miles from both Drayton and Hellesdon, across the Wensum. See p. 35, n. 5.

[3] That is, the hundred court.

will do break your tenants' houses in Hellesdon, and take
as much as they could find therein; and if they be letted
thereof—which shall never lie in your power for to do,
for the Duke of Suffolk is able to keep daily in his house
more men than Daubeney had hairs in his head if him list
('and as for Daubeney, he is a lewd fellow, and so he shall
be served hereafter, and I would that he were here')—and
therefore, he said, if ye take upon you to let them so for
to do, that then they would go into any livelode that ye
had in Norfolk or Suffolk and to take a distress in like wise
as they would do at Hellesdon; and other answer could
they none get, and so they departed. Richard Calle asked
the parson and Stermyn if they would take an action for
their cattle, and the parson said he was aged and sicklow
and he would not be troubled hereafter; he said he had
liefer lose his cattle, for he wist well if he did so he should
be indicted and so vexed with them that he should never
have rest by them. As for Stermyn, he said at that time
he durst not take no suit against them neither, but after
that Richard was ridden I spake with him and he said he
would be ruled as ye would have him, and I found him
right hearty and well-disposed in that matter. . . .

Skipwith[1] went with me to the Bishop of Norwich,[2] and
I let him have knowledge of the riotous and evil disposition of Master Philip, desiring his Lordship that he would
see a mean that a correction might be had, inasmuch as
he was chief justice of the peace and his ordinary, and
inasmuch as he was a priest and under his correction that
he should have understanding of his disposition; and I
made Daubeney to tell him all the matter how it was.
And he said he would send for him and speak with him

[1] William Skipwith, gentleman, of Norwich and of Utterby,
Lincolnshire, was M.P. for Norwich in 1463–5, J.P. for Norfolk in
1469–70, and on commissions. He died in 1487.
[2] See p. 62, n. 5.

and he told me of divers things of the demeaning of him whereby I understood he liked not by his disposition nor demeaning in this matter nor in none other, for it seemed he had proved him what he is in other matters. My lord said to me that he would right fain that ye had a good conclusion in your matters, and said by his troth that he ought you right good will and would right fain that ye were come home, and said to me that it should be a great comfort to your friends and neighbours, and that your presence should do more amongst them than a hundred of your men should do in your absence; and more, your enemies would fear to do against you if ye might be at home and stirring amongst them; and said full plainly in many other things it were too long to write at this time, as Skipwith shall tell you when he cometh to you. I pray you thank Skipwith of his good will, for he was right well-willed to go with me and give me his advice; methinketh he is right well-willed to you.

Item, I pray you send hastily word how that ye will that we be guided with this place, for as it is told me it is like to stand in as great jeopardy in haste as other don. On Thursday all day there were kept in Drayton lodge into 60 persons,[1] and yet, as it is told me, there be within daily and nightly into a 16 or 20 persons.

Item, it is told me that Thomas Ellis[2] of Norwich, which now is chosen mayor, said at Drayton that if my Lord of Suffolk need a hundred men he would purvey him thereof, and if any men of the town would go to Paston he would do lay them fast in prison. I would your men might have a *supersedeas*[3] out of the Chancery and be out of the danger of their men here, and I pray you let not Will Naunton be forgot therein. Richard Calle and other can tell you of his

---

1 Followers of the Duke of Suffolk.
2 See p. 61, n. 5.
3 A writ ordering the stay of legal proceedings.

demeaning, and I pray you that ye be not displeased for his abiding with me, for in good faith he hath been a great comfort to me sin ye departed hence, as I will let you wit hereafter. I pray you if his brother come to you for a release of his land let him none have unto the time that ye see his father's will, the which I wot where it is, and that it like you to desire him to be good brother to him.

Item, I have left John Paston the older at Caister to keep the place there, as Richard can tell you; for I had liefer, an it pleased you, to be captainess here than at Caister. Yet I was nothing purposed to abide here when [I] came from home but for a day or two; but I shall abide here till I hear tidings from you. . . .

Item, my mother[1] told me that she thinketh right strange that she may not have the profits of Clere's place[2] in peaceable wise for you.[3] She saith it is hers and she hath paid most therefor yet, and she saith she will have the profits thereof, or else she will make more folk to speak thereof. She saith she knoweth not what right ne title that ye have therein but if ye list to trouble with her, and that should be no worship to you; and she saith she will be there this summer and repair the housing there. In good faith I hear much language of the demeaning between you and her. I would right fain, and so would many mo of your friends, that it were otherwise between you than it is; and if it were I hope ye should have the better speed in all other matters.

I pray God be your good speed in all your matters, and give you grace to have a good conclusion of them in haste; for this is too weary a life to abide for you and all your.

---

[1] Agnes Paston.
[2] Probably part of the estate of Robert Clere, who died in 1446. See p. 22, n. 2, and cf. p. 130.
[3] 'for you' = 'because of you'.

Written in haste at Hellesdon the 10 day of May. The
cause that I send to you this hastily is to have an answer
in haste from you.

Yours, M. P.

58. *Margaret Paston to John Paston I*

1465, 20 May

Please it you to wit that on Saturday last your servants
Naunton, Wykes, and other were at Drayton, and there
took a distress for the rent and farm that was to pay to the
number of 77 neat, and so brought them home to Hellesdon and put them in the pinfold, and so kept them still
there from the said Saturday morning into Monday[1] at
3 at clock at afternoon. First on the same Saturday the
tenants followed upon and desired to have their cattle
again, and I answered them if they would do pay such
duties as they ought for to pay to you that then they
should have their cattle delivered again, or else if they
were not a power to pay ready money that then they to
find sufficient surety to pay the money at such a day as
they might agree with me, and thereto to be bounden to
you by obligation. And that they said they durst not for
to take upon them for to be bounden, and as for money
they had none for to pay at that time; and therefore I kept
still the beasts. Harleston[2] was at Norwich and sent for

---

[1] This was the day the letter was written.

[2] William Harleston, esq., of Denham, Suffolk, a retainer of the
Duke of Suffolk and under-steward of the Duchy of Lancaster. He
was escheator of Norfolk and Suffolk in 1445 and 1461, on various
commissions from 1455 to 1476, J.P. for Suffolk in 1470, and died
in 1480. He married Philippa Stonor of Oxfordshire, whose family
left another important collection of letters of this period (*Stonor
Letters and Papers*, Camden Society, 1919).

the tenants the said Saturday at afternoon, and there by
the means of the bailiff of Cossey[1] put the tenants in such
fear, saying that if they would pay such duties, or else for
to be bounden to pay, that then they would put them out
of such lands as they held bondly of the lordship and so
to distrain them and trouble them that they should be
weary of their part; and that put them such fear that they
durst neither pay nor be bounden. And on the same day
at evensong time Harleston came to me to Hellesdon,
desiring me that I would deliver again the said distress,
and as for such distresses as they had taken here of your
tenants should be delivered again in like form. And I said
I would not deliver them so, and told them that I would
deliver them as is written afore, and otherwise not; and
otherwise I would not deliver them but by the form of
law. And other communication was had between us at
that time of divers matters which were too long to write
at this time, but ye shall have knowledge thereof in haste.

And on Monday next after at 9 at clock there came
Pinchmore to Hellesdon with a replevin[2] which was made
in Harleston's name as under-steward of the Duchy,[3] saying that the beasts were taken upon the Duchy fee, wherefore he desired me to make him liv[er]y of the said beasts
so taken; and I said I would not deliver them unto the
time that I had examined the tenants of the truth. And so
I sent thither Wykes with Pinchmore to understand what
they would say; and the tenants said that there was taken
none upon the Duchy at their knowledge, save only Piers
Warren the younger and Painter said that their cattle was
taken upon the Duchy, which they cannot prove by none

---

[1] See p. 112, n. 2.

[2] A writ ordering the restitution of distrained goods.

[3] The Duchy of Lancaster, created for Henry of Grosmont in
1351 with the status of a palatinate, and regranted to John of Gaunt,
his son-in-law, in 1362. It included much land outside Lancashire.

record save only by their own saying. And so we would
not obey that replevin, and so they departed; and at 3 at
clock at afternoon Pinchmore came to Hellesdon again
with two men which brought with them a replevin from
the sheriff,[1] whose names be John Wycherley and Robert
Ranson, which required me by the same replevin to make
them delivery of the said beasts taken at Drayton. And
so I, seeing the sheriff's replevin under his seal, bade my
men deliver them, and so they were delivered.

And as for all other matters that ye have written to
[me] of, I will speed me to send you a answer as hastily as
I may, for I may no leisure have to write no more to you
at this time. The Blessed Trinity have you in his keeping.
Written at Hellesdon the 20 day [of May].[2]

By yours, M. P.

59. *John Paston I to Margaret Paston,*
John Daubeney, and Richard Calle

1465, 27 June

⟨I⟩ recommend me to you, and have received a letter from
you. . . .

Item, as for your son:[3] I let you weet I would he did well,
but I understand in him no dispo[si]tion of policy ne of
governance, as man of the world ought to do, but only
liveth, and ever hath, as man dissolute, without any provision; ne that he busieth him nothing to understand
such matters as a man of livelode must needs understand;
ne I understand nothing of what disposition he purposeth

---

[1] Alexander Cressener. See p. 41, n. 1.
[2] The last two words were read by Fenn, but are now obliterated
by a repair to the paper.
[3] John Paston II.

to be, but only I can think he would dwell again in your house and mine, and there eat and drink and sleep. Therefore I let you weet I would know him ere he know mine intent, and how well he hath occupied his time now he hath had leisure. Every poor man that hath brought up his childer to the age of twelve year waiteth then to be holp and profited by his childer; and every gentleman that hath discretion waiteth that his kin and servants that liveth by him and at his cost should help him forthward. As for your son, ye know well he never stood you ne me in profit, ease, or help to value of one groat, saving at Caldecott Hall[1] when [he] and his brother kept it one day against Debenham,[2] and yet it was at thrice the cost that ever Debenham sons put him to; for by their policy they keep Cotton[3] at my cost and with the profits of the same. Wherefore give h(i)m[4] no favour till ye feel what he is and will be.

Item, Calle sendeth me word that Master Philip[5] hath entered in Drayton in my Lord of Suffolk's name, and hath other purpose to enter in Hellesdon, and he asketh mine advice; which is that ye comfort my tenants and help them till I come home, and let them weet I shall not lose it, and that the Duke of Suffolk that last died[6] would have bought it of Fastolf, and, for he might not have it so, he claimed the manor, saying it was one Pole's, and for his name was Pole he claimed to be heir. He was answered that he came nothing of that stock, and whosomever were kin to tho Poles that ought it, it hurt not for it was lawfully bought and sold; and he never claimed it after.

Item, I am in purpose to take assize against them at this

[1] Near Fritton in Suffolk, another of Fastolf's manors.
[2] Paston's title to Caldecott was contested by Gilbert Debenham and his son. See p. 85, n. 4.
[3] See p. 80, n. 3.
[4] Manuscript *hem*, evidently a slip; cf. p. 67, n. 2.
[5] See p. 112, n. 1.   [6] See no. 14.

time, and ell I would have sent thither straight by a letter of attorney to enter in my name. Nevertheless ye be a gentlewoman, and it is worship for you to comfort your tenants; wherefore I would ye might ride to Hellesdon and Drayton and Sparham,[1] and tarry at Drayton and speak with them, and bid them hold with their old master till I come, and that ye have sent me word but late, wherefore ye may have none answer yet. And inform them as I ha writ to you with, and say openly it is a shame that any man should set any lord on so untrue a matter, and special a priest, and let them weet as soon as I am come home I shall see them. . . .

God keep you. Writ the Thursday before Saint Peter's Day. . . .

60. *Richard Calle to John Paston I*

1465, 10 July

Pleaseth it your mastership to wit of the rule and disposition of the Master Philip and the bailiff of Cossey, with other of my Lord of Suffolk's men.[2] On Monday last past at afternoon [they] were at Hellesdon, with the number of 300 men, for to have entered, notwithstanding they said that they came not for to enter; but without doubt, an they had been strong enough for us they would have entered, and that we understand now; but we, knowing of their coming, (had)[3] purveyed so for them that we were strong enough. We had 60 men within the place, and guns and such ordnance so that if they had set

1 A manor some 13 miles north-west of Norwich, inherited by Margaret Paston from her father. She gave it to John III on his marriage; see no. 125.

2 See nos. 57 and 58.

3 Manuscript *and*, probably by confusion of constructions.

upon us they had be destroyed. And there my mistress
was within, and my master Sir John, and hath gotten him
as great worship for that day as any gentleman might do,
and so is it reported of their party and in all Norwich. . . .

And now my Lord's of Suffolk men come from Claxton[1]
to Norwich, and face us and fray upon us daily. There fell
upon me before Swain door twelve of his men, eight of
them in harness, and there they would have mischiefed
me; and the sheriff letted them, and other, and they make
their avaunt where that I may be gotten I shall die, and
so they lie in await for to mischief me, Daubeney, and
Wykes; and so I dare not ride out alone without a man
with me.

And I understand there is comen an *oyer determiner*[2] to
inquire of all riots, and my Lord of Suffolk and Yelverton
be commissioners; and so they say as many of us as can
be taken shall be indicted and hanged forthwith, and so
the people here are dismayed with this rule. Wherefore
that it like you to send word how my mistress shall do at
Hellesdon, and we in all other matters; and whether ye
will that we fetch again the flock of Hellesdon, for they
are now driven to Cawston[3] and there go they on the
heath. And my Lord of Suffolk will be at Drayton on
Lammas Day, and keep the court there; wherefore ye
must seek some remedy for it, or ell it will not do well.

If my Lord of Norfolk[4] would come, he should make all
well, for they fear him above all things; for it is noised
here that my Lord of Norfolk hath taken party in this
matter, and all the country is glad of it, saying that if he

[1] About 8 miles south-east of Norwich near the south bank of the
Yare. The manor belonged to Alice, dowager Duchess of Suffolk.

[2] A **writ** of *oyer and terminer*, a commission empowering justices to
hear and determine indictments on specified offences such as riot and
treason.

[3] Cawston Heath, some 4 miles south-west of Aylsham.

[4] See p. 98, n. 1.

come they will wholly go with him. And meseemeth it
were well done to move my lord in it, though ye should
give him the profits of Hellesdon and Drayton for the
keeping, and some money beside; for ye must seek some
other remedy than ye do, or ell in my conceit it shall go
to the devil and be destroyed, and that in right short time.
And therefore, at the reverence of God, take some appointment with Master Yelverton, such as ye think should
most hurt.

I beseech you to pardon me of my writing, for I have
pity to see the tribulation that my mistress hath here, and
all your friends, &c. Almighty Jesu preserve and keep you.
Written the Wednesday next Saint Thomas' Day.[1]

Your poor servant and bedeman, RICHARD CALLE

61. *Margaret Paston to John Paston I*

1465, 12 July

Right worshipful husband, I recommend me to you, praying you heartily that ye will seek a mean that your servants may be in peace, for they be daily in fear of their
lives. The Duke of Suffolk's men threaten daily Daubeney,
Wykes, and Richard Calle that wheresoever they may get
them they should die, and affrays have been made on
Richard Calle this week so that he was in great jeopardy
at Norwich among them.[2] And great affrays have been
made upon me and my fellowship here on Monday last
past, of which Richard Calle telleth me that he hath sent
you word of in writing more plainly than I may do at this
time, but I shall inform you more plainly hereafter.

---

[1] Since Lammas (1 August) is not far ahead, this must be the
Translation of St. Thomas of Canterbury, 7 July, which in 1465 fell
on a Sunday. For another use of this feast in dating, see p. 110, n. 4.

[2] See no. 60. This letter is in Calle's hand.

I suppose there shall be great labour again you and your servants at the assizes and sessions here, wherefore meseemeth, saving your better advice, it were well do that ye should speak with the justices ere they come here; and if ye will that I complain to them or to any other, if God fortune me life and health, I will do as ye advise me to do, for in good faith I have been simply entreated among them. And what with sickness and trouble that I have had, I am brought right low and weak; but to my power I will do as I can or may in your matters.

The Duke of Suffolk and both the Duchesses[1] shall come to Claxton[2] this day, as I am informed, and this next week he shall be at Cossey. Whether he will come farther hitherward or not I wot not yet. It is said that he should come hither,[3] and yet his men said here on Monday that he claimed no title to this place. They said their coming was but to take out such riotous people as was here within this place, and such as were the King's felons and indicted and outlawed men. Nevertheless they would show no warrants whereby to take none such, though there had been such here. I suppose if they might have come in peaceably they would have made another cause of their coming.

When all was do and they should depart, Harleston[4] and other desired me that I should come and see mine old lady,[5] and sue to my lord, and if anything were amiss it should be amended. I said if I should sue for any remedy that I should sue farther, and let the King and all the lords of this land to have knowledge what hath be done to us, if so were that the Duke would maintain that hath

---

[1] The Duke's mother Alice and his wife Elizabeth.

[2] See p. 121, n. 1.

[3] This use of 'should' indicates that the writer does not vouch for the accuracy of the prediction reported; for a similar modal use in the past tense see p. 18, n. 3.   [4] See p. 116, n. 2.

[5] The dowager Duchess; see p. 93, n. 3.

be done to us by his servants, if ye would give me leave. I pray you send me word if ye will that I make any complaint to the Duke or the Duchess; for, as it is told me, they know not the plainness that hath been done in such things as hath been done in their names.

I should write much more to you but for lack of leisure. . . . The Trinity have you in keeping. Written the Friday next after Saint Thomas.

By your M. P.

62. *John Paston I to Margaret Paston*

1465, 13 July

I recommend me to you, and thank you of your labour and business with the unruly fellowship that came before you on Monday last past, whereof I heard report by John Hobbs; and in good faith ye acquit you right well and discreetly, and heartily to your worship and mine and to the shame of your adversaries. And I am well content that ye avowed that ye kept possession at Drayton, and so would do, wherefore I pray you make your word good if ye may, and at the least let mine adversaries not have it in peace if ye may.

John Hobbs telleth me that ye be sickly, which me liketh not to hear; praying you heartily that ye take what may do your ease and spare not, and in any wise take no thought ne too much labour for these matters, ne set it not so to your heart that ye fare the worse for it.

And as for the matter, so they overcome you not with force ne boasting I shall have the manor surelier to me and mine than the Duke shall have Cossey, doubt ye not. And in case I come not home within three weeks, I pray you come to me; and Wykes hath promised to keep the place in your absence. Nevertheless, when ye come set it in such rule as ye seem best and most sure, both for Caister and Hellesdon, if the war hold. In case ye have peace send me word.

As for that it is desired I should show my title and evidence to the Duke, methinketh he had evil counsel to enter in upon me trusting I should show him evidence. An ye seem it may do you good or ease, let my Lord of Norwich[1] weet that the manor of Drayton was a merchant's of London called John Hellesdon long ere any of the Poles, that the said Duke cometh of, were born to any land in Norfolk or Suffolk; and if they were at that time born to no land, how may the said Duke claim Drayton by that pedigree? As for the said John Hellesdon, he was a poor man born, and from him the said manor descended to Alice his daughter, whose estate I have; and I suppose the said Duke cometh not of them.

Item, as for the pedigree of the said Duke, he is son to William Pole, Duke of Suffolk, son to Michael Pole, Earl of Suffolk, son to Michael Pole, the first Earl of Suffolk of the Poles, made by King Richard sith my father was born; and the said first Michael was son to one William Pole of Hull, which was a worshipful man grow by fortune of the world, and he was first a merchant, and after a knight, and after he was made banneret. And if any of these had the manor of Drayton, I will lose £100 so that any person for the Duke will be bound in as much to prove the contrary; and I wot well the said Duke's council will not claim the said manor by the title of the father of the said William Pole. And what the father of the said William was, as by the pedigree made in the said last Duke's father's days, I know right well, whereof I informed Harry Butler[2] to tell my old Lady of Suffolk, because he is of her

---

[1] The Bishop; see p. 62, n. 5.

[2] Henry Butler, recorder of Coventry from 1455 until his death in

council; and more will I not tell in this matter but if I be desired or compelled.

Item, let my Lord of Norwich weet that it is not profitable, nor the common weal of gentlemen, that any gentleman should be compelled by an entry of a lord to show his evidence or title to his land; nor I nill not begin that example ne thraldom of gentlemen nor of other. It is good a lord take sad counsel ere he begin any such matter.

And as for the Poles that ought Drayton, if there were 100 of them living, as there is none, yet have they no title to the said manor.

God keep you. Writ the Saturday, &c.

Your JOHN PASTON

I pray you be as merry with your fellowship as ye can. . . .

I send you home writ of replevin for the sheep and the horse that were take, and advise you let the writs be delivered before my Lord of Norwich, and good record; and if ye may make men with force to take the cattle again by warrant of replevin, spare not rather than fail.

63. *Margaret Paston to John Paston I*

1465, 7 August

Right worshipful husband, I recommend me to you. Please it you to weet that I sent on Lammas Day to Drayton Thomas Bond[1] and Sir James Gloys to hold the court in your name and to claim your title; for I could get none other body to keep the court, nor that would go thither, but the said Thomas Bond, because I suppose

1490. He was long J.P. for Warwickshire and on many commissions, and often M.P. for Coventry. He acted as lawyer for John, Duke of Suffolk, in 1468. [1] See p. 60, n. 4.

they were afeared of the people that should be there of
the Duke of Suffolk's part. The said Thomas and James,
as the Duke of Suffolk's men—that is to say Harleston,
the parson of Sall Master Philip, and William Yelverton[1]
the which was steward, with a 60 persons or more by
estimation, and the tenants of the same town, some of
them having rusty pole-axes and bills—camen into the
manor yard to keep the court, met with them and told
them that they were comen to keep the court in your
name and to claim your title. Wherefore the said Harleston,
without any more words or occasion given of your men,
committed the said Thomas Bond to the keeping of the
new bailie of Drayton, William Docket, saying that he
should go to my lord and do his errand himself, notwithstanding that Sir James did the errands to them and had
the words; wherefore they took the said Thomas without
occasion. They would have made the said Thomas to
have had the words, and the said James told them that he
had them, because he was the more peaceable man; whom
afterward they bade avoid, and sithen led forth Thomas
Bond to Cossey, and bound his arms behind him with
whipcord like a thief, and should have led him forth to
the Duke of Suffolk nor had be that I had spoken with the
judges in the morn ere they yede to the shire house, and
informed them of such riots and assaults as they had made
upon me and my men; the bailie of Cossey and all the
Duke of Suffolk's council being there present and all the
learned men of Norfolk, and William Jenney[2] and m⟨uch⟩
people of the country, the judge calling the bailie of
Cossey before them all and gave him a great rebuke,
commanding the sheriff to see what people they had
gathered at Drayton; which came after to Hellesdon to
see the people there, with which [peo]ple he held him

[1] Evidently a son of the judge; see p. 49, n. 5 and p. 171.
[2] See p. 80, n. 5.

well content. And fro thence he rode to Drayton to see there people which were avoided ere he came, and there he desired to have delivered the said Thomas Bond to him; and they excused them and said they had sent him to the Duke of Suffolk. Notwithstanding afterward they sent him to Norwich to him, desiring him that he should deliver him not without he made a fine because he troubled the King's leet . . .; and the judges were greatly ⟨. . .⟩ with the Duke's men, and forthwith commanded the sheriff to deliver the said Bond without any fine m[ade], saying that he ought none to make. And in good faith I found the judges right gentle and forbearable to me in my matters, notwithstanding the Duke's council had made their complaint to them ere I came in their worst wise, noising us of great gathering of people and many riotous things done by me and your men; and after I informed the judges of their untruth and of their guiding, and of our guiding in like wise, and after the judges understood the truth he gave the bailie of Cossey before me and many other a passing great rebuke, saying without he amended his condition and governance they w⟨ould⟩ inform the King and help that he should be punished. . . .

Item, on Tuesday next coming shall the sessions of the peace be at Walsingham. What shall be do there I wot not yet, for as for any indictments that we should labour against them, it is but waste work, for the sheriff nor the jurors will nothing do against them. . . .

Item, as for the price of malt, it is fallen here sore, for it is worth but 2*s.* 8*d.* a quarter at Yarmouth.

Item, as for your wool, I may sell a stone for 40*d.* so that I will give half year day of payment. I pray you send me word how I shall do in this matter and in all other, &c. And God keep you. Written in haste the Wednesday next after Lammas Day.

Your M. PASTON

64. *Margaret Paston to John Paston I*

1465, 18 August

Right worshipful husband, I recommend me to you.
Please it you to wit that I received a letter from you sent
by Laurence Rede on Friday last past, whereby I understand that ye had no tidings from me at that time that
your letter was written; whereof I marvel, for I sent you
a letter by Chittock's son, that is prentice in London, the
which was delivered to him upon the Thursday next after
Lammas Day,[1] and he promised to ride forward the same
day and that ye should have it as hastily as he might after
his coming to London; and in the said letter was of the
demeaning at the assizes at Norwich and of divers other
matters. I pray you send me word if ye have it.

As for the replevins, Richard Calle saith he hath sent
you an answer of them, and also the copies of them. As
for the high sheriff, he demeaned him right well here to
me and he said to me as for the replevins he would ask
counsel of learned men what he might do therein, and as
largely as he might do therein, or in any other matter
touching you, saving himself harmless, he will do for you
and for yours that he might do.

The cause that I wrote to you none ere than I did after
the sessions was because that Yelverton held sessions at
Dereham and Walsingham the next week after the assises,
and to have knowledge what labour that was made there
and to have sent you word thereof. There was great
labour made by the bailie of Cossey and other for to have
indicted your men both at Dereham and at Walsingham,
but I purveyed a mean that their purpose was letted at
those two times. . . .

Item, as for my coming to you, if it please you that I

---

[1] This is no. 63.

come I hope I shall purvey so for all things ere I come that it shall be safe enough, by the grace of God, till I come again. But at the reverence of God, if ye may, purvey a mean that ye may come home yourself, for that shall be most profitable to you; for men cut large thongs here of other men's leather.[1]

I shall write to you again as hastily as I may. God have you in his keeping. Written in haste at Hellesdon the Sunday next after the Assumption of Our Lady.[2]

Item, my cousin Elisabeth Clere[3] is at Ormesby,[4] and your mother purposeth to be at her place at Caister this week, for the pestilence is so fervent in Norwich that they dare no lenger abide there, so God help. Methinketh by my mother that she would right fain that ye did well and that ye might speed right well in your matters, and methinketh by my cousin Clere that she would fain have your good will and that she hath sworn right faithfully to me that there shall no default be found in her, nor not hath be if the truth might be understand, as she hopeth it shall be hereafter. She saith there is no man alive that she hath put her trust in so much as she hath done in you. She saith she wot well such language as hath be reported to you of her, otherwise than she hath deserved, causeth you to be otherwise to her than ye should be. She had to me this language weeping, and told me of divers other things the which ye shall have knowledge of hereafter.

By yours, M. P.

---

[1] Forms of this proverb are found from about 1300.
[2] 15 August.
[3] See p. 22, n. 2.
[4] About 5 miles north of Yarmouth, and about 2 from Caister.

65. *John Paston III to Margaret Paston*

1465, 14 September[1]

After all humble and most due recommendation, as lowly as I can I beseech you of your blessing. Please it you to wit that I have sent to my father to have an answer of such matters as I have sent to him for in haste, of which matters the greatest of substance is for the manor of Cotton; beseeching you to remember him of the same matter, that I may have an answer in the most hasty wise. Also I pray you that mine aunt Poynings[2] may be desired to send me an answer of such matters as she wotteth of by him that shall bring me an answer of the matter of Cotton.

Also, mother, I beseech you that there may be purveyed some mean that I might have sent me home by the same messenger two pair hose, one pair black and another pair of russet, which be ready made for me at the hosier's with the crooked back next to the Black Friars'[3] gate within Ludgate; John Pamping[4] knoweth him well enow, I suppose. An the black hose be paid for he will send me the russet unpaid for. I beseech you that this gear be not forgot, for I have not an whole hose for to do on. I trow they shall cost both pair 8*s*.

My brother and my sister Anne and all the garrison of Hellesdon fare well, blessed be God, and recommend them to you every one. I pray you visit the Rood of North

---

[1] This letter is addressed 'To my mistress Margaret Paston be this delivered in haste at London', so that it evidently falls between no. 64, when Margaret wrote of going to London, and no. 66, when she had been.

[2] Elizabeth Paston, now widow of Robert Poynings. See p. 47, n. 2.

[3] The great Dominican priory, begun in 1279, was immediately east of Ludgate.

[4] See p. 80, n. 1.

Door,[1] and St. Saviour at Bermondsey[2] among, while ye
abide in London, and let my sister Margery go with you
to pray to them that she may have a good husband ere
she come home again.

And now I pray you send us some tidings, as ye were
wont to command me. And the Holy Trinity have you
in keeping, and my fair mistress of the Fleet.[3] Written at
Norwich on Holy Rood Day.[4]

Your son and lowly servant, J. PASTON the youngest

66. *John Paston I to Margaret Paston*

1465, 20 September

Mine own dear sovereign lady,[5] I recommend me to you,
and thank you of the great cheer that ye made me here,
to my great cost and charge and labour. No more at this
time, but that I pray you ye will send me hither two eln
of worsted for doublets to hap me this cold winter, and
that ye inquire where William Paston bought his tippet
of fine worsted, which is almost like silk. And if that be
much finer than that ye should buy me after 7 or 8*s*., then
buy me a quarter and the nail thereof for collars, though

[1] The ancient crucifix at the north door of St. Paul's Cathedral
was a famous object of pilgrimage. It was said to be the work of
Joseph of Arimathea, and was believed to work miracles.

[2] The Abbey of St. Saviour in Bermondsey, founded as a Cluniac
priory in 1082 (according to its annals) and made an abbey in 1399,
is commemorated by the modern Abbey Street. It possessed a rood said
to work miracles, claimed by the annals to have been found near the
Thames in 1117. The abbey at this time was very influential; the
widows of both Henry V and Edward IV died there.

[3] See p. 87, n. 2. John I was in prison, as no. 66 shows.

[4] The Exaltation of the Cross, 14 September.

[5] This mode of address, a commonplace of the terminology of
courtly love, is found nowhere else in the letters of the usually prosaic
John I.

it be dearer than the tother; for I would make my doublet all worsted, for worship of Norfolk,[1] rather than like Gunnor's[2] doublet.

Item, as for the matter of the £180 asked by my Lady of Bedford[3] for the manor of West Thurrock,[4] whereas Sir Thomas Howes saith that he hath no writing thereof but that Sir John Fastolf purchased the said manor and paid certain money in earnest, and afterward granted his bargain to the Duke of Bedford, and so the money that he took was for the money that he had paid, peradventure Sir Thomas hath writing thereof and knoweth it not; for if there be any such money paid upon any bargain he shall find it in Kirtling's books, that was Sir John Fastolf's receiver,[5] and it was about such time as the Duke of Bedford was last in England, which as it is told me was the eighth year of King Harry the Fifth or the eighth year of King Harry the Sixth,[6] and the sum that he paid for the said bargain was 300 mark. Also he shall find the twenty-second year of King Harry or thereabout,[7] in the accounts of one of Fastolf's receivers at London, that there was take of Sir Thomas Tyrell[8] and of the Duchess of Exeter

---

[1] Worsted takes its name from the town, now only a village, of Worstead, 3 miles south-east of North Walsham in Norfolk. The name of the cloth is recorded from the thirteenth century.

[2] See p. 15, n. 3.

[3] Jacquette of Luxembourg, second wife of John, Duke of Bedford (see p. 45, n. 2). After his death the Duchess married (before 23 March 1437) Sir Richard Wydevill, who was made Lord Rivers (see p. 56, n. 2), and their daughter Elizabeth became Edward IV's queen.

[4] In Essex, 20 miles east of London.

[5] John Kirtling, clerk, was Fastolf's receiver-general until July 1436—'my right trusty chaplain and servant domestical thirty winter and more'.

[6] The eighth year of Henry VI must have been meant, for Bedford last visited England in 1433–4; but in fact that was 11–12 Henry VI.

[7] 22 Henry VI was 1 September 1443–31 August 1444.

[8] Of East Thorndon (now Horndon), Essex, a soldier who had

that was wife to Sir Lewis John,[1] farmers of the said manor, certain money for repayment of part of the said 300 mark. Also he shall find in years after that, or in that year or thereabouts, that Sir John Fastolf received money of my Lord Rivers that now is,[2] by the name of Richard Wydevill, for his own debt due to Sir John Fastolf; wherefore if Sir Thomas be true to his master let him do his devoir to make that Worcester,[3] which is uphold by him with the dead's goods, to be true to his master, or else it is time for Sir Thomas to forsake him and help to punish him, or men must say that Sir Thomas is not true. And moreover let Sir Thomas examine what he can find in this matter that I sent him word of, which matter he shall find in the said receiver's books if he list to seek it.

Item, weet of him whether any writ of subpoena came to him therefor.

Item, I send him a bill which Edmond Carville for Robert Otley asketh of Sir John Fastolf, of which, as well as of a bill asked by one Frances for making of houses in Southwark,[4] let send hither an answer; for an I could answer them I would not send to him. And that Richard Calle, or whosoever go to him of my servants, let him understand that such brethels as be about Sir Thomas ween that I sent to him for matters of mine own and that I might not forbear his friendship, which is nothing so; and if it lay in his power to avail me £100, as he cannot avail me 20s., I would [not] send to him while he is coupled

served in France under Bedford, and afterwards until 1450. He was often J.P. and M.P. for Essex, sheriff 1440–1 and 1444–5, and was knighted in 1447–8. He died in 1476.

[1] Anne, daughter of the third Earl of Salisbury, married as her second husband Sir Lewis John of West Horndon, Essex. After his death in 1442 she married John Holand, third Duke of Exeter, as his third wife. He died in 1447, she in 1457.

[2] See p. 133, n. 3.   [3] See p. 44, n. 2.

[4] Fastolf held land in Southwark to the value of £102 per annum.

with such fellowship as he is. Wherefore he that should speak with him were best to meet with him at a sudden, where he were with some substantial man that could inform him what were his truth to do in the matter, for it grieveth me full evil to send often to him till he be of a sadder demeaning.

Item, if any answer I shall have in this matter I must have it at the farthest by that time as James Gresham[1] shall come hither; for that time must I give an answer, and if ye can get it ere, send it.

Item, if the said Sir Thomas be of good disposition, let him be spoke to that he beware of the evidence of Dedham.[2] He told John Pamping that he had bid John Russe deliver them me, and now he is turned and keepeth them still, and I doubt lest by such as be about him it shall rather be apaired than amended. For this twenty winter hath Worcester used to buy and sell evidence; an ye can get them of him, take them.

Item, get you copies of the inquisitions take before Master John Selot[3] for Drayton church, and before Edmond Clere,[4] escheator, if any such were taken; and also inquire what day Edmund Clere sat, for he is bound to put in the inquisition within a month after it is taken in the pain of £40.

Item, I sent you word ye should inquire what bribes or rewards Edmund Clere took of outlawed men in Norfolk, or any other false prats that he hath done. Doubt ye not he will not answer of half the good that he hath taken of outlawed men, if it were well inquired. James Gresham shall con tell where ye shall best inquire, and such as ye can know send me justly word.

Item, that the expense made by Daubeney for mine

[1] See p. 12, n. 3.   [2] See p. 74, n. 4.
[3] An official of the diocese of Norwich.
[4] See p. 41, n. 5.

household be made up, and that Daubeney be charged with all such sums as ye or I or Richard Calle have paid for him, and ye for that he hath paid for you. As for that I paid of that was Daubeney's charge, I took Calle thereof a bill, whereof let Calle send me again a copy. And also send me the copy of the bill of your receipts which ye have home with you from hence, and that Daubeney and ye and Calle send me a remembrance of the expenses of mine household and yours, your children and the college[1] and all other foreign payments. . . .

Also the maltster must answer of the increase of malting, according to old accounts of Fastolf's, and if Calle cannot understand that well then ye may send for Barker,[2] and ye shall, when ye have made all thing read(y) to the account, for 40d. have him a day or two, and he can as good skill thereon as Bernard can on his shield.[3] Notwithstanding the precedents of Fastolf's accounts can tell it as well as he, if there were any man could understand it. . . .

Item, let your son John the younger weet that I received his letters and bills for the thing that he searched for, under his seal. Nevertheless I remember I fail certain writings and scrows on paper and parchment touching the same matter, and in especial of the obits and buryings of divers of the Poles,[4] and of one Pole was a wool merchant paid great customs to the King; but I am in doubt whether your said son looked not justly there in the box and bag that I bade him, or else that it were meddled with some other scrows in the same, or else that it be in a bag of like matters in my red chest at Caister; wherefore if he may easily come thereto, without tarrying of his greater matters, let him essay.

Item, he shall find a deed how my father was enfeoffed

---

[1] See p. 106, n. 1.   [2] See p. 109, n. 5.
[3] This simile is used again by John II in 1473 (see p. 221). The point of it is obscure.   [4] Cf. no. 62.

in the manor of Hellesdon and Drayton which I suppose be among the evidence of Hellesdon, where I will have the copy.

Item, he sendeth me word that there is a priest called ¹ told Sir William Barbour² that he hath special evidence longing to the manor of Drayton, and that he said he would I had them, but he would speak with me. Wherefore I pray you let Sir William Barbour, with some other friend of yours, go speak with the said priest and to find the mean that he would deliver you the said evidence, and in case he will not deliver them till [he] hath spoke with me, then desire ye with some friend of yours to see them, and if ye seem they be likely desire him to come to London with one of my men, and to pay for his costs to come hither to me, and quit his labour. But an ye may, take them of him, though ye appoint to take them him again or else to agree with him therefor. Nevertheless, in the beginning let him be told that ye marvel that he should have any evidence of that manor, for ye heard me say that I had all the evidence of the manor; and let this be do betimes and wittily, and beware that this be not do of a subtlety, to feel whether that I would inquire after any evidence, for failing.

Item, I pray you remember and read often my bill of errands and this letter till it be done, and all such matters or articles as ye speed hereof, cross them that ye may know them from tho that be not sped; and send me answer of your good speed. . . . Though I write right certainly, if ye look them lightly and see them seld they shall soon be forgot.³

¹ Name left blank, space for about fifteen letters.
² Evidently a priest dependent on the Pastons. In 1468 John II wrote that he 'would full fain be discharged' of him and another.
³ 'Seldom seen, soon forgotten' is a proverb found often from the mid-fourteenth century onwards.

Item, I shall tell you a tale:
Pamping and I have picked your mail
and taken out pieces five,
for upon trust of Calle's promise we may soon un-
    thrive.
And if Calle bring us hither twenty pound
ye shall have your pieces again good and round;
or else, if he will not pay you the value of the pieces
    there,
to the post do nail his ear,
or else do him some other sorrow,
for I will no more in his default borrow;
and but if the receiving of my livelode be better plied
he shall [have] Christ's curse and mine clean tried.
And look ye be merry and take no thought,
for this rhyme is cunningly wrought.
My Lord Percy[1] and all this house
recommend them to you, dog, cat, and mouse,
and wish ye had be here still,
for they say ye are a good gill.
No more to you at this time,
but God him save that made this rhyme.
Writ the Vigil of St. Matthew.

                    By your true and trusty husband, J. P.

67. *Margaret Paston to John Paston I*

                                    1465, 27 September

Right worshipful husband, I recommend me to you, desiring heartily to hear of your welfare, thanking you of your
great cheer that ye made me and of the cost that ye did
on me. Ye did more cost than mine will was that ye should

---

[1] Henry Percy, son and heir of the Earl of Northumberland who
was killed at Towton in 1461 and attainted (see no. 35 and p. 68, n. 1).

do, but that it pleased you to do so; God give me grace to do that may please you.

Please it you to wit that on Friday after mine departing from you I was at Sudbury, and spake with the sheriff,[1] and Richard Calle took him the two writs. And he brake them, and Richard hath the copies of them; and he said he would send the writs to his undersheriff, and a letter therewith charging him that he should do therein as largely as he ought to do. And I and Richard informed him of the demeaning of his undersheriff, how partial he had be with the other party both in that matter and also for the actions being in the shire; and he was nothing well pleased of the demeaning of his undersheriff, and he hath written to him that he should be indifferent for both parties according to the law, both for that matte(r) and for all other. What the undersheriff will do therein I wot ne'er, for he is not yet spoken with.

Item, as for Cotton, I entered into the place as on Sunday last was, and there I abode till on Wednesday last past. I have left there John Paston the younger, Wykes, and other twelve men, for to receive the profits of the manor; and against the day of keeping of the court I hope there shall be more to strength them if it need. John Paston hath be with mine Lord of Norfolk[2] sith we entered, and desired his good lordship to strength him with his household men and other if need be, and he hath promised he would do so. And I sent Richard Calle on Tuesday to Knyvett[3] desiring him that he would send to his bailie and tenants at Mendlesham that they should be

---

[1] Cressener. See p. 41, n. 1.
[2] John III had been in Norfolk's service; see nos. 50 and 69.
[3] The Knyvetts of Buckenham Castle were a well-known Suffolk family with property in Suffolk also. John Knyvett, esq., succeeded to his father's lands in 1459, and died in 1490 seised, *inter alia*, of Mendlesham, Suffolk, which is about 2 miles east of Cotton. Cf. p. 72, n. 2.

ready to come to John Paston when he sent for them; and
he sent a man of his forthwith, charging them in any wise
that they should do so. And he sent me word by Richard,
and his son also, if we were not strong enough that either
he or his son, or both if need were, would come with such
fellowship as they could get about them, and that they
would do as faithfully as they could for you, both in that
matter and in all other.

Item, on Saturday last was Jenney[1] did warn a court at
Caldecott to be hold there in his name as on Tuesday last
was, and Debenham[2] did charge another court there the
Sunday next after, to be hold there the same Tuesday in
his name. And Daubeney had knowledge thereof, and he
did send on Sunday at night to your elder son for to have
some men fro thence, and so he sent Wykes and Berney[3]
to him on Monday in the morning. And as soon as they
were come to Caister they sent for men there in the
country, and so they got them into a three score men;
and Daubeney and Wykes and Berney rode to Caldecott
the same Monday at night with their fellowship, and
there kept them privy in the place so that none of all the
tenants knew them there save Rising's wife and her
household till the Tuesday at 10 of the clock. And then
Sir Thomas Brews,[4] Debenham the father and the knight
his son, Jenney, Micklefield, young Jermyn[5] and young
Jerningham[6] and the bailie of Mutford,[7] with other to the
number of a three score persons come fro the sessions at
Beccles the which they had kept there on the day before,

1 See p. 80, n. 5.
2 See p. 119, n. 2.
3 See p. 106, n. 4.
4 See p. 232, n. 3.
5 Presumably the son of John Jermyn; see p. 29, n. 4.
6 See p. 73, n. 6.
7 About 4 miles east-south-east of Beccles in Suffolk. The manor
belonged to the Duke of Suffolk.

came to St. Olave's[1] and there they tarried and dined; and when they had dined Sir Gilbert Debenham came to Caldecott with twenty horse for to wit what fellowship there was in the place. And then Wykes espied them coming, and he and Berney and two with them rode out to a spoke with them; and when Sir Gilbert espied them coming he and his fellowship fled and rode again to St. Olave's. And then they sent young Jerningham and the bailie of Mutford to your men, letting them weet that the justice of the peace were come down with Debenham and Jenney to see that the peace should be kept, and that they should enter and keep the court in peaceable wise. And your men answered and said that they knew no man was possessed therein, nor had no right therein, but ye; and so in your name and in your right they said they would keep it. And so they yede again with this answer, and were put from their purpose that day; and all the tenants' beasts were put fro Caldecott fee, and shall be till other remedy may be had. Your men would not keep there a court that day because it was warned by the tother part, but we will do warn a court and keep it, I hope, in haste. Ye will laugh for to hear all the process of the demeaning there, which were too long to write at this time. . . .

Item, I have do spoke for your worsted,[2] but ye may not have it till Hallowmas,[3] and then I am promised ye shall have as fine as may be made. Richard Calle shall bring it up with him.

Written the Friday next before Michaelmas Day.

---

[1] Caldecott Hall is about 8 miles north-east of Beccles, and St. Olave's is on the way, about 1½ miles short of it.

[2] See no. 66, first paragraph.

[3] All Saints' Day, 1 November.

68. *John Paston III to John Paston I*

1465, 3 October

After all humble and most due recommendation, as lowly
as I can I beseech you of your blessing. Please it you to
have knowledge that as on Sunday[1] next before Michaelmas Day as my mother came fro London ward she came
homeward by Cotton, and she sent for me to Hellesdon
to come to her thither; and so I have been in the place
ever sithen. And as soon as Michaelmas Day was past
I began to distrain the tenants, and gathered some silver,
as much I trow as will pay for our costs. And yet I keep
here right a good fellowship, and more were promised me
which that came not to me, whereby I was near deceived;
for when Debenham heard say how that I began to gather
silver he raised many men within one day and an half, to
the number of three hundred men, as I was credibly
ascertained by a yeoman of the chamber of my lord's[2]
that conneth me good will, which yeoman as soon as he
had seen their fellowship rode straight to my lord and
informed him of it. And also he informed my lord how
that I had gathered another great fellowship, which fellowship he named more than we were by one hundred and
an half and yet more; and he said unto my lord and my
lady and to their council that without that my lord took
a direction in the matter that there were like to be do
great harm on both our parties, which were a great disworship to my lord, considering how that he taketh us
both for his men and so we be known well enow; upon
which information and disworship to my lord, that twain
of his men should debate so near him,[3] contrary to the

---

[1] 22 September.
[2] The Duke of Norfolk.
[3] Cotton is some 14 miles from Framlingham, the Duke's seat.

King's peace, considered of my lord and my lady and their council, my lord sent for me and Sir Gilbert Debenham to come to him to Framlingham both. And as it fortuned well, my mother came to me to Cotton not half an hour before that the messenger came to me fro my lord, which was late upon Tuesday last past at night; and the next day on the morning I rode to my lord to Framlingham, and so did Sir Gilbert also. And as soon as we were come we were sent for to come to my lord; and when we came to my lord he desired of us both that we should neither gather no fellowship, but such men as we had gathered that we should send them home again, and that the court should be continued into the time that my lord, or such as he would assign, had spoke both with you and Yelverton and Jenney, and that one indifferent man chosen by us both should be assigned to keep the place into the time that ye and they were spoke with. And then I answe[re]d my lord and said how that at that time I had my master within the manor of Cotton, which was my mother, and into the time that I had spoke with her I could give none answer. And so my lord sent Richard Fulmerston, bearer hereof, to my mother this day for an answer; which answer he should bring to my lord to London, for my lord rode to London ward as yesterday, and the sooner because he trusted to have a good end of this matter and all other betwixt you, which he taketh for a great worship to him ward and a great advantage both an he could bring this matter about, for then he would trust to have your service all, which were to him great treasure and advantage. And this was the answer that my mother and I gave him, that at the instance of my lord and my lady we would do thus much as for to put the court in continuance and no more to receive of the profits of the manor than we had and had distressed for, till into the time that she and I had word again fro my lord and you, if so were that they would neither make entries nor distrain the tenants nor keep no court more than we would do.

And we told Richard Fulmerston that this my mother and I did at the instance and great request of my lord, because my lord intended peace, which reasonably we would not be against; and yet we said we knew well that we should have no thank of you when ye knew of it, without it were because we did it at my lord's instance. But before this answer we had received as much silver, full nigh, as Richard Calle sent us books of for to gather it by. And as for the possession of the place, we told him that we would keep it, and Sir Gilbert agreed so that Yelverton and Jenney would do the same; for it was time for him to say so for my lord told him that he would set him fast by the feet else, to be sure of him that he should make none insurrections into the time that my lord came again fro London. I ween, and so doth my mother both, that this appointment was made in good time, for I was deceived of better than an hundred men and an half that I had promise of to have come to me when I sent for them—this promise had I before that I sent to you the last letter the day after St. Michael.

Jenney heard say how that I keeped Cotton, and he rode to Nacton[1] and there held a court and received the profits of the manor. I beseech you that I may have knowledge in haste fro you how ye will that I be demeaned in this matter and in all other, and I shall apply me to fulfil your intent in them to my power, by the grace of God, whom I beseech have you in guiding and send you your heart's desire. Written at Hempnall Hall in Cotton the Thursday next before St. Faith.[2]

My mother recommendeth her to you and prayeth you to hold her excused that she writeth not to you at this time, for she may have no leisure.

---

[1] See p. 81, n. 2.   [2] 6 October.

The bearer hereof shall inform you whether Jenney will agree to this appointment or not. I think he dare do none otherwise.

Your son and lowly servant, JOHN PASTON

69. *The Duke of Norfolk to John Paston III*

1465, 12 October

The Duke of Norfolk

Right well-beloved servant, I greet you heartily well, certifying that we shall be at full age[1] on Friday next coming. Wherefore, well counselled by the lords of our council and other of our council that ye, one of our servants of household, with other, be with us at London on Friday or Saturday next coming at the furthest, to accompany us then to our worship; for we shall have then livery[2] of our lands and offices. And that ye fail us not as ye will have our good lordship in time coming; and also that ye do warn our feed men and servants, such as be nigh to you, that they be there then in our livery. I writen the 12 day of October.

NORFOLK

[1] The inquisition *post mortem* on John Mowbray, third Duke of Norfolk, who died in 1461, states that his son John was 17 years of age on St. Luke's Day (18 October) of that year. He would thus be 21 on Friday, 18 October 1465.

[2] The legal handing over of possessions to a tenant in chief of the Crown, for which an heir had to wait until he was of full age. This practice ceased in 1660. (The word is used at the end of the letter in its commoner sense of 'servant's uniform'.)

70. *Margaret Paston to John Paston I*

1465, 17 October

On Tuesday[1] in the morwen was John Butler, otherwise called John Palmer, and Davy Arnald your cook, and William Malthouse of Aylsham[2] taken at Hellesdon by the bailiff of Eye,[3] called Bottesforth, and led for[th] to Cossey, and there they keep them yet without any warrant or authority of justice of peace. And they say they will carry them forth to Eye prison, and as many as they may get more of your men and tenants that they may know that owe you good will or hath be to you ward, they be threat to be slain or prisoned.

The Duke[4] came to Norwich on Tuesday at 10 of clock with the number of five hundred men, and he sent after the mayor[5] and alderman with the sheriffs, desiring them in the King's name that they should take an inquirance of the constables of every ward within the city what men should a go on your party to have holpen or succoured your men at any time of these gatherings, and if any they could find, that they should take and arrest him and correct him, and also certify him the names on Wednesday by 8 of clock; which the mayor did, and will do anything that he may for him and his. And hereupon the mayor hath arrested one that was with me called Robert Lovegold, brazier, and threat him that he shall be hanged by the neck; wherefore I would that there might come down a writ to remove him, if ye think it be to do. He was not with me not save that Harleston and other made the assault upon me (at)[6] Lammas; he is right good and faithful unto you, and therefore I would he had help. I have

---

[1] 15 October.   [2] Twelve miles north of Norwich.
[3] In Suffolk, one of the Duke of Suffolk's manors.
[4] Suffolk.   [5] Ellis; see p. 61, n. 5.
[6] Manuscript &.

none man at this time to await upon me that dare be avowed but Little John. William Naunton[1] is here with me, but he dare not been avowed for he is sore threat. It is told me the old lady and the Duke is set fervently again us by the information of Harleston, the bailie of Cossey, and Andrews,[2] and Dogget the bailie's son, and such other false shrews the which would have this matter borne out for their own pleasure, the which causeth an evil noise in this country and other places.

And as for Sir John Heveningham,[3] Sir John Wingfield,[4] and other worshipful men, [they] been made but their dogbolts, the which I suppose will turn them to disworship hereafter. I spake with Sir John Heveningham and informed him with the truth of the matter, and of all our demeaning at Drayton; and he said he would that all thing were well, and that he would inform my lord as I said to him, but Harleston had all the words and the rule with the Duke here, and after his advice and Doctor Aleyn's[5] he was advised here at this time.

The lodge[6] and the remnant of your place was beaten

[1] See no. 43.

[2] John Andrews, esq., of Baylham, Suffolk, a lawyer of Lincoln's Inn and an associate of John Heydon (see p. 15, n. 2). He was M.P. several times, J.P. for Suffolk 1445–60 and for Norfolk in 1463.

[3] Son of the Sir John of nos. 13 and 19. He was knighted by 1463, was J.P. for Suffolk 1465–97 and for Norfolk 1471–4, and sheriff in 1469–70. The Duke of Norfolk made him one of his captains at the siege of Caister in 1469 (see nos. 87–90). He died in 1499.

[4] Of Letheringham, Suffolk; sheriff 1454–5 and 1471–2, J.P. often, and M.P. in 1478. He died in 1481.

[5] John Aleyn, LL.D., of Norwich and Cambridge, appears in several letters as an opponent of Fastolf and a friend of Heydon. He was clerk of the signet to the Queen in 1465, lieutenant for the Constable in judging overseas cases in 1469 and 1475–6, and several times M.P. He died in 1490.

[6] The ruins of a brick-built lodge still exist near Drayton (see H. D. Barnes, 'Drayton Lodge', *Norfolk Archaeology*, xxix (1946), 228–37). But though it seems to be of the fifteenth century and is indeed

down on Tuesday and Wednesday, and the Duke rode
on Wednesday to Drayton, and so for[th] to Cossey, while
the lodge at Hellesdon was in the beating down. And this
night at midnight Thomas Sleaford, Green, Porter, and
the bailie of Eye and other had a cart and fetched away
feather beds and all the stuff that was left at the parson's
and Thomas Water's house to be kept of ours. I shall send
you bills hereafter as near as I may what stuff we have
forborne.

I pray you send me word how ye will that I be demeaned, whether ye will that [I] abide at Caister or come
to you to London. I have no leisure to write no more.
God have you in his keeping. Written at Norwich on
St. Luke's Even.

M. P.

71. *Margaret Paston to John Paston I*

1465, 27 October

Right worshipful husband, I recommend me to you. . . .
I was at Hellesdon upon Thursday last past and saw the
place there, and in good faith there will no creature think
how foul and horribly it is arrayed but if they saw it.
There cometh much people daily to wonder thereupon,
both of Norwich and of other places, and they speak
shamefully thereof. The Duke had be better than £1000
that it had never be done, and ye have the more good will
of the people that it is so foul done. And they made your
tenants of Hellesdon and Drayton, with other, to help to
break down the walls of the place and the lodge both,

probably one of the lodges known to have been built at Hellesdon and
Drayton by Fastolf, it is likely to be the lodge of the Drayton rather
than the Hellesdon manor, and so not the building destroyed on this
occasion.

God knoweth full evil against their wills, but that they durst none otherwise don for fear. I have spoken with your tenants of Hellesdon and Drayton both, and put them in comfort as well as I can.

The Duke's men ransacked the church and bare away all the good that was left there, both of ours and of the tenants, and left not so much but that they stood upon the high altar and ransacked the images, and took away such as they might find, and put away the parson out of the church till they had done, and ransacked every man's house in the town five or six times. And the chief masters of robbing was the bailie of Eye, the bailie of Stradbroke,[1] Thomas Sleaford; and Sleaford was the chief robber of the church, and he hath most of the robbery next the bailie of Eye. And as for lead, brass, pewter, iron, doors, gates, and other stuff of the house, men of Cossey and Cawston have it, and that they might not carry they have hewn it asunder in the most despitous wise. If it might be, I would some men of worship might be sent from the King to see how it is, both there and at the lodge, ere than any snows come, that they may make report of the truth; else it shall not mow be seen so plainly as it may now.

And at the reverence of God, speed your matters now, for it is too horrible a cost and trouble that we have now daily, and must have till it be otherwise; and your men dare not go about to gather up your livelode, and we keep here daily more than three hundred persons for savation of us and the place, for in very truth an the place had not be keeped strong the Duke had come hither.

The mayor of Norwich did arrest the bailie of Normand's,[2] Lovegold,[3] Gregory Cordoner, and Bartholomew

---

[1] In Suffolk, 6 miles east of Eye.

[2] This manor does not appear elsewhere in the letters. It may be Norman's Spital manor in Norwich.   [3] See no. 70.

Fuller withouten any authority save only he saith that he hath a commandment of the Duke to do so; and he will not let them out of prison till he had surety for each of them in £80 for to answer to such matters as the Duke and his council will put against them at any time that they be called, and so will he do to other, as many as he may get, that owe you any good will. And also the mayor would have had them sworn that they should never be against the Duke nor none of his, which they would not do in no wise. . . .

At the reverence of God, if any worshipful and profitable mean may be take in your matters, forsake it not in eschewing of our trouble and great costs and charges that we have and may grow hereafter. It is thought here that if my Lord of Norfolk would take upon him for you, and that he may have a commission for to inquire of such riots and robberies as hath be done to you and other in this country, that then all the country will await upon him and serve your intent, for the people loveth and dreadeth him more than any other lord except the King and my Lord of Warwick,[1] &c. . . .

And I pray you heartily send me word how ye do and how ye speed in your matters in haste, and that I may have knowledge how your sons doth. I came home this night late, and shall be here till I hear other tidings from you. Wykes came home upon Saturday, but he met not with your sons. God have you in his keeping, and send us good tidings from you. Written in haste upon the Saint Simon and Jude's Even.

By yours, M. P.

[1] Cf. p. 56, n. 2.

72. *Agnes Paston to John Paston I*

Perhaps 1465, 29 October[1]

Son, I greet you well, and let you weet that, forasmuch as your brother Clement letteth me weet that ye desire faithfully my blessing, that blessing that I prayed your father to give you the last day that ever he spake, and the blessing of all saints under heaven, and mine, mote come to you all days and times. And think verily none other but that ye have it, and shall have it with that that I find you kind and willing to the weal of your father's soul, and to the welfare of your brethren.

By my counsel, dispose yourself as much as ye may to have less to do in the world. Your father said, 'In little business lieth much rest.' This world is but a thorough-fare, and full of woe;[2] and when we depart therefro, right naught [we] bear with us but our good deeds and ill. And there knoweth no man how soon God will clepe him, and therefore it is good for every creature to be ready. Whom God visiteth, him he loveth.[3]

And as for your brethren, they will I know certainly labouren all that in them lieth for you.

[1] The date of this letter is uncertain, but it would best suit an attempt by John I to heal the strained relations with his mother mentioned by Margaret in the penultimate paragraph of no. 57 (p. 115).

[2] Both these maxims appear in Chaucer: *Truth* (the theme of which, 'Flee fro the press', is close to Agnes's meaning here), l. 10, 'Gret reste stant in litel besinesse'; *Knight's Tale*, A. 2847, 'This world nys but a thurghfare ful of wo.' Skelton also used the former, and Lydgate wrote a poem with the latter as refrain.

[3] These remarks are ultimately derived from passages such as 1 Tim. vi. 7, 'For we brought nothing into this world, and it is certain we can carry nothing out'; Matt. xxiv. 44, 'Therefore be ye also ready: for in such an hour as ye think not the Son of man cometh'; Heb. xii. 6, 'For whom the Lord loveth he chasteneth'. These are quoted in the words of the 1611 Bible. The Wyclif and other early versions differ, but not in the same way as these passages.

Our Lord have you in his blessed keeping, body and soul. Written at Norwich the 29 day of October.

By your mother, A. P.

73. *J. Payn to John Paston I*

1465

Right honourable and my right entirely beloved master, I recommend me unto you with all manner of due reverence in the most lowly wise, as me ought to do, evermore desiring to hear of your worshipful state, prosperity, and welfare, the which I beseech God of his abundant grace increase and maintain to his most pleasance and to your heart's desire.

Pleaseth it your good and gracious mastership tenderly to consider the great losses and hurts that your poor petitioner hath and hath ihad ever sith the commons of Kent came to the Black Heath,[1] and that is at fifteen year past, whereas my master Sir John Fastolf, knight, that is your testator, commanded your beseecher to take a man, and two of the best horse that were in his stable, with him to ride to the commons of Kent to get the articles[2] that they came for. And so I did; and also soon as I came to the Black Heath the captain made the commons to take me. And for the savation of my master's horse I made

---

[1] The insurrection of the commons of Kent under Jack Cade, the 'captain of Kent', began at the end of May 1450. The rebels camped on Blackheath on 11 June, retired on 18 June before a royal force, but defeated it and returned to Blackheath by 29 June. They seized Southwark on 2 July, so Payn's mission to them was probably on 30 June.

[2] The complaints of the rebels were mainly against the abuses and incompetence of government which had lost France, though they demanded also the abolition of the Statute of Labourers which governed the wages and movement of workmen.

my fellow to ride away with the two horses, and I was
brought forthwith before the captain of Kent. And the
captain demanded me what was my cause of coming
thither, and why that I made my fellow to steal away
with the horse. And I said that I came thither to cheer
with my wife's brethren and other that were mine allies
and gossips of mine that were present there. And then
was there one there and said to the captain that I was one
of Sir John Fastolf's men, and the two horse were Sir John
Fastolf's; and then the captain let cry treason upon me
throughout all the field, and brought me at four parts of
the field with a herald of the Duke of Exeter[1] before me
in the Duke's coat of arms, making four *Oyes* at four parts of
the field, proclaiming openly by the said herald that I was
sent thither for to espy their puissance and their habiliments of war, fro the greatest traitor that was in England
or in France, as the said captain made proclamation at
that time, fro one Sir John Fastolf, knight, the which
minished all the garrisons of Normandy and Mans and
Maine, the which was the cause of the losing of all the
King's title and right of an heritance that he had beyond
sea. And moreover he said that the said Sir John Fastolf
had furnished his place with the old soldiers of Normandy
and habiliments of war to destroy the commons of Kent
when that they came to Southwark.[2] And therefore he
said plainly that I should lose my head.

And so forthwith I was taken and led to the captain's
tent, and an axe and a block was brought forth to have
smitten off mine head. And then my master Poynings,
your brother,[3] with other of my friends, came and letted
the captain, and said plainly that there should die a

---

[1] See p. 68, n. 6. The herald had presumably been captured by the
rebels when they attacked the royal army.

[2] For Fastolf's property in Southwark see no. 29 and p. 134, n. 4.

[3] See p. 47, n. 2. Poynings was Cade's 'carver and sword-bearer'.

hundred or two that in case be that I died. And so by that
mean my life was saved at that time, and then I was sworn
to the captain and to the commons that I should go to
Southwark and array me in the best wise that I could, and
come again to them to help them; and so I got th'articles
and brought them to my master, and that cost me more
amongst the commons that day than 27s.

Whereupon I came to my master Fastolf and brought
him th'articles and informed him of all the matter, and
counselled him to put away all his habiliments of war and
the old soldiers; and so he did, and went himself to the
Tower and all his meinie with him but Betts and one
Matthew Brain; and had not I been,[1] the commons would
have burned his place and all his tenantries, wherethrough
it cost me of mine own proper goods at that time more
than 6 mark in meat and drink. And notwithstanding the
captain that same time let take me at the White Hart in
Southwark, and there commanded Lovelace to despoil me
out of mine array, and so he did; and there he took a fine
gown of musterdevillers furred with fine beavers, and a
pair of brigandines covered with blue velvet and gilt nail,
with leg harness, the value of the gown and the
brigandines £8.

Item, the captain sent certain of his meinie to my chamber in your rents, and there brake up my chest and took
away an obligation of mine that was due unto me of £36
by a priest of Paul's, and another obligation of a knight of
£10, and my purse with five rings of gold and 17s. 6d.
of gold and silver, and a harness complete of the touch of
Milan,[2] and a gown of fine perse blue furred with martens,
and two gowns, one furred with bogey and another lined
with frieze; and there would have smitten off mine head

---

[1] The medieval idiom for 'had it not been for me'.
[2] Milan was famous for its armour, and the 'touch' is its standard
of quality.

when that they had despoiled me at the White Hart. And there my master Poynings and my friends saved me, and so I was put up till at night that the battle was at London Bridge.[1] And then at the night the captain put me out into the battle at the bridge, and there I was wounded and hurt nearhand to death, and there I was six hours in the battle and might never come out thereof. And four times before that time I was carried about through Kent and Sussex, and there they would have smitten off my head.

And in Kent, there as my wife dwelled, they took away all our goods movable that we had, and there would have hanged my wife and five of my children, and left her no more good but her kirtle and her smock. And anon after that hurling the Bishop Ross[2] apeached me to the Queen, and so I was arrested by the Queen's commandment into the Marshalsea,[3] and there was in right great duress and fear of mine life, and was threatened to have been hanged, draw, and quartered; and so [they] would have made me to have peached my master Fastolf of treason. And because that I would not they had me up to Westminster and there would have sent me to the coal-house[4] at Windsor, but my wife's and a cousin of mine own that were yeomen of the Crown,[5] they went to the King and got grace and a charter of pardon.

Par le vostre, PAYN J.

---

[1] The night of 5 June.

[2] Richard Clerk, Bishop of Ross, co. Cork, was suffragan in the diocese of London 1434–41 and also in Canterbury until his death in 1465, acting for the Archbishop in many things. He was Rector of Shoreham in Kent.

[3] This prison, in Southwark, first appears in history when it was attacked by Wat Tyler's rebels in 1381. It was closed in 1842.

[4] This appears to be the first mention of the use of coal-stores as prisons, which Bishop Bonner made notorious during the Marian persecutions.

[5] Officials of the Royal Household, first mentioned in 1450.

74. *Margaret Paston to John Paston* II

1466, 29 October[1]

I greet you well, and send you God's blessing and mine, desiring you to send me word how that ye speed in your matters, for I think right long till I hear tidings from you. And in all wise I advise you for to beware that ye keep wisely your writings that been of charge, that it come not in their hands that may hurt you hereafter. Your father, whom God assoil, in his trouble season set more by his writings and evidence than he did by any of his movable goods. Remember that if tho were had from you ye could never get no mo such as tho be for your part, &c.

Item, I would ye should take heed that if any process come out against me, or against any of tho that were indicted afore the coroner, that I might have knowledge thereof, and to purvey a remedy therefor.

Item, as for you father's will, I would ye should take right good counsel therein, as I am informed it may be proved though no man take no charge this twelvemonth. Ye may have a letter of ministration to such as ye will, and minister the goods and take no charge. I advise you that ye in no wise take no charge thereof till ye know more than ye do yet, for ye may verily know, by that your Uncle Will[2] said to you and to me, that they will lay the charge upon you and me for mo things than is expressed in your father's will, the which should be too great for you or me to bear. But as for me, I will not be too hasty to take it upon me, I ensure you.

And at the reverence of God, speed your matters so this term that we may be in rest hereafter, and let not for no

---

[1] John Paston I had died in May 1466.
[2] William Paston II. From this time there was ill-feeling between him and John II, and later John III, over inheritance.

labour for the season; and remember the great cost and charge that we have had hithertoward, and think verily it may not long endure. Ye know what ye left when ye were last at home, and wit it verily, there is no more in this country to bear out no charge with. I advise you to inquire wisely if ye can get any more there as ye be, for else by my faith I fear else it will not be well with us; and send me word in haste how ye do, and whether ye have your last deeds that ye failed, for plainly they are not in this country.

It is told me in counsel that Richard Calle hath near conquered your Uncle Will with fair promise touching his livelode and other things, the which should prevail him greatly, as he saith. Beware of him and of his fellow, by mine advice.

God send you good speed in all your matters. Written at Caister the morn next after Simon and Jude, where as I would not be at this time but for your sake, so mote I thee.

                                        By your mother

75. *John Paston III to John Paston II*

                                        1467, 27 January

Sir, liketh it you to wit that this day my mother sent me your letters, whereby I understand, blessed be God, all thing standeth in good way. Also I understand by your letter sent to my mother and me that ye would have your livelode gathered as hastily as we might do it. Sir, as to that, an other folk do no worse their devoir in gathering of other manors than we have done in Caister, I trust to God that ye shall not be long unpaid; for this day we had in the last comb of barley that any man oweth in Caister town, notwithstanding Hugh Austin and his men hath cracked many a great word in the time that it hath been in gathering. And twenty comb Hugh Austin's men had done carted, ready for to have led it to Yarmouth; and when I heard thereof I let slip a certain of whelps, that gave the cart and the barley such a turn that it was fain to take covert in your bakehouse cistern at Caister Hall; and it was wet within an hour after that it came home, and is nigh ready to make of good malt ale, ho ho![1]

William Yelverton hath been at Guton,[2] and hath set in a new bailie there and hath distrained the tenants, and hath given them day till Candlemas[3] to pay such money as he asketh of them. Also the said Yelverton hath been at Saxthorpe,[4] and hath distrained the farmer there and taken of him surety to pay him. And this day the said Yelverton and eight men with him, with jacks and trussing doublets all the fellowship of them, were ready to ride; and one of the same fellowship told to a man that saw them all ready that they should ride to take a distress in certain manors that were Sir John Fastolf's. Wherefore I suppose verily that they be to Guton and Saxthorpe, wherefore tomorrow I purpose to send Daubeney thither to wit what they do, and to command the tenants and farmers that they pay no money to nobody but to you.

John Grey, otherwise called John de Les Bay, and John Burgess, they be Yelverton's captains, and they ride and go daily, as well in Norwich as in other places of yours and other men's in the country, in their trussing doublets, with bombards and cannons and chassevilains, and do whatsoever they will in the country. There dare no poor

---

[1] These last words seem likely to be the refrain of a drinking song.
[2] In Brandiston, 10 miles north-west of Norwich; a manor of Fastolf's, claimed by Yelverton.   [3] 2 February.
[4] About 6 miles north of Brandiston. The manor of Loundhall in Saxthorpe was Fastolf's.

man displease them, for whatsoever they do with their swords they make it law, and they take distresses out of men's houses, horse or cattle or what they will, though it be not on that fee that they ask the duty for.

Wherefore methinks with easy means ye might get a privy seal of the King to be directed to the mayor of Norwich,[1] as for the town of Norwich, and for the country another privy seal direct to me and to some other good fellow (Sir William Calthorp,[2] for he hateth Grey) for to arrest the said fellows for such riot, and to bring them to the next prison, there to abide without bail till such time as the King sendeth otherwise word; and they that the privy seal shall be direct to to be charged upon pain of their allegiance to execute the King's commandment. And this done, I warrant your livelode that my lord[3] deals not with shall be gathered peaceably. As to that livelode that my lord claims, I shall do my devoir, our lodging kept,[4] to take as much profit of it as I may, by the grace of God, whom I pray send you the accomplishment of your heart's desire, and other poor fools theirs. All my fellowship are merry and well at ease, blessed be God, and recommendeth them all unto you. Written the Tuesday next before Candlemas.

Your brother, J. P.

I pray you let me and my fellowship not be long without tidings from you.

1 Roger Best, grocer, was sheriff of Norwich in 1460 and mayor in 1467 and 1472.

2 See p. 66, n. 8.

3 The Duke of Norfolk, who claimed Caister and seized it in 1469.

4 Apparently 'provided we can keep our lodging there'.

76. *John Paston II to John Paston III*

1467, March

Right worshipful and verily well-beloved brother, I heartily commend me to you, thanking you of your labour and diligence that ye have in keeping of my place at Caister so surely, both with your heart and mind, to your great business and trouble; and I againward have had so little leisure that I have not sped but few of your errands, nor cannot before this time.

As for my Lady Boleyn's[1] disposition to you wards, I cannot in no wise find her agreeable that ye should have her daughter, for all the privy means that I could make; insomuch I had so little comfort by all the means that I could make that I disdained in mine own person to common with her therein. Nevertheless I understand that she saith, 'What if he and she can agree, I will not let it; but I will never advise her thereto in no wise.' And upon Tuesday last past she rode home into Norfolk; wherefore as ye think ye may find the mean to speak with her yourself, for without that, in mine conceit, it will not be. And as for Crosby, I understand not that there is no marriage concluded between them; nevertheless there is great language that it is like to be.

Ye be personable, and peradventure your being once in the sight of the maid, and a little discovering of your good will to her, binding her to keep it secret, and that ye can find in your heart, with some comfort of her, to find the mean to bring such a matter about as shall be her pleasure and yours, but that this ye cannot do without

---

[1] Anne, daughter of Lord Hoo and Hastings and widow of Geoffrey Boleyn, citizen and mercer of London, who was sheriff of London in 1446–7, M.P. 1449, alderman 1452–63, and mayor 1457–8. He died in 1463. They had three surviving daughters, of whom the youngest, Alice, is concerned here; see no. 77.

some comfort of her in no wise—. And bear yourself as lowly to the mother as ye list, but to the maid not too lowly, nor that ye be too glad to speed nor too sorry to fail. And I always shall be your herald, both here if she come hither and at home when I come home, which I hope hastily within forty days at the farthest.

My mother hath a letter which can tell you more, and ye may let Daubeney see it.

JOHN PASTON, K.

I suppose an ye call well upon R. Calle he shall purvey you money. I have written to him enow.

77. *John Paston III to John Paston II*

1467, April

Sir, pleaseth you to weet that my mother and I commoned this day with Friar Mowth[1] to understand what his saying shall be in the court when he cometh up to London, which is in this wise. He saith at such time as he had shriven Master Brackley,[2] and houselled him both, he let him weet that he was informed by divers persons that the said Master Brackley ought for to be in great conscience for such things as he had done and said, and caused my father, whom God assoil, for to do and say also, in proving of Sir John Fastolf's will; to whom the said Master Brackley answered thus again: 'I am right glad that it cometh to you in mind for to move me with this matter in discharging of my conscience against God', saying furthermore to the said Friar Mowth, by the way

---

[1] Friar John Mowth, or Molet, LL.D., was Prior of the Cathedral Priory, Norwich, from 1453 to 1471.

[2] See p. 33, n. 2.

that his soul should to,[1] that the will that my father put
into the court was as verily Sir John Fastolf's will as it
was true that he should once die.

This was said on the Sunday, when the said Brackley
weened to have died. Then on the Monday he revived
again, and was well amended till on the Wednesday. And
on the Wednesday he sickened again, supposing to have
died forthwith; and in his sickness he called Friar Mowth,
which was confessor unto him, of his own motion, saying
unto him in this wise: 'Sir, whereas of your own motion
ye moved me the last day to tell you after my conscience
of Sir John Fastolf's will likewise as I knew, and now of
mine own motion and in discharging of my soul, for I
know well that I may not escape but that I must die in
haste, wherefore I desire you that [ye] will report after
my death that I took it upon my soul at my dying that
that will that John Paston put in to be proved was Sir
John Fastolf's will.' And the said Brackley died the same
Wednesday.

And whereas ye would have had Richard Calle to you
as on Sunday last past, it was this Tuesday ere I had your
letter; and whereas it pleaseth you for to wish me at
Eltham[2] at the tourney for the good sight that was there,
by troth I had liefer see you once in Caister Hall than to
see as many kings tourney as might be betwixt Eltham
and London.

And, sir, whereas it liketh you to desire to have know-

[1] The infinitive of a verb of motion is often omitted after an
auxiliary, so that this could mean 'should *go* to'; but with *way* this is
scarcely appropriate, and *to* may be miswritten for *te*, 'draw', 'go'; but
the latest records of this are about 1450, and it is more likely to be a
mistake for *take* or *go*.

[2] In Kent, about 8 miles from London, where there was a royal
palace. A letter from John II, now known only from a copy made in
1674, had reported a tournament there in which he had taken part on
the King's side, and said, 'I would that you had been there and seen it.'

ledge how that I have done with the Lady Boleyn, by my
faith I have done nor spoken naught in that matter, nor
not will do till time that ye come home, an ye come not
this seven year. Notwithstanding, the Lady Boleyn was
in Norwich in the week after Eastern, fro the Saturday till
the Wednesday, and Heydon's wife and Mistress Alice
both;[1] and I was at Caister and wist not of it. Her men
said that she had none other errand to the town but for
to sport her; but so God help me I suppose that she
weened I would have been in Norwich for to have seen
her daughter.

I beseech you with all my heart, hie you home, though
ye should tarry but a day; for I promise you your folk
think that ye have forgotten them, and the most part of
them must depart at Whitsuntide[2] at the farthest, they
will no lenger abide.

Your J. PASTON

And as for R. Calle, we cannot get half a quarter the
money that we pay for the bare household, beside men's
wages. Daube[3] nor I may no more without coinage.

78. *John Paston III to John Paston II*

Probably 1468, March[4]

Sir, &c., it is so that without ye have hasty reparation
done at Caister ye be like to have double cost in haste,

---

[1] Anne, second daughter of Geoffrey Boleyn, had married Henry,
son of John Heydon; see p. 15, n. 2. Alice was the youngest daughter.
She in fact married John Fortescue, esq., nephew of the chief justice
of the same name.

[2] Whit Sunday was 17 May.   [3] Daubeney.

[4] The date is evidently earlier than Norfolk's seizure of Caister in
September 1469 (see no. 90). A reference, in the part not printed, to
releases suggests that it is not long after Fastolf's executors released

for the rain hath so moisted the walls in many places that they may not tile the houses till the walls be repaired; or else ye shall have double cost for to untile your houses again at such time as ye shall amend the walls. And if it be not do this year many of the walls will lie in the moat ere long to. Ye know the feebleness of the utter court of old. John Pamping hath had home to Caister as good as 10,000 tile fro the place at Yarmouth, and it were pity that the tile were lost, and the lenger that it lieth unlaid the worse it will be. I have this day bespoke as much lime as will serve for the tile, wherefore I pray you remember the cost of the workmanship and purvey the money by o mean or other, what shift soever ye make. . . .

I pray you hie you home hastily and see your own profit yourself. Pamping and I shall clout up your houses as we may with the money that we have till more come, but ye should do better yourself. I pray read this bill once on a day till ye have sped these matters written herein. Though it be to your pain to labour them, remember your profit.

No more, &c., but God keep you this Lent fro lollardy of flesh. Written at Norwich the Tuesday next after that I departed fro you.

J. P.

79. *John Paston III to Margaret Paston*

1468, 8 July[1]

Right reverend and worshipful mother, I recommend me unto you as humbly as I can think, desiring most heartily

Caister to John II, which they did in January 1468. Ash Wednesday in that year was 2 March.

[1] The two eldest Paston brothers went to Bruges in 1468 in the retinue of Princess Margaret, youngest sister of Edward IV, for her marriage to Charles the Bold, Duke of Burgundy. John II perhaps

to hear of your welfare and heart's ease, which I pray God send you as hastily as any heart can think. Please it you to wit that at the making of this bill my brother and I and all our fellowship were in good heal, blessed be God.

As for the guiding here in this country, it is as worshipful as all the world can devise it, and there were never Englishmen had so good cheer out of England that ever I heard of.

As for tidings here, but if it be of the feast, I can none send you, saving that my Lady Margaret was married on Sunday last past[1] at a town that is called The Damme, three mile out of Bruges, at 5 of the clock in the morning. And she was brought the same day to Bruges to her dinner, and there she was received as worshipfully as all the world could devise, as with procession with ladies and lords best beseen of any people that ever I saw or heard of.[2] And many pageants were played in her way in Bruges to her welcoming, the best that ever I saw. And the same Sunday my lord the Bastard[3] took upon him to answer 24 knights and gentlemen within eight days at jousts of peace;[4] and when that they were answered they 24 and himself should tourney with other 25 the next day after, which is on Monday next coming. And they that have jousted with him into this day have been as richly beseen, and himself

owed his place to his acquaintance with Lord Scales (see p. 166), John III to the Duchess of Norfolk, who was the Princess's chief lady attendant on this occasion.

[1] 3 July.

[2] The court of Burgundy at this time was recognized as the most sumptuous and most elaborately ceremonious in western Europe. Its master of ceremonies, Olivier de la Marche, included in his memoirs a long account of the festivities he organized on this occasion.

[3] Anthony, Count de la Roche, natural son of Philip the Good, Duke of Burgundy, Charles's father. He had negotiated the marriage in London the previous year.

[4] A tournament in which the contestants used blunt weapons so that injuries would not be fatal.

also, as cloth of gold and silk and silver and goldsmiths' work might make them; for of such gear, and gold and pearl and stones, they of the Duke's court, neither gentlemen nor gentlewomen, they want none; for without that they have it by wishes, by my troth I heard never of so great plenty as here is.

This day my Lord Scales[1] jousted with a lord of this country, but not with the Bastard, for they made promise at London that none of them both should never deal with other in arms. But the Bastard was one of the lords that brought the Lord Scales into the field; and of misfortune an horse struck my lord Bastard on the leg, and hath hurt him so sore that I can think he shall be of no power to accomplish up his arms,[2] and that is great pity, for by my troth I trow God made never a more worshipful knight.

And as for the Duke's court, as of lords, ladies, and gentlewomen, knights, squires, and gentlemen, I heard never of none like to it save King Arthur's court. By my troth, I have no wit nor remembrance to write to you half the worship that is here; but that lacketh, as it cometh to mind I shall tell you when I come home, which I trust to God shall not be long to; for we depart out of Bruges homeward on Tuesday next coming, and all folk that came with my Lady of Burgoyne out of England, except such as shall abide here still with her, which I wot well shall be but few.

We depart the sooner, for the Duke hath word that the French king is purposed to make war upon him hastily, and that he is within four or five days' journey of Bruges; and the Duke rideth on Tuesday next coming forward to meet with him. God give him good speed, and all his, for by my troth they are the goodliest fellowship that ever I came among, and best can behave them, and most like gentlemen.

[1] See p. 59, n. 2.   [2] 'complete his series of jousts'.

Other tidings have we none here, but that the Duke of Somerset[1] and all his band departed well beseen out of Bruges a day before that my lady the Duchess came thither; and they say here that he is to Queen Margaret that was,[2] and shall no more come here again nor be holpen by the Duke.

No more, but I beseech you of your blessing as lowly as I can, which I beseech you forget not to give me every day once; and, mother, I beseech you that ye will be good mistress to my little man, and to see that he go to school.[3] I sent my cousin Daubeney 5*s*. by Calle's man for to buy for him such gear as he needeth. And, mother, I pray you this bill may recommend me to my sisters both,[4] and to the master,[5] my cousin Daubeney, Sir James,[6] Sir John Still,[7] and to pray him to be good master to little Jack and to learn him well; and I pray you that this bill may recommend me to all your folks and my well-willers.

And I pray God send you your heart's desire. Written at Bruges the Friday next after Saint Thomas.[8]

Your son and humble servant, J. PASTON the younger

[1] Edmund Beaufort, brother of the third duke, who was beheaded in 1464 and attainted (see p. 68, n. 5). He was pardoned in 1464 for acts against Edward IV and went to join Queen Margaret, who had been in exile in Burgundy and France since 1463. He later fought at Barnet and at Tewkesbury, where he was captured and executed on 6 May 1471.

[2] Queen Margaret lived at St. Mihiel in her father's duchy of Bar in eastern France.

[3] The identity of this child is obscure. John III was not married until 1477.

[4] Margery, who married Richard Calle in the following year, and Anne, who married William Yelverton in 1477.

[5] Of the college of priests and poor men; see p. 106, n. 1.

[6] Gloys.

[7] Another priest in the service of the Pastons, from this date until 1472; see p. 80, n. 1, and no. 92.

[8] 7 July, as in nos. 56 and 60.

80. *William Ebsham[1] to John Paston II*

1468, between July and end of October

My most worshipful and most special master, with all my
service most lowly I recommend [me] unto your good
mastership, beseeching you most tenderly to see me
somewhat rewarded for my labour in the great book[2]
which I write unto your said good mastership. I have
oftentimes written to Pamping, according to your desire,
to inform you how I have laboured in writings for you;
and I see well he speaks not to your mastership of it, and
God knoweth I lie in sanctuary[3] at great cost and amongst
right unreasonable askers. I moved this matter to Sir
Thomas[4] late, and he told me he would move your
mastership therein; which Sir Thomas desired me to
remember well what I have had in money at sundry times
of hym, which parcels here ensuen:

[1] Ebsham, who also spelt his name *Ebesham* (common medieval
forms of *Epsom*), was a professional scribe employed occasionally by
John Paston II and his uncle William. Many manuscripts written by
him have been identified; see A. I. Doyle, *Rylands Library Bulletin*,
xxxix (1957), 298–325.
  This letter was written after the brothers returned from Bruges
('beyond the sea'), but before the end of October 1468 because a later
account records the receipt of 3s. 4d. on 30 Oct. of that year.
[2] The later account shows that the 'great book' contained treatises
on the coronation, knighthood, war, challenges, and acts of arms, as
well as 'Othea Pistill', presumably Scrope's translation of the *Épître
d'Othéa* (see p. 22, n. 3), and *De Regimine Principum*, a verse rendering
by Lydgate and Burgh of the pseudo-Aristotelian *Secreta Secretorum*.
The greater part of the book survives as British Museum MS.
Lansdowne 285.
[3] Ebsham seems to have taken sanctuary in Westminster from his
creditors.
[4] The account shows this to be Thomas Lyndes, a priest who
appears under the Pastons' patronage from 1466 until his death; see
p. 191, n. 2.

First I had for half the writing of the privy seal[1]
    with Pamping   8d.

Also for the writing of the privy seal another
    time in paper   20d.

Also for the writing of the little book of physic   20d.

Also for the great witnesses[2] at the first time,
    eight in parchment   10s.

Also Calle set me a writing at time of your
    being beyond the sea: two times the privy
    seal in paper, and then clearly in parchment;
    and three of the said greatest witnesses
    written then again, for which he promised
    me 10s. for my labour, for I watched greatly
    for it, he desired it so hastily, and gave me
    but   4s. 8d.

                                caret[3]   5s. 4d.

So, sir, if it please you, there is owing me for
    two quires' writing of the said witness in
    paper, which quires contain 28 leaves, after
    14 leaves in a quire, 2d. a leaf   3s.

Item, for 7 quires of the great book wherein is
    contained the third part of the said book,
    I wot well, for the remnant will be in five   14s.

And in especial I beseech you to send me for alms one
of your old gowns, which will countervail much of the
premisses, I wot well. And I shall be yours while I live,
and at your commandment. I have great mister of it, God

---

    [1] This is probably the licence, dated 10 September 1464, granted
by Edward IV to John Paston I authorizing him to found a college
at Caister according to Fastolf's will (see p. 106, n. 1). A copy of it,
written in Pamping's hand, survives in the British Museum.
    [2] The witnesses called during the inquiry into the title to Fastolf's
property, held in 1464–7; cf. no. 77. Copies of such evidence exist in
the Bodleian and the British Museum, but not in Ebsham's hand.
    [3] 'is wanting'.

knows, whom I beseech preserve you from all adversity. I am somewhat acquainted with it.

Your very man, W. EBSHAM

81. *John Paston II to John Paston III*

1468, 9 November

Right well-beloved brother, I commend me to you, letting you weet that I have waged, for to help you and Daubeney to keep the place at Caister, four well-assured and true men to do all manner of thing, what that they be desired to do, in safeguard or enforcing of the said place. And moreover they be proved men, and cunning in the war and in feats of arms, and they can well shoot both guns and crossbows, and amend and string them, and devise bulwarks or any things that should be a strength to the place; and they will, as need is, keep watch and ward. They be sad and well-advised men, saving one of them which is bald and called William Penny, which is as good a man as goeth on the earth saving a little he will, as I understand, be a little cupshotten; but yet he is no brawler, but full of courtesy, much upon James Halman. The other three be named Peryn Sale, John Chapman, Robert Jackson; saving that as yet they have none harness comen, but when it cometh i(t) shall be sent to you. And in the meanwhile I pray you and Daubeney to purvey them some. Also a couple of beds they must needs have, which I pray you by the help of my mother to purvey for them till that I come home to you.

Ye shall find them gentlemanly, comfortable fellows, and that they will and dare abide by their tackling. And if ye understand that any assault should be towards, I send you these men because that men of the country there

about you should be fraid for fear of loss of their goods;
wherefore if there were any such thing towards, I would
ye took of men of the country but few, and that they were
well-assured men; for else they might discourage all the
remnant.

And as for any writing fro the King, he hath promised
that there shall come none; and if there do his unwares,[1]
your answer may be this, how the King hath said, and so
to delay them till I may have word, and I shall soon purvey
a remedy. . . .

I shall send you tiding of other things in haste, with the
grace of God, who, &c. Written on Wednesday next before
Saint Martin.[2]

JOHN PASTON . . .

82. *Margaret Paston to John Paston II*

1469, 12 March[3]

I greet you well and send you God's blessing and mine,
desiring you to recommend me to my brother William[4]
and to common with him and your council in such matters
as I write to you, that there may be purveyed by some
writing fro the King that my Lord of Norfolk and his
council cease of the waste that they don in your lordships
and in especial at Hainford,[5] for they have felled all the
wood and this week they will carry it away, and let run
the waters and take all the fish.

And Sir William Yelverton and his son William, John

---

[1] 'without his knowledge'. [2] 11 November.
[3] The year appears from the Duke of Norfolk's interference with
lands claimed by Paston. Yelverton, Howes, and Jenney, as feoffees of
Sir John Fastolf, enfeoffed Norfolk in the manor of Caister and others
in October 1468. [4] William Paston II.
[5] A Fastolf manor, 6 miles north of Norwich.

Grey, and Burgess, Will Yelverton men, have been at
Guton and taken distresses, and without that they will
pay them they shall not set out no plough to till their
land.... They set not so soon a plough out at their gates
but there is a fellowship ready to take it. And they ride
with spears and lancegays like men of war, so that the
said tenants arn afeared to keep their own houses. Therefore purvey a ready remedy, or ell ye lose the tenants'
hearts and ye greatly hurt; for it is great pity to hear the
sweamful and pitous complaints of the poor tenants that
come to me for comfort and succour, sometime by six or
seven together. Therefore for God's love see that they
been holpen, and desire my brother William to give you
good counsel herein.

Also it is told me that my Lady of Suffolk hath promised
you her good will if your bargain of the marriage[1] holdeth,
to do as largely as she shall be desired or largelier, if there
be any appointment taken atwixt you for any matters
atwixt her and you. An they would advise you to give
any money to her to make her refuse or disclaim her title,
meseemeth ye may well excuse you by the money that
she had last, and by the wrongs that were done by her
and her men in felling of wood and pulling down of your
place and lodge at Hellesdon, and taking away of the
sheep and your father's goods which were taken away at
the pulling down of the said place; which well considered,
she were worthy to recompense you. An the King and the
lords were well informed they would consider the readilier
your hurts.

It seemeth this Sir William Yelverton hath comfort,

---

[1] A marriage had been arranged between John II and Anne Haute,
daughter of William Haute of Kent and his wife Jane Wydevill, and
so a cousin of the Queen and of Lord Scales. A letter written by Scales
on 10 April of this year says 'marriage is fully concluded betwixt the
said Sir John Paston and one of my nearest kinswomen'; but it never
took place. See no. 110.

that he is so bold; for [he] hath right proud and foul language and right slanderous to the tenants, as they have reported to me. Therefore be right ware that ye bind not yourself nor make none ensurance till ye be sure of a peaceable possession of your land. For oftentime rape rueth;[1] and when a man hath made such a covenant he must keep it, he may not choose there. Be not too hasty till your land be clear, and labour hastily a remedy for these premisses, or ell Sir John Fastolf's livelode, though ye enter it peaceably, shall not be worth to you a groat this year without ye will undo your tenants.

I pray you remember a kerchie of cremil for your sister Anne.

Remember to labour some remedy for your father's will[2] while my Lord of Canterbury[3] liveth, for he is an old man and he is now friendly to you; and if he happed to die who should come after him ye wot never. And if he were a needy man, inasmuch as your father was noised of so great value he will be the more strange to entreat;[4] and let this be not forgot. For [if] there were one that ought us no good will he might call us up to make account of his goods, and if we had not for to show for us whereby we have occupied he might send down a sentence to curse us in all the diocese and to make us to deliver his goods, which were to us a great shame and a rebuke. Therefore purvey hastely and wisely therefor while he liveth, and do not, as ye did while my Lord of York[5] was chancellor, make

---

[1] 'Haste brings regret', a proverb recorded in this form from *c.* 1300. Margaret uses it again in no. 108—the last known occurrence.

[2] Probate of John I's will was not granted until 1473, so that Margaret and John II could not legally administer his property until then.

[3] Bourchier; see p. 40, n. 1. He was evidently only about 57, for a papal indult of 1427 says he was then in his sixteenth year.

[4] 'difficult to deal with'.

[5] George Neville, younger brother of the Earl of Warwick, was

delays; for if ye had laboured in his time as ye have do sith, ye had be through in your matters. Beware by that, and let sloth no more take you in such default. Think of afterclaps and have prevision in all your work, and ye shall do the better.

God keep you. Written on Mid-Lent Sunday in haste.

By your mother, M. P.

83. *Margaret Paston to John Paston II*

1469, 3 April

I greet you well, and send you God's blessing and mine, thanking you for my seal that ye sent me; but I am right sorry that ye did so great cost thereupon, for one of 40*d.* should have served me right well. Send me word what it cost you and I shall send you money therefor.

I sent you a letter by a man of Yarmouth.[1] Send me word if ye have it, for I marvel ye sent me none answer thereof by Juddy.[2]

I have none very knowledge of your ensurance, but if ye have ensured I pray God send you joy and worship together, and so I trust ye shall have if it be as it is reported of her. And anemps God ye arn as greatly bound to her as ye were married, and therefore I charge you upon my blessing that ye be as true to her as she were married unto you in all degrees, and ye shall have the more grace and the better speed in all other things. Also I would that ye should not be too hasty to be married till

Bishop of Exeter from 1456 to 1465 and Archbishop of York from 1465 to 1476. He had been made chancellor after Warwick's victory at Northampton in 1460 and held office until June 1467.

1 From the similarity of the next paragraph to the fourth paragraph of no. 82, that was probably the letter in question.

2 Employed by the Pastons from perhaps 1467 to 1473.

ye were more sure of your livelode, for ye must remember what charge ye shall have; and if ye have not to maintain it[1] it will be a great rebuke. And therefore labour that ye may have releases of the lords, and be in more surety of your land ere than ye be married.

The Duchess of Suffolk is at Ewelme in Oxfordshire,[2] and it is thought by your friends here that it is do that she might be far and out of the way, and the rather feign excuse because of age or sickness if that the King would send for her for your matters.[3]

Your enemies be as bold here as they were before, wherefore I cannot think but that they have some comfort. I sent to Caister that they should beware in keeping of the place, as ye did write to me. Haste you to speed your matters as speedily as ye can, that ye may have less fellowship at Caister; for the expenses and costs be great and ye have no need thereof an ye remember you well what charges ye have beside and how your livelode is despoiled and wasted by your adversaries.

Also I would ye should purvey for your sister[4] to be with my Lady of Oxford[5] or with my Lady of Bedford[6] or in some other worshipful place where as ye think best, and I will help to her finding; for we be either of us weary of other. I shall tell you more when I speak with you. I pray you do your devoir herein as ye will my comfort

---

[1] That is, 'if you have not the means to maintain it'.

[2] The dowager Duchess had inherited the manor of Ewelme from her mother. She died there in 1475, and her splendid alabaster tomb, with a fine effigy, is in the church.

[3] Edward IV visited Norwich in June 1469.

[4] Margery, for the last paragraph shows that Anne was already living away from home. Cf. the arrangements made for Elizabeth Paston in no. 26.

[5] Margaret, Countess of Oxford, wife of John de Vere, the thirteenth earl (see p. 185, n. 3). She was a daughter of Richard Neville, Earl of Salisbury, and sister of the late Earl of Warwick.

[6] See p. 133, n. 3.

and welfare and your worship, for divers causes which ye shall understand afterward, &c.[1]

I spake with the Lord Scales at Norwich and thanked him for the good lordship that he had showed to you, and desired his lordship to be your continual good lord. And he swore by his troth he would do that he might do for you, and he told me that Yelverton the justice had spoke to him in your matter, but he told me not what; but I trow an ye desired him to tell you, he would. Ye arn beholding to my lord of his good report of you in this country, for he reported better of you than I trow ye deserve. I felt by him that there hath be proffered him large proffers on your adversaries' part again you. Send me word as hastely as ye may after the beginning of the term[2] how ye have sped in all your matters, for I shall think right long till I hear some good tidings. . . .

I pray you forget not to send me a kerch[3] of cremil for neckerches for your sister Anne, for I am shent of the good lady that she is with because she hath none, and I can none get in all this town. I should write more to you but for lack of leisure. God have you in his keeping and send you good speed in all your matters. Written in haste on Eastern Monday.

By your mother[4]

---

[1] The reference is probably to Margery's attachment to Richard Calle, which caused the family much distress soon after this; see no. 86. This part of the letter is in Gloys's hand, and Margaret may not have wished to confide fully in him.

[2] The Easter law term began on the second Sunday after Easter, 16 April in 1469.

[3] This repeats the reminder in no. 82 (p. 173).

[4] The last paragraph and the subscription are written on the back of the sheet in the hand of Edmond Paston.

84. *John Paston III to John Paston II*

1469, May

Sir, pleaseth it to understand that I conceive by your letter which that ye sent me by Juddy[1] that ye have heard of R. C.[2] labour which he maketh by our ungracious sister's assent. But whereas they write that they have my good will therein, saving your reverence they falsely lie of it, for they never spake to me of that matter, nor none other body in their name. Lovell asked me once a question whether that I understood how it was betwixt R. C. and my sister. I can think that it was by Calle's means, for when I asked him whether C. desired him to move me that question or not, he would have gotten it away by hums and by hays.[3] But I would not so be answered, wherefore at the last he told me that his oldest son desired him to speer whether that R. C. were sure of her or not, for he said that he knew a good marriage for her. But I wot he lied, for he is whole with R. Calle in that matter; wherefore, to that intent that he nor they should pick no comfort of me, I answered him that an my father, whom God assoil, were alive and had consented thereto, and my mother and ye both, he should never have my good will for to make my sister to sell candle and mustard in Framlingham;[4] and thus, with more which were too long to write to you, we departed.

And whereas it pleaseth you in your letter to cry me mercy for that ye sent me not such gear as I sent you money for, I cry you mercy that I was so lewd to encumber you with any so simple a matter, considering the great matters and weighty that ye have to do; but need

---

[1] See p. 174, n. 2.
[2] Richard Calle. See p. 176, n. 1.
[3] The first record of this expression.
[4] See p. 61, n. 3.

compelled me, for in this country is no such stuff as I sent
to you for.

Also, whereas it pleaseth you to send to Richard Calle
to deliver me money, so God help me I will none ask him
for myself, nor none had I of him, nor of none other man
but of mine own, sin ye departed; but that little that I
might forbear of mine own I have delivered to Daubeney
for household, and paid it for you in men's wages. And
therefore whoever sends you word that I have spent you
any money sin ye went hence, they must give you another
reckoning, saving in meat and drink, for I eat like an
horse[1] of purpose to eat you out at the doors;[2] but that
needeth not, for ye come not within them, wherefore, so
God help me, the fellowship here thinks that ye have forgotten us all. Wherefore, an anything be ill ruled when ye
come home, wite it yourself for default of oversight. . . .

I pray you find the means that my lord[3] may have some
reasonable mean proffered so that he and my lady may
understand that ye desire to have his good lordship. I
promise you it shall do you ease, and your tenants both.
And God preserve.

J. P.

85. *Richard Calle to Margery Paston*

1469

Mine own lady and mistress, and before God very true
wife, I with heart full sorrowful recommend me unto you,
as he that cannot be merry nor naught shall be till it be
otherwise with us than it is yet; for this life that we lead

---

1 This simile is otherwise first recorded in 1707.
2 This expression is next recorded from 1659.
3 The Duke of Norfolk, who at this time was claiming Caister,
where this letter was written.

now is neither pleasure to God nor to the world, considering the great bond of matrimony that is made betwixt us, and also the great love that hath be, and as I trust yet is, betwixt us, and as on my part never greater. Wherefore I beseech Almighty God comfort us as soon as it pleaseth him, for we that ought of very right to be most together are most asunder; meseemeth it is a thousand year ago sin that I spake with you. I had liefer than all the good in the world I might be with you. Alas, alas, good lady, full little remember they what they do that keep us thus asunder. Four times in the year are they accursed that let matrimony.[1] It causeth many men to deem in them they have large conscience in other matters as well as herein. But what, lady, suffer as ye have do and make you as merry as ye can, for iwis, lady, at the long way God will of his righteousness help his servants that mean truly and would live according to his laws, &c.

I understand, lady, ye have had as much sorrow for me as any gentlewoman hath ⟨ha⟩d in the world; as would God all that sorrow that ye have had had rested upon m⟨e s⟩o that ye had be discharged of it, for iwis, lady, it is to me a death to hear that ye be entreated otherwise than ye ought to be. This is a painful life that we lead; I cannot live thus without it be a great displeasure to God. . . .

My lad told me that my mistress your mother asked him if he had brought any letter to you, and many other things she bare him on hand, and among all other at the last she said to him that I would not make her privy to the beginning, but she supposed I would at the ending. And

<hr />

[1] This refers to the 'Great Sentence', a list of about twenty excommunications first promulgated in 1222 and ordered to be published in church on Christmas Day, Easter Day, Whit Sunday, and All Saints' Day. Archbishop Chichele in 1434 issued an abbreviated version in English, of which the relevant clause is: 'Also [they are accursed that] wittingly bring forth in judgement false witness, to let rightful matrimony.'

as to that, God knoweth she knew it first of me and none other. I wot not what her mistressship meaneth, for by my troth there is no gentlewoman alive that my heart tendereth more than it doth her, nor is loather to displease, saving only your person, which of very right I ought to tender and love best, for I am bound thereto by the law of God, and so will do while that I live, whatsomever fall of it.

I suppose an ye tell them sadly the truth, they would not damn their souls for us. Though I tell them the truth they will not believe me as well as they will do you. And therefore, good lady, at the reverence of God, be plain to them and tell the truth, and if they will in no wise agree thereto, betwixt God, the Devil, and them be it; and that peril that we should be in I beseech God it may lie upon them and not upon us. I am heavy and sorry to remember their disposition. God send them grace to guide all things well, as well as I would they did. God be their guide and send them peace and rest, &c. . . .

Mistress, I am afeared to write to you, for I understand ye have showed my letters that I have sent you before this time; but I pray you let no creature see this letter. As soon as ye have read it let it be burnt, for I would no man should see it in no wise. Ye had no writing from me this two year, nor I will not send you no more; therefore I remit all this matter to your wisd⟨om⟩.

Almighty Jesu preserve, keep, and [give] you your heart's desire, which I wot well should be to God's pleasure, &c. This letter was written with as great pain as ever wrote I thing in my life, for in good faith I have be right sick, and yet am not verily well at ease, God amend it, &c.

86. *Margaret Paston to John Paston II*

1469, about 10 September

I greet you well, and send you God's blessing and mine, letting you weet that on Thursday last was, my mother[1] and I were with my Lord of Norwich,[2] and desired him that he would no more do in the matter touching your sister[3] till that ye and my brother[4] and other that wern executors to your father might been here together; for they had the rule of her as well as I. And he said plainly that he had be required so often for to examine her that he might not, nor would, no lenger delay it, and charged me in pain of cursing that she should not be deferred, but that she should appear beforn him the next day. And I said plainly that I would neither bring her nor send her; and then he said that he would send for her himself, and charged that she should be at her liberty to come when he sent for her. And he said by his troth that he would be as sorry for her an she did not well as he would be an she were right near of his kin, both for my mother's sake and mine, and other of her friends; for he wost well that her demeaning had sticked sore at our hearts.

My mother and I informed him that we could never understand by her saying, by no language that ever she had to him, that neither of them were bound to other, but that they might choose both. Then he said that he would say to her as well as he could before that he examined her; and so it was told me by divers persons that he did as well and as plainly as she had be right near to him, which were too long to write at this time. Hereafter ye shall weet, and who were labourers therein; the

---

[1] Agnes Paston.

[2] The Bishop; see p. 62, n. 5.

[3] Margery Paston's betrothal to Richard Calle, which her family were trying to break off.   [4] William Paston II.

chancellor was not so guilty therein as I weened he had been.

On Friday the Bishop sent for her by Ashfield and other that arn right sorry of her demeaning. And the Bishop said to her right plainly, and put her in remembrance how she was born, what kin and friends that she had, and should have mo if she were ruled and guided after them; and if she did not, what rebuke and shame and loss it should be to her if she were not guided by them, and cause of forsaking of her for any good or help or comfort that she should have of them; and said that he had heard say that she loved such one that her friend[s] were not pleased with that she should have, and therefore he bade her be right well advised how she did, and said that he would understand the words that she had said to him, whether it made matrimony or not. And she rehearsed what she had said, and said if tho words made it not sure she said boldly that she would make it surer ere than she went thence; for she said she thought in her conscience she was bound, whatsoever the words wern. These lewd words grieve me and her grandam as much as all the remnant. And the Bishop and the chancellor both said that there was neither I nor no friend of hers would receive her.

And then Calle was examined apart by himself, that her words and his accorded, and the time and where it should a be done. And then the Bishop said that he supposed that there should be found other things against him that might cause the letting thereof, and therefore he said he would not be too hasty to give sentence thereupon, and said that he would give over day till the Wednesday or Thursday after Michaelmas, and so it is delayed. They would an had their will performed in haste, but the Bishop said he would none otherwise than he had said.

I was with my mother at her place when she was

examined, and when I heard say what her demeaning was I charged my servants that she should not be received in mine house. I had given her warning, she might a be ware afore if she had a be gracious. And I sent to one or two more that they should not receive her if she came. She was brought again to my place for to a be received, and Sir James[1] told them that brought her that I had charged them all, and she should not be received; and so my Lord of Norwich hath set her at Roger Best's,[2] to be there till the day beforesaid, God knoweth full evil again his will and his wife's, if they durst do otherwise. I am sorry that they arn acumbered with her, but yet I am better paid that she is there for the while than she had been in other place, because of the sadness and good disposition of himself and his wife, for she shall not be suffered there to play the brethel.

I pray you and require you that ye take it not pensily, for I wot well it goeth right near your heart, and so doth it to mine and to other; but remember you, and so do I, that we have lost of her but a brethel, and set it the less to heart; for an she had be good, whatsoever she had be it should not a been as it is, for an he were dead at this hour she should never be at mine heart as she was.

As for the divorce that ye writ to me of, I suppose what ye meant, but I charge you upon my blessing that ye do not, nor cause none other to do, that should offend God and your conscience; for an ye do, or cause for to be do, God will take vengeance thereupon, and ye should put yourself and other in great jeopardy; for wot it well, she shall full sore repent her lewdness hereafter, and I pray God she mote so. I pray you, for mine heart's ease, be ye of a good comfort in all things. I trust God shall help right well, and I pray God so do in all our matters. . . .

---

[1] Gloys.   [2] See p. 159, n. 1.

87. *Margaret Paston to John Paston II*

1469, 12 September

I greet you well, letting you weet that your brother and his fellowship stand in great jeopardy at Caister, and lack victual; and Daubeney and Berney[1] be dead, and divers other greatly hurt, and they fail gunpowder and arrows, and the place sore broken with guns of the tother part; so that, but they have hasty help, they be like to lose both their lives and the place, to the greatest rebuke to you that ever came to any gentleman, for every man in this country marvelleth greatly that ye suffer them to be so long in so great jeopardy without help or other remedy.

The Duke hath be more fervently set thereupon, and more cruel, sith that Writtle,[2] my Lord of Clarence man, was there than he was before, and he hath sent for all his tenants from every place, and other, to be there at Caister on Thursday next coming, that there is then like to be the greatest multitude of people that came there yet. And they purpose then to make a great assault, for they have sent for guns to Lynn and other place by the sea's side, that with their great multitude of guns, with other shoot and ordnance, there shall no man dare appear in the place. They shall hold them so busy with their great people that it shall not lie in their power within to hold it again them, without God help them or [they] have hasty succour from you. Therefore, as ye will have my blessing, I charge you

[1] Osbern; see p. 106, n. 4. This report was false; he was not killed at Caister, and lived for many years after. Margaret left him a legacy in her will.

[2] Walter Writtle, gentleman, of White Roding, Essex, in this year sheriff of Essex and Hertfordshire. He was in the service of George, Duke of Clarence (see p. 93, n. 1), through whom John Paston II was seeking to come to terms with the Duke of Norfolk. He was a clerk of the Exchequer from 1455 to 1472, often J.P. and M.P., and sheriff again in 1471. He died in 1475.

and require you that ye see your brother be holpen in haste. And if ye can have none mean, rather desire writing fro my Lord of Clarence, if he be at London, or ell of my Lord Archbishop of York,[1] to the Duke of Norfolk that he will grant them that be in the place their lives and their goods;[2] and in eschewing of insurrections, with other inconvenience that be like to grow within the shire of Norfolk, this troublous world, because of such conventicles and gatherings within the said shire for cause of the said place, they shall suffer him to enter upon such appointment, or other like taken by the advice of your counsel there at London, if ye think this be not good, till the law hath determined otherwise; and let him write another letter to your brother to deliver the place upon the same appointment. And if ye think, as I can suppose, that the Duke of Norfolk will not agree to this, because he granted this aforn and they in the place would not accept it, then I would the said messenger should with the said letters bring fro the said Lord of Clarence, or ell my Lord Archbishop, to my Lord of Oxford[3] other letters, to rescue them forthwith, though the said Earl of Oxford should have the place during his life for his labour. Spare not this to be done in haste, if ye will have their lives and be set by in Norfolk, though ye should lose the best

[1] See p. 173, n. 5.

[2] When Norfolk finally took Caister he issued a safe-conduct, on 26 September 1469, for John Paston III and the other defenders, saying in the preamble that he did so at the instance of the Archbishop of Canterbury, the Duke of Clarence, and others.

[3] John de Vere, thirteenth Earl of Oxford (1462–1513), a prominent Lancastrian. He was imprisoned in the Tower for a time in 1468, took a leading part in the temporary restoration of Henry VI in 1470–1, and after it went into exile. He seized St. Michael's Mount in September 1473 and held it for some months, but was forced to surrender and was imprisoned for ten years. In Henry VII's time John Paston III became a member of his council and William Paston III was in his service; see no. 141.

manor of all for the rescue. I had liefer ye lost the livelode
than their lives. Ye must get a messenger of the lords or
some other notable man to bring these letters.

Do your devoir now, and let me send you no more
messengers for these matters; but send me by the bearer
hereof more certain comfort than ye have do by all other
that I have sent before. In any wise, let the letters that
shall come to the Earl of Oxford comen with the letters
that shall comen to the Duke of Norfolk, that if he will
not agree to the tone that ye may have ready your rescue,
that it need no more to send therefor.

God keep you. Written the Tuesday next before Holy
Rood Day[1] in haste.

By your mother

88. *John Paston II to Margaret Paston*

1469, 15 September

Mother, upon Saturday last was, Daubeney and Berney
were alive and merry, and I suppose there came no man
out of the place to you sin that time that could have
ascertained to you of their deaths.[2] And as touching the
fierceness of the Duke or of his people showed sin that
time that Writtle departed, I trow it was concluded that
truce and abstinence of war should be had ere he departed,
which shall dure till Monday next coming.[3] And by that
time I trow that truce shall be taken till that day sevennight after, by which time I hope of a good direction shall
be had.

And whereas ye write to me that I should sue for letters
from my Lords of Clarence and York, they be not here;
and if they wrote to him, as they have done two times,

---

[1] 14 September.   [2] This letter answers no. 87.

[3] 18 September.

I trow it would not avail. And as for to labour those letters and the rescue together, they been two sundry things, for when the rescue is ready that the cost thereof is done—for if I be driven thereto to rescue it ere they come there that should do it, it shall cost 1,000 escutes, and as much after; which way were hard for me to take while that I may do it otherwise. But as to say that they shall be rescued, if all the land that I have in England, and friends, may do it, they shall, an God be friendly, and that as shortly as it may goodlily and well be brought about.

And the greatest default earthly is money, and some friends and neighbours to help; wherefore I beseech you to send me comfort, what money ye could find the means to get or chevish upon surety sufficient, or upon livelode to be in mortgage or yet sold, and what people by likelihood, your friends and mine, could make upon a short warning, and to send me word in all the haste as it is needful.

But, mother, I feel by your writing that ye deem in me I should not do my devoir without ye wrote to me some heavy tidings; and, mother, if I had need to be quickened with a letter in this need I were of myself too slow a fellow. But, mother, I ensure you that I have heard ten times worse tidings sin the assiege began than any letter that ye wrote to me, and sometime I have heard right good tidings both. But this I ensure you, that they that be within have no worse rest than I have, nor casteth more jeopardy. But whether I had good tidings or ill, I take God to witness that I have done my devoir as I would be done for in case like, and shall do till there be an end of it.

I have sent to the King to York,[1] and to the lords, and

---

[1] Edward IV had been taken prisoner by Warwick at the end of July 1469, and kept at Warwick Castle and at Middleham in Yorkshire. In September he was allowed to go to York, and by 19 September was at Pontefract.

hope to have answer from them by Wednesday at the farthest; and after that answer shall I be ruled, and then send you word, for till that time can I take none direction. And to encomfort you, despair you not for lack of victual nor of gunpowder, nor be not too heavy nor too merry therefor; for an heaviness or sorrow would have been the remedy thereof, I knew never matter in my life that I could have been so heavy or sorry for. With God's grace it shall be remedied well enow; for by my troth I had liefer lose the manor of Caister than the simplest man's life therein if that may be his savation. Wherefore I beseech you to send me word what money and men ye think that I am like to get in that country, for the hasty purchase of money and men shall be the getting and rescue of it, and the savation of most men's lives, if we take that way. . . .

Writ the Friday next after Holy Rood Day.

JOHN PASTON, K.

89. *John Paston II to John Paston III*

1469, 18 September

I recommend me to you, and promise you that I have and shall labour and find the mean that ye shall have honour of your dealing, as ye have hithertowards, as all England and every man reporteth. And moreover, I am in way for it by many divers ways, whereof there shall be one executed by this day fourteennight at the farthest, and peradventure within seven days; and if ye may keep it so long I would be glad. And after that, if ye have not from me other writing, that then ye do therein for your safeguard and your fellowship only, and to your worships;

and as for the place, no force therefor. Ye know this hand, therefore needeth no mention from whom it cometh.[1]

And moreover, they that be about you[2] be in obloquy of all men, and moreover they have been written to by as special writing as might be, after the world that now is, and [I] promise you that the Duke's council would that they had never begun it. And moreover, they be charged in pain of their lives that, though they gat the place, they should not hurt one of you. There is neither ye nor none with you but, an he knew what is generally reported of him, he or ye—and God fortune you well—may think him four times better in reputation of all folk than ever he was.

Beware whom ye make a counsel to this matter. Also, I let you weet that I am in much more comfort of you than I may write, and they that be about you have cause to be more feared than ye have. And also beware of spending of your stuff of quarrels, powder, and stone, so that if they assault you ere we come, that ye have stuff to defend you of one,[3] and then of my life ye get no more; and that your fellowship be ever occupied in renewing of your stuff.

Written the Monday next after Holy Rood Day.

I trow, though ye be not privy thereto, there is taken a truce new till this day sevennight.

---

[1] The letter is in John II's own hand, and is addressed 'To John Paston and to none other'.

[2] The besiegers, who were led by Sir John Heveningham (see p. 147, n. 3), Sir Thomas Wingfield, younger brother of Sir John (see p. 147, n. 4), Sir Gilbert Debenham (see p. 85, n. 4), and Sir William Brandon (see p. 216, n. 1).

[3] That is, from one assault.

90. *John Paston III to John Paston II*

1469, about 25 September

Right worshipful sir, I recommend me unto you. And as for the certainty of the deliverance of Caister, John Chapman[1] can tell you how that we were enforced thereto as well as myself. As for John Chapman and his three fellows, I have purveyed that they be paid each of them 40*s.* with the money that they had of you and Daubeney, and that is enow for the season that they have done you service. I pray you give them their thank, for by my troth they have as well deserved it as any men that ever bare life; but as for money, ye need not to give them without ye will, for they be pleased with their wages.

Writtle promised me to send you the certainty of the appointment. We were, for lack of victual, gunpowder, men's hearts, lack of surety of rescue, driven thereto to take appointment.

If ye will that I come to you, send me word and I shall purvey me for to tarry with you a two or three days. By my troth, the rewarding of such folks as hath been with me during the siege hath put me in great danger for the money. God preserve you, and I pray you be of good cheer till I speak with you; and I trust to God to ease your heart in some things.

J. PASTON[2]

---

[1] See no. 81, p. 170.
[2] On the back of the letter, in a panel shown by soiling to have been folded outside, is the following note in a hand unlike John III's: 'Caister yielded. J.P.'

91. *Margaret Paston to John Paston II*

1469, 22–30 September

I greet you well, and send you God's blessing and mine, letting you weet that methink by the letter[1] that ye sent me by Robin that ye think that I should write to you fables and imaginations. But I do not so. I have written as it have be informed me, and will do. It was told me that both Daubeney and Berney were dead; but for certain Daubeney is dead, God assoil his soul, whereof I am right sorry, an it had pleased God that it might a be otherwise.

Remember you ye have had two great losses within this twelvemonth, of him and of Sir Thomas.[2] God visiteth you as it pleaseth him in sundry wises. He would ye should know him and serve him better than ye have do before this time, and then he will send you the more grace to do well in all other things. And for God's love, remember it right well, and take it patiently, and thank God of his visitation; and if anything have be amiss any other wise than it ought to have been before this, either in pride or in lavish expenses or in any other thing that have offended God, amend it and pray him of his grace and help, and intend well to God and to your neighbours; and though your power hereafter be to acquit them of their malice, yet be merciful to them, and God shall send you the more grace to have your intent in other things. . . .

---

[1] No. 88.

[2] This probably means Thomas Lyndes; see p. 168, n. 4. John II had recommended him to his father in 1465 for the living of Mautby, saying 'I and he have been much acquainted together', and in his will of 1477 he left money for prayers to be said for the souls of Lyndes and Daubeney. The first clear mention of him as dead is in February 1470, but its terms are not such as to exclude his having died say six months earlier. Thomas Howes (see p. 50, n. 7) certainly died between October 1468 and May 1469; but he seems unlikely to have been so greatly mourned by the Pastons.

I would ye should [send] your brother word, and some other that ye trust, to see to your own livelode, to set it in a rule and to gather thereof that may be had in haste, and also of Sir John Fastolf's livelode that may be gathered in peaceable wise; for as for Richard Calle, he will no more gather it but if ye command him, and he would fain make his account and have your good mastership, as it is told me, and deliver the evidence of Beckham[1] and all other things that longeth to you, that he trusteth that ye will be his good master hereafter. And he saith he will not take none new master till ye refuse his service. . . .

This letter was begun on Friday was sevennight, and ended this day next after Michaelmas Day. God keep you and give you grace to do as we⟨ll⟩ as I would ye did. And I charge you beware that ye set no land to mortgage, for if any advise you thereto they arn not your friends. . . .

92. *John Paston III to John Paston II*

1469, 5 October

Right worshipful sir, I recommend [me] unto you, praying you that ye will in all haste send me word how that ye will that Sir John Still,[2] John Pamping,[3] W. Milsent,[4] Nicholas Mondonet, T. Tomson, shall be ruled, and whether that they shall seek them new services or not; and Matthew,[5]

---

[1] This manor, a few miles west of Gresham, had been in the Paston family since the judge's day. The deeds were evidently left in Calle's charge.

[2] See p. 167, n. 7.

[3] See p. 80, n. 1.

[4] Milsent remained in the Paston service until at least 1474; see especially no. 94.

[5] These two words are written in the margin with no clear indication where they are to be inserted.

and Bedford[1] also, for he hath be with me this season and is fro my mother. And if so be that ye will have these to abide with you, or any of them, send word which that they be; for betwixt this and Hallowmas my mother is agreed that they shall have meat and drink of her for such a certain weekly as my mother and ye and I can accord when we meet. Notwithstanding if ye could get Berney, or any of these said folks which that ye will not keep, any service in the mean season it were more worship for you than to put them from you like masterless hounds, for by my troth they are as good men's bodies as any live, and specially Sir John Still and John Pamping. An I were of power to keep them, and all these before rehearsed, by troth they should never depart fro me while I lived.

If ye send me word that I shall come to you to London for to common with you of any matter, so God help me I have neither money to come up with, nor for to tarry with you when I am there, but if ye send me some; for by my troth these works have caused me to lay out for you better than £10 or £12 beside that money that I had of my mother, which is about an £8. God amend defaults; but this I warrant you, without that it be Matthew, which ye sent word by John Thresher that ye would have to await on you, there is no man that was hired for the time of this siege that will ask you a penny. . . .

I will not make me masterfast with my Lord of Norfolk nor with none other till I speak with you. An ye think it be to be done, get me a master. . . .

Written on Saint Faith's Even.

J. Paston

I pray you in all haste possible send me answer of everything in this bill, for it requireth haste. . . .

---

[1] William Bedford appears several times about this date. A bill and a bow of his are listed in an inventory of goods plundered by the Duke of Suffolk's men from Hellesdon in 1465.

By Saint George, I and my fellowship stand in fear of my Lord of Norfolk men, for we be threat sore, notwithstanding the safeguards that my fellowship have. As for me I have none, nor none of your household men, nor none will have—it were shame to take it.

93. *John Paston III to Margaret Paston*

1470, 12 October[1]

After humble and most due recommendation, as lowly as I can I beseech you of your blessing. Please it you to wit that, blessed be God, my brother and I be in good heal and I trust that we shall do right well in all our matters hastily. For my Lady of Norfolk hath promised to be ruled by my Lord of Oxford[2] in all such matters as belong to my brother and to me; and as for my Lord of Oxford, he is better lord to me, by my troth, than I can wish him in many matters, for he sent to my Lady of Norfolk by John Bernard only for my matter and for none other cause, mine unwitting[3] or without any prayer of me, for when he sent to her I was at London and he at Colchester; and that is a likelihood he remembereth me. The Duke and the Duchess[4] sue to him as humbly as ever I did to them, insomuch that my Lord of Oxford shall have the rule of them and theirs by their own desires and great means.

As for the offices that ye wrote to my brother for, and to me, they be for no poor men; but I trust we shall speed of other offices meetly for us, for my master the Earl of Oxford biddeth me ask and have. I trow my brother Sir

---

[1] This letter was written in the disturbed time of the brief restoration of Henry VI in 1470. Warwick, with Clarence and several Lancastrian magnates including the Earl of Oxford, landed at Dartmouth in September, forced Edward IV to flee abroad on 2 October, and enthroned Henry VI in St. Paul's on 13 October.

[2] See p. 185, n. 3.   [3] 'without my knowledge'.

[4] Of Norfolk.

John shall have the constableship of Norwich Castle with £20 of fee. All the lords be agreed to it.[1]

Tidings, the Earl of Worcester[2] is like to die this day or tomorrow at the farthest. John Pilkington, Master W. Attcliff, and Fowler are taken and in the castle of Pomfret, and are like to die hastily, without they be dead.[3] Sir T. Montgomery[4] and John Donne[5] be taken; what shall fall of them I cannot say.

The Queen that was,[6] and the Duchess of Bedford,[7] be

[1] This hoped-for appointment was never made.

[2] John Tiptoft, who had been constable of England since 1462 and was notorious for his ferocious treatment of captured opponents. One of his first acts in 1462 had been the execution of the Earl of Oxford, the present Earl's father. On Henry VI's restoration Oxford was made constable, and one of his first acts was to condemn Tiptoft, who was executed on 18 October 1470. See p. 96, n. 7.

[3] None of these was in fact put to death. Pilkington had been a squire of the King's body since 1461, sheriff of Lancashire, and J.P. for Northamptonshire and the West Riding. He fought and was knighted at Tewkesbury in 1471, and was later knight of the body, M.P. for Yorkshire, and chamberlain of the Exchequer. He died in 1479. William Attcliff (more usually spelt Hatcliff), doctor of medicine, had been physician to Henry VI and continued in the same function for Edward IV, becoming also King's secretary in 1466. He took part in many diplomatic missions both before this time (e.g. the negotiations for the marriage of Princess Margaret to the Duke of Burgundy in 1468 (see no. 79)) and after Edward's restoration in 1471. He died in 1480. Thomas Fowler, a London fishmonger, had been J.P. and alderman of Oxford. He later became squire of the body, M.P., and sheriff of Buckinghamshire and Bedfordshire. He died in 1496.   [4] See p. 89, n. 3.

[5] From 1461 Donne had been usher of the chamber, constable of Aberystwyth Castle, and sheriff of Carmarthen and Cardigan. He received grants 'for good service to the King's father Richard, late Duke of York, in England, France, and Ireland, and against Henry VI' and became squire of the body in 1465. He was knighted at Tewkesbury in 1471, was sent on embassies to France and Flanders in 1477, and was on many Buckinghamshire commissions from 1488 to 1503. He was dead by 1506.

[6] Elizabeth Wydevill, queen of Edward IV.

[7] Queen Elizabeth's mother; see p. 133, n. 3.

in sanctuary at Westminster. The Bishop of Ely[1] with other bishops are in St. Martin's. When I hear more I shall send you more.

I pray God send you all your desires. Written at London on Saint Edward's Even.

Your son and humble servant, J. P.

Mother, I beseech you that Brome[2] may be spoken to to gather up my silver at Guton[3] in all haste possible, for I have no money. Also that it like you that John Milsent[4] may be spoken to to keep well my grey horse, an he be alive, and that he spare no meat on him, and that he have cunning leeches to look to him. As for my coming home, I know no certainty; for I tarry till my Lady of Norfolk come to go through with tho matters, and she shall not be here till Sunday.

94. *John Paston II to Margaret Paston*

1471, 18 April[5]

Mother, I recommend me to you, letting you weet that, blessed be God, my brother John is alive and fareth well, and in no peril of death. Nevertheless he is hurt with an arrow on his right arm beneath the elbow, and I have sent him a surgeon, which hath dressed him, and he telleth me that he trusteth that he shall be all whole within right

---

[1] William Gray, bishop 1454–78.

[2] Edmund Brome, gentleman, of Reedham, had been one of the defenders of Caister in 1469.   [3] See p. 158, n. 2.

[4] Evidently a brother of William Milsent, in Paston's service at the same time; see p. 192, n. 4. He was reported killed at Barnet in 1471 (see no. 94), but is mentioned again in 1472.

[5] This was written just after the battle of Barnet on 14 April 1471, in which Edward IV defeated the Lancastrians under Warwick and recovered the throne. The two Paston brothers fought on the losing side.

short time. It is so that John Milsent[1] is dead, God have mercy on his soul, and William Milsent is alive, and his other servants all be escaped, by all likelihood.

Item, as for me, I am in good case, blessed be God, and in no jeopardy of my life if me list myself, for I am at my liberty if need be.

Item, my Lord Archbishop[2] is in the Tower. Nevertheless I trust to God that he shall do well enough. He hath a safeguard for him and me both. Nevertheless we have been troubled since, but now I understand that he hath a pardon; and so we hope well.

There was killed upon the field, half a mile from Barnet, on Eastern Day, the Earl of Warwick, the Marquis Montagu,[3] Sir William Tyrrell,[4] Sir Lewis John,[5] and divers other esquires of our country, Godmanston[6] and Booth.[7] And on the King Edward's party, the Lord Cromwell,[8] the Lord Say,[9] Sir Humphrey Bourchier[10] of our country, which is a sore moaned man here, and other people of both parties to the number of more than a thousand.

As for other tidings, [it] is understand here that the Queen Margaret is verily landed,[11] and her son, in the west

---

[1] See p. 196, n. 4.

[2] George Neville; see p. 173, n. 5.

[3] John Neville; see p. 68, n. 1.

[4] Of Essex; J.P. and M.P. often from 1443 to 1466, knighted 1460.

[5] Of Essex; sheriff of Essex and Hertfordshire 1457–8, M.P. 1459, J.P. from 1465.

[6] William Godmanston, esq., of Frinton, Essex.

[7] Richard Booth, esq., sheriff of Essex and Hertfordshire 1455–6, and of Norfolk and Suffolk 1456–7.

[8] Humphrey, son of Henry Lord Bourchier, Earl of Essex (see p. 74, n. 3); created Lord Cromwell in 1461.

[9] William Fiennes, whose father was executed by Cade's rebels in 1450. He had served with Warwick at the battle of Northampton in 1460 and accompanied Edward IV into exile in 1470.

[10] Son of Lord Berners (see p. 68, n. 2).

[11] Margaret of Anjou landed at Weymouth on the day of the

country, and I trow that as tomorrow or else the next day
the King Edward will depart from hence to her ward to
drive her out again.

Item, I beseech you that I may be recommended to my
cousin Lomnor,[1] and to thank him for his good will to me
wards if I had had need, as I understood by the bearer hereof.
And I beseech you on my behalf to advise him to be well
ware of his dealing or language as yet, for the world, I
ensure you, is right queasy, as ye shall know within this
month. The people here feareth it sore. God hath showed
himself marvellously, like him that made all and can undo
again when him list; and I can think that by all likelihood
shall show himself as marvellous again, and that in short
time, and as I suppose ofter than once in cases like.

Item, it is so that my brother is unpurveyed of money.
I have holpen him to my power and above, wherefore, as
it pleaseth you, remember him, for [I] cannot purvey for
myself in the same case. Written at London the Thursday
in Eastern week. I hope hastily to see you. All this bill
must be secret.

Be ye not adoubted of the world, for I trust all shall be
well. If it thus continue I am not all undone, nor none of
us; and if otherwise, then, &c.

95. *John Paston III to Margaret Paston*

1471, 30 April

After humble and most due recommendation, in as humble
wise as I can I beseech you of your blessing, praying God
to reward you with as much pleasure and heart's ease as
I have lateward caused you to have trouble and thought.
And, with God's grace, it shall not be long to ere than

battle. Her forces were destroyed at Tewkesbury on 4 May and she
herself was captured on 7 May.   [1] See p. 26, n. 2.

my wrongs and other men's shall be redressed, for the world was never so like to be ours as it is now; wherefore I pray you let Lomnor no[t] be too busy as yet.

Mother, I beseech you, an ye may spare any money, that ye will do your alms on me and send me some in as hasty wise as is possible, for by my troth my leechcraft and physic, and rewards to them that have kept me and condite me to London, hath cost me sith Eastern Day more than £5. And now I have neither meat, drink, clothes, leechcraft, nor money but upon borrowing, and I have essayed my friends so far that they begin to fail now in my greatest need that ever I was in.

Also, mother, I beseech you, an my horse that was at leechcraft at the Holt[1] be not taken up for the King's hawks, that he may be had home and kept in your place, and not to go out to water nor nowhither else, but that the gate be shut, and he to be chased after water within your place, and that he have as much meat as he may eat. I have hay enow of mine own, and as for oats, Dollis will purvey for him, or who that doth it I will pay. And I beseech you that he have every week three bushel of oats, and every day a pennyworth of bread. . . .

And if it please you to have knowledge of our royal person, I thank God I am whole of my sickness, and trust to be clean whole of all my hurts within a sevennight at the farthest, by which time I trust to have other tidings. And those tidings once had, I trust not to be long out of Norfolk, with God's grace, whom I beseech preserve you and your for my part.

Written the last day of April. The bearer hereof can tell you tidings such as be true for very certain.

Your humblest servant, J. OF GELSTON[2]

---

[1] Presumably Holt, 22 miles north-west of Norwich.

[2] Geldeston; see p. 6, n. 6. Since Margaret was living there in 1444, and John III was born in that year, it seems likely that he was

96. *John Paston II to John Paston III*

1471, 15 September

Right well-beloved brother, I commend me to you, letting
you weet that I am in welfare, I thank God, and have been
ever since that I spake last with you; and marvel sore that
ye sent never writing to me since ye departed. I heard
never sin that time any word out of Norfolk. Ye might at
Bartholomew Fair¹ have had messengers enow to London,
and if ye had sent to Wykes² he should have conveyed it
to me.

I heard yesterday that a worsted³ man of Norfolk, that
sold worsteds at Winchester, said that my Lord of Norfolk and my Lady were on pilgrimage at Our Lady⁴ on
foot, and so they went to Caister; and that at Norwich
one should have had large language to you and called you
traitor, and picked many quarrels to you. Send me word
thereof. It were well do that ye were a little surer of your
pardon than ye be. Advise you; I deem ye will hereafter
else repent you.

I understand that Bastard Fauconberg is either headed
or like to be,⁵ and his brother both. Some men say he
would have deserved it, and some say nay. I purpose to

born there and that he used this fact as a kind of private code which
his mother would understand but which would conceal his identity
from strangers who might read the letter. This letter is exceptional
in bearing no address on the outside, which again suggests that it was
intended to be confidential.

¹ This fair was held annually from 1133 at West Smithfield, London, on St. Bartholomew's Day, 24 August, the day before and the
day after. After the Restoration it was extended to a fortnight, and
remained so until it was suppressed in 1855.

² See p. 78, n. 4.

³ See p. 133, n. 1.   ⁴ See p. 6, n. 1.

⁵ Thomas Neville, natural son of William, Lord Fauconberg, uncle
of Warwick, Earl of Kent from 1461. He was beheaded at Middleham
in Yorkshire on 22 September.

be at London the first day of the term.[1] Send me word whether ye shall be there or not.

Item, I would weet whether ye have spoken with my Lady of Norfolk or not, and of her disposition, and the household's, to me and to you wards, and whether it be a possible to have Caister again, and their good wills, or not. And also I pray you understand what fellowship and guiding is in Caister, and have a spy resorting in and out; so may ye know the secrets among them.

There is much ado in the north, as men sayn. I pray you beware of your guiding, and in chief of your language, so that fro henceforth by your language no man perceive that ye favour any person contrary to the King's pleasure. . . .

Item, I pray you send me word if any of our friends or well-willers be dead, for I fear that there is great death in Norwich and in other borough towns in Norfolk; for I ensure you it is the most universal death that ever I wist in England, for by my troth I cannot hear by pilgrims that pass the country, nor none other man that rideth or goeth any country, that any borough town in England is free from that sickness. God cease it when it pleaseth him. Wherefore, for God's sake, let my mother take heed to my young brethren, that they be not in none place where that sickness is reigning, nor that they disport not with none other young people which resorteth where any sickness is; and if there be any of that sickness dead or infect in Norwich, for God's sake let her send them to some friend of hers into the country, and do ye the same by mine advice. Let my mother rather remove her household into the country. . . .

Written at Waltham[2] beside Winchester the day next Holy Rood Day.   J. P., K.

[1] The Michaelmas law term began on 6 October, the octave.
[2] Bishop's Waltham, the residence of the Bishop of Winchester. The

97. *Margaret Paston to John Paston III*

1471, 5 November

I greet you well and send you God's blessing and mine, letting you weet that mine cousin Clere[1] hath sent to me for the 100 mark that I borrowed of her for your brother. It fortuned so that a friend of her late hath lost better than 300 mark, and he sent to her for money and she had none that she might comen by, and therefore she sent to me for the said 100 mark; and I know not how to do therefor, by my troth, for I have it not nor I cannot make shift therefor an I should go to prison therefor. Common with your brother hereof and send me word how that he will make shift therefor in haste, for I must ell needs sellen all my woods and that shall disavail him better than 200 mark if I die; and if I should sell them now there would none man give for them so much by near an 100 mark as they be worth, because there be so many wood sales in Norfolk at this time. And therefore let him make purveyance therefor in haste, as he will have mine good will and that I save him the said woods to the better avail in time coming. And send me an answer thereof in haste if ye will my welfare, for I shall never been in quiet till I know an end in this; for she hath therefor an obligation of £100, and it is not kept close—there been many persons now knowen it, which meseemeth a great rebuke to me that I departed so largely with your brother that I reserved not to pay that I was in danger for him,[2] and so have

Bishop was Wainfleet (see p. 42, n. 5), whom John II had doubtless gone to see about Caister. Wainfleet and other of Fastolf's trustees had released it to him in 1468, but he was still deprived of it by Norfolk. In 1472 John III reported from Framlingham that 'the matter of Caister . . . hath be moved to my lady's good grace by the Bishop of Winchester' (p. 217).   [1] See p. 22, n. 2.

[2] 'I gave your brother so generous a share of my money that I did not keep back enough to pay the debt I had incurred on his account.'

divers said to me which of late have known it. And when I remember it it is to mine heart a very spear, considering that he never gave me comfort therein, nor of all the money that he hath received will never make shift there-for. . . .

As for tidings, my cousin Berney of Witchingham,[1] Veil's wife, London's wife, and Pickard of Tombland[2] be passed to God, God have their souls. All this household and this parish arn safe, blessed be God. We liven in fear, but we wot not whither to flee for to be better than we arn here.

I send you 5s. to buy with sugar and dates for me. I would have 3 or 4 lb. of sugar, and beware the remnant in dates, and send them to me as hastily as ye may. And send me word what price a pound of pepper, cloves, maces, ginger, cinnamon, almonds, rice, raisins of currants, galingale, saffron, grains, and comfits—of each of these send me word what a pound is worth, and if it be better cheap at London than it is here I shall send you money to buy such stuff as I will have. . . .

Written in haste on Saint Leonard's Even. I warn you keep this letter close and lose it not, rather burn it.[3]

By your mother

98. *Edmond Paston II to John Paston III*

1471, 18 November

Right worshipful brother, I recommend me to you, pray-ing you heartily that ye will remember such matters as I write to you. I send you now by the bringer hereof

[1] See p. 70, n. 6.
[2] The square facing the entrance to Norwich Cathedral close.
[3] This is one of the very few letters extant in both draft and fair copy. The text is taken from the fair copy, which contains a few pas-sages, including this sentence, not in the draft.

money, which money I pray you that [ye] bestow it as I write to you. I weened a done it myself, but considering costs and other divers things I may not bring it about; wherefore I pray you heartily to take the labour upon you, and I trust to deserve it.

I pray you bestow this money thus: to Christopher Hanington 5*s*.; to the Principal of Staple Inn[1] 5*s*., in part of payment; also, I pray you to buy me three yards of purple chamlet, price the yard 4*s*.; a bonnet of deep murrey, price 2*s*. 4*d*.; an hose cloth of yellow kersey of an ellen, I trow it will cost 2*s*.; a girdle of plunket ribbon, price 6*d*.; four laces of silk, two of one colour and two of another, price 8*d*.; three dozen points, white, red, and yellow, price 6*d*.; three pair of pattens—I pray you let William Milsent purvey for them. I was wont to pay but 2½*d*. for a pair, but I pray you let them not be left behind though I pay more. They must be low pattens; let them be long enow, and broad upon the heel. . . .

Also, sir, my mother greets you well, and send you God's blessing and hers, and prays you that ye will buy her a runlet of malmsey out of the galley; and if ye have no money she bid that ye should borrow of my brother Sir John, or of some other friend of yours, and send her word as hastily as ye have it and she shall send you money. And if that ye send it home, she bid that it should be wound in a canvas, for broaching of the carriers,[2] for she saith that she hath known men served so before. . . .

All the court recommends them to you. I pray you, an ye can get me any profitable service, essay. My brother Sir John was moved of my aunt Poynings[3] to have been with her. I would have right an easy service till I were out of debts.

---

1 In Holborn, one of ten Inns of Chancery; see p. 8, n. 3.
2 'to prevent the carriers from broaching it'.
3 Elizabeth Paston; see p. 47, n. 2.

God have you in his keeping. Written at Norwich the Monday next before Saint Edmund the King.[1]

EDMOND PASTON

99. *Margaret Paston to John Paston III*

1471, 29 November

I greet you well, and send you God's blessing and mine, letting you weet that I have a letter from your brother whereby I understand that he cannot, nor may, make no purveyance for the 100 mark,[2] the which causeth me to be right heavy, and for other things that he writ to me of that he is in danger for; remembering what we have had before this, and how simply it hath be spent, and to little profit to any of us, and now arn in such case that none of us may well help other without that we should do that were too great a disworship for us to do—either to sell wood, or land, or such stuff that were necessary for us to have in our houses. So mote I answer afore God, I wot not how to do for the said money, and for other things that I have to do of charge, and my worship saved.[3] It is a death to me to think upon it.

Methinketh by your brother's writing that he thinketh that I am informed by some that be about me to do and to say as I have before this; but by my troth he deemeth amiss. It needeth me not to be informed of no such things. I construe in my own mind, and conceive enow, and too much; and when I have broken my conceit to some that in hap he deemeth it to, they have put me in comfort more than I could have by any imagination in my own conceit.

---

[1] 20 November.   [2] See no. 97, first paragraph.

[3] 'without dishonour'.

He writeth to me also that he hath spent this term £40. It is a great thing. Methinketh by good discretion there might much thereof a been spared. Your father, God bless his soul, hath had as great matters to do as I trow he hath had this term, and hath not spent half the money upon them in so little time, and hath do right well. At the reverence of God, advise him yet to beware of his expenses and guiding, that it be no shame to us all. It is a shame, and a thing that is much spoken of in this country, that your father's gravestone is not made. For God's love, let it be remembered and purveyed for in haste. There hath be much more spent in waste than should have made that.

Methinketh by your brother that he is weary to write to me, and therefore I will not acumber him with writing to him. Ye may tell him as I write to you. . . .

As for my runlet of wine,[1] I should send you money therefor, but I dare not put it in jeopardy, there be so many thieves stirring. John Loveday's man was robbed into his shirt as he came homeward. I trow an ye essay Townshend[2] or Playter[3] or some other good countryman of ours to lend it you for me till they come home, they will do so much for me, and I shall content them again.

Item, James Gresham[4] hath been passing sick, and is yet. Juddy[5] telleth me that your brother is advised for to sue him. For God's sake, let no unkindness be showed to him, for that would soon make an end of him. Remember how kind and true-hearted he hath been to us, to his power, and he had never take that office upon him that he

---

[1] See no. 98, third paragraph.

[2] Roger Townshend of Raynham, Norfolk, a lawyer of Lincoln's Inn who became serjeant in 1477 and a judge of the Common Pleas in 1484. He was often J.P., M.P. 1467-8 and 1472-5, knighted in 1486, died in 1493. He acted for the Pastons in 1470, and they borrowed money from him at various times.

[3] See p. 55, n. 1.   [4] See p. 12, n. 3.

[5] See p. 174, n. 2.

is in danger for ne had be[1] for our sakes. He hath sold a great part of his land therefor, as I suppose ye have knowledge of. Let it be remembered, and else our enemies will rejoice it and there will no worship be therein at long way.

I should write more, but I have no leisure at this time. I trow ye will soon come home, and therefore I write the less. God keep you and send you good speed, &c. Written the Friday, Saint Andrew Eve.

By your mother

100. *Margaret Paston to John Paston III*

Probably 1471, 7 December

I greet you well and send you God's blessing and mine, desiring you to send me word how that your brother doth. It was told here that he should have be dead,[2] which caused many folks, and me bothen, to be right heavy. Also it was told me this day that ye were hurt by affray that was made upon you by fellows disguised. Therefore in any wise send me word in haste how your brother doth and ye bothen, for I shall not been well at ease till I know how that ye do. And for God's love let your brother and ye beware how that ye walken, and with what fellowship ye eaten or drinken and in what place, for it was said here plainly that your brother was poisoned.

And this week was one of Drayton[3] with me, and told me that there were divers of the tenants said that they wost not what to do if that your brother came home; and there was one of the Duke of Suffolk's men by, and bade

---

[1] 'had it not been'; cf. p. 154, n. 1.
[2] See p. 18, n. 3.   [3] See p. 109, n. 4.

them not fearen for his way should be shorted an he should come there. Wherefore in any wise beware of yourself, for I can think they give no force what to do to be venged and to put you fro your intent, that they might have their will in Sir John Fastolf's land ⟨ . . . ⟩.[1] I had liefer ye had never know the land. Remember it was the destruction of your father.

Trust not much upon promises of lords nowadays that ye should be the surer of the favour of their men; for there was a man, and a lord's son, said but late and took it for an example that Sir Robert Harcourt[2] had the good will of the lords after their coming in, and yet within short time after their men killed him in his own place. A man's death is little set by nowadays. Therefore beware of simulation, for they will speak right fair to you that would ye fared right evil.

The blessed Trinity have you in his keeping. Written in great haste the Saturday next after Saint Andrew. Let this letter be burnt when ye have understand it. . . .

By your mother

101. *Margaret Paston to John Paston II*

1472, 5 June

I greet you well and send you God's blessing and mine, letting you wit that I spake with friends of mine within

1 Half a line of writing is lost here through decay of the paper.

2 Of Stanton Harcourt, Oxfordshire; M.P. 1447, 1450–1, 1460–1, often J.P., sheriff of Warwickshire and Leicestershire 1444–5, of Oxfordshire and Berkshire 1455–6. By 1463 he had become a leading Yorkist, was rewarded for his part in the siege of Alnwick in 1464, and went on embassy to Rouen in 1467 with Thomas Colt (see p. 63, n. 1). 'The lords' restored Henry VI in October 1470 (see p. 194, n. 1), and on 14 November Harcourt was murdered by the bastard son of Sir Humphrey Stafford, with whom he had a long-standing feud.

this few days that told me that I am like to be troubled for Sir John Fastolf's goods which were in your father's possession. And as for me, I had never none of them; wherefore I pray you send me a copy of the discharge which ye have of my Lord of Winchester[1] that ye told me that ye had, both for my discharge and yours, whatsomever that be called upon of either of us hereafter.

Item, it is told me that Harry Heydon[2] hath bought of the said lord both Saxthorpe and Titchwell,[3] and hath take possession therein. We beat the bushes and have the loss and the disworship, and other men have the birds.[4] My lord hath false counsel and simple that adviseth him thereto. And as it is told me Guton[5] is like to go the same way in haste, and as for Hellesdon and Drayton[6] I trow it is there it shall be. What shall fall of the remnant God knoweth: I trow as evil, or worse. We have the loss among us. It ought to be remembered, and they that be defaulty to have conscience therein. And, so mote I thrive, it was told me but late that it is said in counsel of them that been at Caister that I am like to have but little good of Mautby[7] if the Duke of Norfolk have possession still in Caister; and if we lose that we lose the fairest flower of our garland, and therefore help that he may be out of possession thereof in haste, by mine advice, whatsoever fortune hereafter. . . .

God keep you. Written in haste on Friday next after Saint Pernel.[8]   By your mother

---

[1] Wainfleet; see p. 201, n. 2. He had been one of Fastolf's trustees and executors, and was eventually recognized as sole executor. An indenture of 14 July 1470 between him and John Paston II set out the terms of an agreement to end the disputes over Fastolf's lands and goods. Most of the lands except Caister were surrendered to Wainfleet.

[2] See p. 163, n. 1.

[3] For Saxthorpe see p. 158, n. 3. Titchwell is about 5 miles east of Hunstanton.   [4] This proverb is recorded from about 1300.

[5] See p. 158, n. 2.   [6] See p. 61, n. 2, and p. 109, n. 4.

[7] See p. 2, n. 5.   [8] St. Petronilla, 31 May.

102. *John Paston III to John Paston II*

1472, 5 June

Right worshipful sir, I recommend me to you. . . . Tidings here, my Lady of Norfolk is with child, she weeneth herself, and so do all the women about her, insomuch she waits the quickening within these six weeks at the farthest. . . .[1]

Also, I pray you to recommend me in my most humble wise unto the good lordship of the most courteous, gentlest, wisest, kindest, most companable, freest, largest, and most bounteous knight, my lord the Earl of Arran, which hath married the King's sister of Scotland.[2] Hereto, he is one the lightest, deliverest, best spoken, fairest archer, devoutest, most perfect, and truest to his lady of all the knights that ever I was acquainted with;[3] so would God my lady liked me as well as I do his person and most knightly condition, with whom I pray you to be acquainted as you seemeth best. He is lodged at the George

[1] Anne Mowbray, the only daughter and heir of the Duke of Norfolk, was born on 10 December 1472. She married Richard, Duke of York, second son of Edward IV, in January 1478. She died in 1481.

[2] Thomas, son of the first Lord Boyd (in the peerage of Scotland), married Lady Mary, sister of James III of Scotland, and was created Earl of Arran in 1467. He was attainted with his father in 1469 and went into exile, where he died before 1474.

[3] The style of this passage seems likely to be indebted to Malory's *Morte Darthur*. There Sir Ector addresses the dead Lancelot in these words: 'And now I dare say, thou Sir Lancelot, there thou liest, that thou were never matched of earthly knight's hand. And thou were the courteoust knight that ever bare shield; and thou were the truest friend to thy lover that ever bestrade horse, and thou were the truest lover of a sinful man that ever loved woman, and thou were the kindest man that ever strake with sword. And thou were the goodliest person that ever came among press of knights, and thou was the meekest man and the gentlest that ever ate in hall among ladies, and thou were the sternest knight to thy mortal foe that ever put spear in the rest' (*Works*, ed. Vinaver (Oxford, 1947), iii. 1259).

in Lombard Street. He ha⟨th⟩ a book of my sister Anne's of the Siege of Thebes.[1] When he hath done with it he promised to deliver it you. I pray you let Portland bring the book home with him; Portland is lodged at the George in Lombard Street also.

And this I promise you, ye shall not be so long again without a bill fro me as ye have been, though I should write how oft the wind changeth; for I see by your writing ye can be wroth an ye will. Written the 5 day of June. . . .

J. PASTON

103. *John Paston III to John Paston II*

1472, 8 July

Right worshipful sir, I recommend me to you. . . .

Item, the proud, peevish, and evil-disposed priest to us all, Sir James,[2] saith that ye commanded him to deliver the book of Seven Sages[3] to my brother Walter, and he hath it. . . .

Item, my mother would ye should in all haste get her acquittance of the Bishop of Winchester for Sir John Fastolf goods.[4] She prayed you to make it sure by the advice of your counsel, and she will pay for the costs. . . .

Item, she would ye should get you another house to lay in your stuff such as came fro Caister; she thinketh one of the Friars' is a fair house. She purposeth to go into the country and there to sojourn once again.[5] Many quarrels

---

[1] A verse narrative by John Lydgate, of which twenty-seven manuscripts survive.   [2] Gloys; see p. 10, n. 2.

[3] 'The Seven Sages of Rome', a collection of tales of which versions exist in many languages. Of the English version there are eight different texts, the oldest dating from early in the fourteenth century.

[4] See no. 101, p. 209.

[5] Margaret did retire to her old home at Mautby by 1474.

are picked to get my brother E.[1] and me out of her house. We go not to bed unchidden lightly. All that we do is ill done, and all that Sir James and Pecock[2] doth is well done. Sir James and I be twain. We fell out before my mother with 'Thou proud priest' and 'Thou proud squire',[3] my mother taking his part, so I have almost beshit the boat as for my mother's house. Yet summer shall be done ere I get me any master.

My mother purposeth hastily to take estate in all her lands, and upon that estate to make her will of the said lands: part to give to my younger brethren for term of their lives and after to remain to you, part to my sister Anne's marriage till £100 be paid, part for to make her aisle at Mautby,[4] part for a priest to sing for her and my father and their ancestors. And in this anger between Sir James and me she hath promised me that my part shall be naught; what your shall be I cannot say. God speed the plough![5]

I'faith ye must purvey for my brother E. to go over[6] with you, or he is undone. He will bring 20 nobles in his purse. My mother will neither give nor lend none of you both a penny forward. Purvey a mean to have Caister again ere ye go over. My lord[7] and my lady—which for certain is great with child[8]—be weary thereof, and all the household also.

If ye will any other thing to be done in this country, send me word and I shall do as well as I can, with God's

---

[1] Edmond.   [2] See p. 76, n. 1.

[3] Cf. p. 10, n. 4.

[4] Margaret directed in her will that she should be buried in the aisle of Mautby church, and that the aisle should be newly roofed, leaded, and glazed, and its walls raised 'conveniently and workmanly'.

[5] The earliest recorded use of this expression appears to be in a song of about 1450 in MS. Arch. Selden B.26 in the Bodleian.

[6] To Calais, where John II went early in 1473.

[7] The Duke of Norfolk.   [8] See the opening of no. 102.

grace, who preserve you. Written the 8 day of July. . . .
I pray burn this bi[ll] for losing.[1]

Your J. P.

104. *John Paston III to John Paston II*

1472, 21 September

Right worshipful sir, I recommend me to you. . . . Sir,
I have been twice at Framlingham[2] sith your departing,
but now the last time the council was there. I saw your
letter, which was better than well indited. R. T.[3] was not
at Framlingham when the council was there, but I took
mine own advice and delivered it to the council, with a
proposition therewith as well as I could speak it. And my
words were well taken, but your letter a thousandfold
better. When they had read it they showed it to my lady.
After that my lady had seen it I spake with my lady,
offering to my lord and her your service, and beside that
ye to do my lord a pleasure,[4] and her a better so as ye
might depart, without any sum specified. She would not
deal in that matter but remitted me again to the council,
for she said an she spake in it till my lord and the council
were agreed they would lay the wite of all the matter on
her, which should be reported to her shame; but this she
promised to be helping, so it were first moved by the
council.

Then I went to the council and offered before them your
service to my lord, and to do him a pleasure, for the having
again of your place and lands in Caister, £40, not speaking

---

[1] 'for fear of losing it'.   [2] See p. 61, n. 3.
[3] Presumably Roger Townshend; see p. 206, n. 2.
[4] That is, give him a present.

of your stuff nor thing else. So they answered me your
offer was more than reasonable, and if the matter were
theirs they said they wist what conscience would drive
them to. They said they would move my lord with it,
and so they did; but then the tempest arose and he gave
them such an answer that none of them all would tell it
me. But when I asked an answer of them they said an
some lords or greater men moved my lord with it the
matter were your (keep counsel),[1] and with this answer
I departed. . . . Discover not this, but in my reason an my
Lord Chamberlain[2] would send my lady a letter with some
privy token betwixt them, and also to move my Lord of
Norfolk when he cometh to the parliament, certainly
Caister is yours. . . .

Written at Norwich the 21 day of September, anno
E. IV 12.[3]

J. P.

105. *John Paston III to John Paston II*

1472, 16 October

Right worshipful sir, I commend me to you. . . . I send
you herewith the indenture betwixt you and Townshend.[4]
My mother hath heard of that matter by the report of old
Wayte,[5] which runneth on it with open mouth in his
worst wise. My mother weepeth and taketh on marvel-

---

[1] These two words are written above the line.

[2] William, Lord Hastings 1461–83, was chamberlain of the Household throughout Edward IV's reign. See p. 63, n. 5.

[3] 'in the 12th year of Edward IV', i.e. 4 March 1472–3 March
1473.

[4] John II had borrowed money from Townshend, giving as security
the manor of Sporle, near Swaffham, which had been in the family
since the judge's day.

[5] Probably the same man as in no. 31; see p. 58, n. 1.

lously, for she saith she wotteth well it shall never be
pledged out; wherefore she saith that she will purvey
for her land that ye shall none sell of it, for she thinks ye
would an it came to your hand. As for her will, and all
such matters as were in hand at your last being here, they
think that it shall not lie in all our powers to let it in one
point.

Sir James is ever chopping at me when my mother is
present, with such words as he thinks wrath me and also
cause my mother to be displeased with me, even as who
saith he would I wist that he setteth not by the best of us.
And when he hath most unsitting words to me, I smile a
little and tell him it is good hearing of these old tales. . . .

Item, I pray you send me some tidings how the world
goeth, and whether ye have sent any of your folk to
Calais. Methinks it costeth you too much money for to
keep them all in London at your charge.

Item, whether ye have anything spoken of my going
to Calais.

Item, as for a goshawk or a tercel, I weened to have had
one of yours in keeping ere this time;[1] but far fro eye, far
fro heart.[2] By my troth, I die for default of labour. An it
may be by any mean possible, for God's sake let one be
sent me in all haste, for if it be not had by Hallowmas the
season shall pass anon. *Memento mei*,[3] and in faith ye shall
not lose on it—nor yet much win on it, by God, who
preserve you.

Written on Saint Michael Day in Monte Tumba.[4]

J. P.

---

[1] John III had several times asked his brother to send him a hawk.
[2] This proverb is recorded from about 1300.
[3] 'Remember me.'
[4] The feast of St. Michael in Monte Tumba was 16 October.

106. *John Paston II to John Paston III*

1472, 4 November

Worshipful and well-beloved brother, I recommend me to you. . . .

Also I pray you feel my Lady of Norfolk's disposition to me wards, and whether she took any displeasure at my language, or mocked or disdained my words which I had to her at Yarmouth, between the place where I first met with her and her lodging. For my Lady Brandon, and Sir William also,[1] asked me what words I had had to her at that time. They said that my lady said I gave her thereof, and that I should have said[2] that my lady was worthy to have a lord's son in her belly, for she could cherish it and deal warely with it. In truth, either the same or words much like I had to her, which words I meant as I said. They lay to that I said she took her ease. Also I should have said that my lady was of stature good, and had sides long and large, so that I was in good hope she should bear a fair child; he was not laced nor braced in to his pain, but that she left him room to play him in. They say that I said my lady was large and great, and that it should have room enow to go out at. And thus whether my lady mock me, or they, I wot not. I meant well, by my troth, to her and to that she is with, as any he that oweth her best will in England.

If ye can by any mean weet whether my lady take it to

---

[1] Sir William Brandon, of Soham, Cambridgeshire, was one of Norfolk's advisers. He was marshal of the King's Bench from 1457, M.P. 1467–8 and 1472–5, and often J.P. He died in 1491. His son William was killed at Bosworth by Richard III; his grandson Charles became Duke of Suffolk in 1514. He had taken a leading part in the siege of Caister in 1469, and John III wrote of him in 1471 as one of his greatest enemies. His wife was Elizabeth, daughter of Sir Robert Wingfield and sister of Sir John of no. 70; see p. 147, n. 4.

[2] See p. 18, n. 3.

displeasure or not, or whether she think I mocked her, or if she wite it but lewdness of myself, I pray you send me word, for I wot not whether I may trust this Lady Brandon or not. . . .

I sent you word of an hawk; I heard not from you since. I do and shall do that is possible in such a need.

Also, I cannot understand that my Lord of Norfolk shall come here this time, wherefore I am in a great agony how is best for me to sue to him for rehaving of my place.[1] That good lord wot full little how much harm he doth me, and how little good or worship it doth him. I pray you send me your advice.

No more to you at this time, but God have you in his keeping. Written at London the 4 day of November anno E. IV 12. . . .

JOHN PASTON, K.

107. *John Paston III to John Paston II*

1472, 18 December

Right worshipful sir, I recommend me to you, thanking you most heartily of your great cost which ye did on me at my last being with you at London, which to my power I will recompense you with the best service that lieth in me to do for your pleasure while my wits be mine own.

Sir, as for the matter of Caister, it hath be moved to my lady's good grace by the Bishop of Winchester[2] as well as he could imagine to say it, considering the little leisure that he had with her; and he told me that he had right an agreeable answer of her, but what his answer was he would not tell me. Then I asked him what answer I should

---

[1] Caister.   [2] See p. 42, n. 5.

send you, inasmuch as ye made me a solicitor to his lordship for that matter. Then he bade me that under counsel I should send you word that her answer was more to your pleasure than to the contrary, which ye shall have more plain knowledge of this next term, at which time both my lord and she shall be at London.

The Bishop came to Framlingham on Wednesday[1] at night, and on Thursday by 10 of the clock before noon my young lady was christened and named Anne. The Bishop christened it and was godfather both, and within two hours and less after the christening was do my Lord of Winchester departed towards Waltham. . . .

Written at Framlingham the Friday next after that I departed fro you. This day my lord is towards Walsingham,[2] and commanded me to overtake him tomorrow at the farthest.

J. P.

108. *Margaret Paston probably to James Gloys*

1473, 18 January

I recommend me to you, and thank you heartily of your letters and diligent labour that ye have had in those matters that ye have written to me of, and in all other, to my profit and worship; and in especial at this sessions touching the matter that I sent you the indenture of. Ye have lighted mine heart therein by a pound, for I was in fear that it would not have been do so hastily without danger.

And as for the letters that Thomas Holler[3] son should

---

[1] 16 December.   [2] See p. 6, n. 1.

[3] Holler, described as 'yeoman', was executor, with John Paston I, of Margaret's uncle John Berney, second son of John Berney of Reedham, whose will was proved in 1461 (see p. 2, n. 5).

have brought me, I see neither him ne the letters that he
should have brought. Wherefore I pray you heartily, if it
be no disease to you, that ye will take the labour to bring
Walter[1] there he should be, and to purvey for him that he
may be set in good and sad rule, for I were loath to lose
him; for I trust to have more joy of him than I have of
them that been older. Though it be more cost to me to
send you forth with him, I hold me pleased, for I wot well
ye shall best purvey for him, and for such things as is
necessary to him, than another should do, after mine
intent. And as for an horse to lead his gear, methink it
were best to purvey one at Cambridge, less than ye can
get any carriers from thence to Oxford more hastily.

And I marvel that the letters came not to me, and
whether I may lay the default to the father or to the son
thereof. And I will Walter should be coupled with a better
than Holler son is, there as he shall be. Howbeit, I will
not that he should make never the less of him, because he
is his countryman and neighbour.

And also I pray you write a letter in my name to Walter,
after that ye have known mine intent before this to him
ward: so that he do well, learn well, and be of good rule
and disposition, there shall nothing fail him that I may
help with, so that it be necessary to him. And bid him
that he be not too hasty of taking of orders that should
bind him, till that he be of 24 year of age or more, though
he be counselled the contrary; for often rape rueth.[2] I will
love him better to be a good secular man than to be a
lewd priest. . . .

God keep you. Written on the Monday next after Saint
Hilary.[3] I have no lenger leisure at this time.

---

[1] Margaret's fourth son.   [2] See p. 173, n. 1.
[3] 13 January.

109. *John Paston II to John Paston III*

1473, 3 June

Right worshipful brother, I commend me to you, letting you weet that this day I was in very purpose to Calais ward, all ready to have gone to the barge, save I tarried for a young man that I thought to have had with me thither, one that was with Rowse, which is in the country. And because I could not get him, and that I have no more here with me but Pamping,[1] Edward, and Jack, therefore Pamping remembered me that at Calais he told me that he purposed to be with the Duchess of Norfolk, my lady and yours; and Edward is sick and seemeth not abiding— he would see what should fall of this world. And so I am as he that saith, 'Come hither, John, my men'.[2]

And as hap was, yesterday Juddy went afore to Calais ward, wherefore I am now ill purveyed, which for aught that I know yet is like to keep me here this Whitsuntide.[3] Wherefore, if ye know any likely men and fair conditioned, and good archers, send them to me, though it be four, and I will have them, and they shall have 4 mark by year and my livery. . . .

I hoped to have been very merry at Calais this Whitsuntide, and am well apparelled and appointed save that these folks fail me so, and I have matter there to make of right excellent. Some man would have hasted him to Calais though he had had no better errand, and some men think it wisdom and profit to be there now, well out of the way. . . .

Written at London the 3 day of June anno E. IV 13.

JOHN P., K.

---

[1] See p. 80, n. 1.
[2] The joke lies in addressing a single servant as 'men'.
[3] Whit Sunday was 6 June.

110. *John Paston II to John Paston III*

1473, 22 November

Right worshipful and heartily beloved brother, I commend me to you, letting you weet that I received a letter that came from you, written *circa* 8 Michael's,[1] wherein ye let me weet of the decease of Sir James, and that my mother is in purpose to be at Norwich; and I am right glad that she will now do somewhat by your advice. Wherefore beware fro henceforth that no such fellow creep in between her and you; and if ye list to take a little labour ye may live right well, and she pleased. It is as good that ye ride with a couple of horse at her cost as Sir James or Richard Calle. . . .

Ye prayed me also to send you tidings how I sped in my matters, and in chief of Mistress Anne Haute.[2] I have answer again fro Rome that there is the well of grace, and salve sufficient for such a sore, and that I may be dispensed with. Nevertheless my proctor there asketh 1,000 ducats, as he deemeth; but Master Lacy, another Rome-runner here, which knoweth my said proctor there, as he saith, as well as Bernard knew his shield,[3] saith that he meaneth but 100 ducats, or 200 at the most; wherefore after this cometh more. . . .

Item, as touching my sister Anne, I understand she hath been passing sick, but I weened that she had been wedded. As for Yelverton,[4] he said but late that he would have her

---

[1] The octave of Michaelmas, 6 October.

[2] See p. 172, n. 1. As late as August 1477 John II was still not released from his engagement. He wrote then to his mother: 'The matter between Anne Haute and me shall, with God's grace, this term be at a perfect end.'   [3] See p. 136, n. 3.

[4] William Yelverton, grandson of the judge (see p. 49, n. 5). He married Anne Paston in 1477. He served on various commissions in Norfolk from 1485 to 1499, and died in 1500. Anne died in 1494–5.

if she had her money, and else not; wherefore methinketh
that they be not very sure. But among all other things
I pray you beware that the old love of Pamping renew
not. He is now fro me; I wot not what he will do.

No more. Written at London the 22 day of November
anno regni regis E. IV 13.[1]

JOHN PASTON, K.

III. *John Paston II to Margaret Paston*

1474, 20 February

Right honourable and most tender good mother, I recommend me to you, beseeching you to have, as my trust is
that I have, your daily blessing; and thank you of your
good motherhood, kindness, cheer, charge, and cost which
I had and put you to at my last being with you, which
God give me grace hereafter to deserve.

Please it you to weet that I think long that I hear not
from you, or from Pecock your servant, for the knowledge
how he hath done in the sale of my farm barley, nor what
is made thereof; wherefore I beseech you, if it be not
answered by that time that this bill cometh to you, to
haste him and it hitherwards. For if that had not tarried
me I deem I had been at Calais by this day, for it is so,
as men say, that the French king with a great host is at
Amiens, but three score mile from Calais;[2] and if he or his
rode before Calais and I not there I would be sorry.

Item, men say that the Earl of Oxford[3] hath been con-
strained to sue for his pardon only of his life, and his body,
goods, lands, with all the remnant, at the King's will; and
so should in all haste now come in to the King. And some

---

[1] 'in the 13th year of the reign of King Edward IV'.
[2] More like four score by modern mileage.
[3] See p. 185, n. 3.

men say that he is gone out of the Mount, men wot not
to what place, and yet left a great garrison there well
furnished in victual and all other thing.

Item, as for the having again of Caister, I trust to have
good tidings thereof hastily. . . .

No more at this time, but Jesu have you in his keeping.
Written at London the 20 day of February anno E. IV 13.

Your son, J. PASTON, K.

112. *John Paston II to John Paston III*

1475, 17 January

I recommend me to you, praying you heartily that I may
have weeting when that my Lord and Lady of Norfolk
shall be at London and how long they shall tarry there,
and in especial my Lord of Norfolk; for upon their coming
to London were it for me to be guided. Nevertheless I
would be sorry to come there but if I needs must. I think
it would be to you over irksome a labour to solicit the
matters atween them and me but if I were there myself;
wherefore if ye think it be convenient that I come thither
I pray you send me word as hastily as ye may, and by
what time ye think most convenient that I should be
there, and of all such comfort as ye find or hear of the
towardness thereof, and when also that ye shall be there
yourself.

For it is so that as tomorrow I purpose to ride into
Flanders to purvey me of horse and harness, and percase
I shall see the assiege at Neuss[1] ere I come again, if I have
time; wherefore if I so do by likelihood it will be a fourteen
days ere I be here again. And after as I hear from you and

---

[1] On the west bank of the Rhine about 10 miles from Düsseldorf,
besieged by Charles the Bold, Duke of Burgundy.

other, then upon that at the next passage, an God will, I purpose to come to London ward, God send me good speed, in chief for the matter above written and secondly for to appoint with the King and my lord[1] for such retinue as I should have now in these wars into France. Wherefore I pray you in Norfolk and other places common with such as ye think likely for you and me that are disposed to take wages in gentlemen's houses and elsewhere, so that we may be the more ready when that need is. Nevertheless at this hour I would be glad to have with me daily three or four more than I have, such as were likely, for I lack of my retinue that I have here so many. I pray you send me some tidings such as ye hear, and how that my brother Edmond doth.

For as for tidings here, there be but few save that the assiege lasteth still by the Duke of Burgoyne afore Neuss, and the Emperor[2] hath besieged also, not far from thence, a castle and another town in like wise wherein the Duke's men been. And also the French king, men say, is comen nigh to the water of Somme with four thousand spears, and some men trow that he will, at the day of breaking of truce or else before, set upon the Duke's countries here. When I hear more I shall send you more tidings. The King's ambassadors, Sir Thomas Montgomery[3] and the Master of the Rolls,[4] be coming homewards from Neuss, and as for me I think that I should be sick but if I see it. . . .

Written at Calais the 17 day of January anno E. IV 14.

[1] Hastings, under whom John II was serving; see p. 63, n. 5.
[2] Frederick III of Austria, King of the Romans 1440–93.
[3] See p. 89, n. 3.
[4] Dr. John Morton became Master of the Rolls in 1473. He was later Bishop of Ely 1478–86, Archbishop of Canterbury from 1486 to his death in 1500, chancellor from 1487, cardinal 1493.

113. *John Paston II to Margaret Paston*

1475, 22 February

Please it you to weet that I received a letter from you written the Saturday[1] next before Candlemas, for answer whereof like it you to weet that, as for the books that were Sir James', God have his soul, I think best that they be still with you till that I speak with you myself. My mind is now not most upon books. . . .

Item, where it pleased you to weet of mine heal and amending, I thank God I am in good case and as good a[s] full whole, both of the fever ague, of mine eye, mine leg, and mine heel, save that I am tender of all these and, were not good rule, full like to feel of each of them right soon. Nevertheless God thank you of your large proffer, whereof I would be right glad if I might, for troubles and other labour that I have taken on me now into France ward. For the good speed of me and that journey I beseech you of your prayers and remembrance; and that journey with God's grace once done, I purpose verily with God's grace thereafter to dance attendance[2] most about your pleasure and ease, and with God's grace soon upon Eastern,[3] ere ever I go forth, I hope to see you and fetch your blessing.

No more at this time, but Jesus have you in his keeping. Written at Calais the 22 day of February anno E. IV 14.

Your son, JOHN PASTON, K.

[1] 28 January.
[2] The first record of this expression.
[3] Easter Day was 26 March.

114. John Paston II to Margaret Paston

1475, 11 September

Right reverend and my most tender and kind mother, I recommend me to you. Please it you to weet that, blessed be God, this voyage of the King's is finished for this time and all the King's host is comen to Calais as on Monday last past, that is to say the 4 day of September;[1] and at this day many of his host be passed the sea into England again, and in especial my Lord of Norfolk and my brethren.

Item, I was in good hope to have had Caister again. The King spake to my Lord of Norfolk for it, and it was full like to have comen; but in conclusion it is delayed till this next term, by which time the King hath commanded him to take advice of his council and to be sure that his title be good, or else the King hath ascertained him that for any favour he must do me right and justice, &c.

And if Caister had comen, by my faith I had comen straight home. Notwithstanding, if I may do you service or ease, as ye and I have commoned heretofore, after as I hear from you, as God help me, I purpose to leave all here and come home to you and be your husband and bailiff, wherein I spake to my brother John to tell you mine advice.

I also mislike somewhat the air here, for by my troth I was in good heal when I came hither, and all whole, and to my weeting I had never a better stomach in my life; and now within eight days I am crazed again.

I suppose that I must be at London at Michaelmas, and there to purvey for payment for mine uncle William, by which time I pray you that I may hear from you, and of

[1] Edward IV had landed at Calais on 4 July, intending to join the Duke of Burgundy in an attack on France. But he was bought off by the French king, whose offer of a pension of 50,000 crowns a year was ratified by the Treaty of Picquigny on 29 August.

your advice and help if anything be grown of Sporle wood;[1]
for had not yet that danger have been, I might yet have
been at home with you at this day or within seven days
after.

No more, but I beseech Jesus have you in keeping.
Written at Calais the 11 day of September.

JOHN PASTON, K.

115. *John Paston III to John Paston II*

1475, 10 October

Right worshipful sir, I recommend me to you, certifying
you that I have commoned with Barnard and other your
well-willers with my Lord of Norfolk, which advise me
that ye should, for your nighest mean to get Caister again,
labour to get a letter fro the King direct to R. Southwell,[2]
James Hobart,[3] and other of my lord's council being, and
to each of them. . . . My lady sweareth, and so doth
Barnard on her behalf, that she would as fain ye had it
as anybody, notwithstanding she said not so to me sith
I came home, for I spake not with her but once sith I saw
you last. Yet she lieth in Norwich, and shall do till she
be delivered.[4] But I have be sick ever sith I came on this
side the sea, but I trust hastily to amend; for all my sick-

---

[1] See p. 214, n. 4. John II had redeemed the manor from Townsend
in 1474, and was now trying to sell the timber. The 'danger' was a
demand by William Paston II for the delivery of pledges by Margaret
Paston as surety for money he was to pay on her behalf.

[2] See p. 52, n. 4.

[3] A lawyer of Lincoln's Inn employed by Norfolk. He was M.P.
for Ipswich in 1467–8, 1478, and 1483, and in 1486 became King's
attorney to Henry VII and privy councillor. He was recorder of
Norwich in 1496, was knighted in 1503, and died in 1517.

[4] There is no record of the birth of a second child to the Duchess of
Norfolk.

ness that I had at Calais, and sith I came over also, came but of cold. But I was never so well armed for the war as I have now armed me for cold; wherefore I advise you take example by me if it happen you to be sick, as ye were when I was at Calais. In any wise keep you warm. . . .

My mother sendeth you God's blessing and hers, and she would fain have you at home with her; and if ye be once met she telleth me ye shall not lightly depart till death depart you.

As I was writing this letter one told me that the King should be at Walsingham this next [week]. If it be so it were best for you to await on the King all the way, and if ye have not men and horse enough I shall send you. Do as ye think best, and as ye will have me to do send me your advice and I shall accomplish it to my power, with God's grace, who preserve you.

Written at Norwich the 10 day of October anno 15 E. IV.

P. J.

116. *John Paston III to John Paston II*

1475, 23 October

After all duties of recommendation, please it you to understand that I have spoken with my lady sith I wrote to you last; and she told me that the King had no such words to my lord for Caister as ye told me,[1] but she saith that the King asked my lord at his departing fro Calais how he would deal with Caister, and my lord answered never a word.

Sir W. Brandon[2] stood by, and the King asked him what my lord would do in that matter, saying that he had commanded him beforetime to move my lord with that

---

[1] See no. 114.   [2] See p. 216, n.1.

matter; and Sir W. Brandon gave the King to answer that he had done so. Then the King asked Sir W. B. what my lord's answer was to him, and Sir W. B. told the King that my lord's answer was that the King should as soon have his life as that place. And then the King asked my lord whether he said so or not, and my lord said yea. And the King said not o word again, but turned his back and went his way; but my lady told me an the King had spoken any word in the world after that to my lord, my lord would not have said him nay. And I have given my lady warning that I will do my lord no more service, but ere we parted she made me to make her promise that I should let her have knowledge ere I fastened myself in any other service; and so I departed and saw her not since, nor not purpose to do till I speak with you. . . .

I have been right sick again sith I wrote to you last, and this same day have I been passing sick; it will not out of my stomach by no mean. I am undone—I may not eat half enough when I have most hunger; I am so well dieted and yet it will not be. God send you heal, for [I] have none three days together, do the best I can.

Written at Norwich the Monday next before Saint Simon and Jude anno E. IV 15.

J. P. . . .

117. *John Paston II to Margaret Paston*

1476, 17 January

Like it you to weet that, not in the most happy season for me, it is so fortuned that whereas my Lord of Norfolk yesterday being in good heal this night died about midnight, wherefore it is for all that loved him to do and help now that that may be to his honour and weal to his soul.

And it is so that this country is not well purveyed of cloth of gold for the covering for his body and hearse; wherefore, every man helping to his power, I put the council of my lord in comfort that I hoped to get one for that day if it were so that it be not broken or put to other use.

Wherefore please it you to send me word if it be so that ye have or can come by the cloth of tissue that I bought for my father's tomb, and I undertake it shall be saved again for you unhurt at my peril. I deem hereby to get great thank and great assistance in time to come; and that either Sim or Mother Brown[1] may deliver it me tomorrow by 7 of the clock.

Item, as for other means, I have sent my servant Richard Turner to London, which I hope shall bring me good tidings again, and within four days I hope to see you.

Written on Wednesday the 17 day of January anno E. IV 15.

JOHN PASTON, K.

118. *John Paston III to John Paston II*

1476, 23 January

After all duties of recommendation, liketh you to weet that I ensure you your sending to Caister is evil taken among my lord's folks, insomuch that some say that ye tendered little my lord's death inasmuch as ye would so soon enter upon him after his decease, without advice and assent of my lord's council. Wherefore it is thought here by such as be your friends in my lord's house that, if my lady have once the grant of the wardship of the child,[2] that she will occupy Caister with other lands, and lay the

---

[1] These both appear elsewhere as household servants of the Pastons.
[2] Her daughter Anne; see p. 210, n. 1.

default on your unkind hastiness of entry without her assent. Wherefore in any wise get you a patent of the King enealed before hers, an ye may by any mean possible.

Also I pray you common with my Lord Chamberlain[1] for me and weet how that he will have me demeaned. It is told me for certain that there is none hay to get at Calais; wherefore if I might be pardoned for any keeping of horse at Calais till midsummer it were a good turn. . . .

Written at Norwich the Tuesday next after your departing thence, 23 die Januarii anno E. IV 15.

JOHN PASTON

119. *John Paston II to John Paston III*

1476, 27 January

I recommend me to you. . . . Item, I have received a letter from you written on Tuesday last.[2] Item, where that some towards my Lady of Norfolk noise that I did unkindly to send so hastily to Caister as I did, there is no discreet person that so thinketh. For if my lord had been as kind to me as he might have been, and according to such heart and service as my grandfather, my father, yourself, and I have ought and done to my Lords of Norfolk that dead been, and yet if I had wedded his daughter, yet must I have done as I did.

And moreover, if I had had any deeming of my lord's death four hours ere he died I must needs, but if I would be known a fool, have entered it the hour before his decease. But in effect they that in that matter have alway meant unkindly to me, they feign that rumour again me; but there is none that meant truly to him that dead is that would be sorry that I had it, and in especial such as love his soul.

Item, where it is deemed that my lady would hereafter be the rather mine heavy lady for that dealing, I think that she is too reasonable so to be; for I did it not unwist to her council. There was no man thought that I should do otherwise; and as to say that I might have had my lady's advice or leave, I might have tarried yet ere I could have spoken with her, or yet have had anybody to have moved her on my behalf. As ye wot, I did what I could. . . .

Item, as for my matter here, it was this day before all the lords of the Council, and among them all it was not thought that in my sending of Whetley[1] thither immediately after the decease of the Duke that I dealt unkindly or unsittingly, but that I was more unreasonably dealt with. Wherefore let men deem what they will, greatest clerks are not alway wisest men;[2] but I hope hastily to have one way in it or other. . . .

Written at London the 27 day of January anno E. IV 15. . . .

120. *Dame Elizabeth Brews*[3] *to John Paston III*

1477, about 10 February

Cousin, I recommend me unto you, thanking you heartily for the great cheer that ye made me and all my folks the

---

[1] A servant of John II's often mentioned in the period 1476–8; see, for example, nos. 125 and 128. Here he had been sent to make a formal claim to Caister in John II's name.

[2] This proverb is found in English from Chaucer onwards, and earlier in medieval Latin.

[3] Second wife of Sir Thomas Brews of Topcroft, 10 miles south of Norwich. (The title 'Dame' was used of the wife of a baronet or knight.) She was a daughter of Gilbert Debenham (see p. 85, n. 4). Brews (see no. 124) was sheriff of Norfolk and Suffolk in 1438–9 and

last time that I was at Norwich. And ye promised me that ye would never break the matter to Margery unto such time as ye and I were at a point. But ye have made her such advocate for you that I may never have rest night nor day, for calling and crying upon to bring the said matter to effect, &c.

And, cousin, upon Friday is Saint Valentine's Day, and every bird chooseth him a make;[1] and if it like you to come on Thursday at night, and so purvey you that ye may abide there till Monday, I trust to God that ye shall so speak to mine husband, and I shall pray that we shall bring the matter to a conclusion, &c. For, cousin, it is but a simple oak that [is] cut down at the first stroke;[2] for ye will be reasonable, I trust to God, which have you ever in his merciful keeping, &c.

> By your cousin DAME ELIZABETH BREWS,
> otherwise shall be called by God's grace.

121. *Margery Brews to John Paston III*

1477, February

Right reverend and worshipful and my right well-beloved Valentine, I recommend me unto you full heartily, desiring to hear of your welfare, which I beseech Almighty God long for to preserve unto his pleasure and your heart's desire. And if it please you to hear of my welfare, I am

---

1442–3, often J.P., M.P, for Suffolk 1435, 1445–6, 1467–8. He died in 1482. John III married Margery Brews before the end of the year.

[1] Very close to Chaucer's lines in *The Parliament of Birds*, 309–10:

> For this was on seynt Valentynes day,
> Whan every foul cometh there to chese his make.

[2] This proverb is recorded from about 1400.

not in good heal of body nor of heart, nor shall be till I hear from you;

> For there wots no creature what pain that I endure,
> And for to be dead, I dare it not discure.

And my lady my mother hath laboured the matter to my father full diligently, but she can no more get than ye know of, for the which God knoweth I am full sorry.

But if that ye love me, as I trust verily that ye do, ye will not leave me therefor; for if that ye had not half the livelode that ye have, for to do the greatest labour that any woman alive might, I would not forsake you.

> And if ye command me to keep me true wherever I go,
> Iwis I will do all my might you to love and never no mo.
> And if my friends say that I do amiss, they shall not me let so for to do,
> Mine heart me bids evermore to love you
> Truly over all earthly thing,
> And if they be never so wroth, I trust it shall be better in time coming.

No more to you at this time, but the Holy Trinity have you in keeping. And I beseech you that this bill be not seen of none earthly creature save only yourself, &c. And this letter was indite at Topcroft with full heavy heart, &c.[1]

By your own M. B.

122. *Margery Brews to John Paston III*

1477, February

Right worshipful and well-beloved Valentine, in my most humble wise I recommend me unto you, &c. And heartily

[1] It was written by her father's clerk, Thomas Kela.

I thank you for the letter which that ye sent me by John Beckerton, whereby I understand and know that ye be purposed to come to Topcroft in short time, and without any errand or matter but only to have a conclusion of the matter betwixt my father and you. I would be most glad of any creature alive so that the matter might grow to effect. And there as ye say, an ye come and find the matter no more toward than ye did aforetime ye would no more put my father and my lady my mother to no cost nor business for that cause a good while after, which causeth mine heart to be full heavy; and if that ye come and the matter take to none effect, then should I be much more sorry and full of heaviness.

And as for myself, I have done and understand in the matter that I can or may, as God knoweth. And I let you plainly understand that my father will no more money part withal in that behalf but £100 and 50 mark, which is right far fro the accomplishment of your desire. Wherefore, if that ye could be content with that good, and my poor person, I would be the merriest maiden on ground. And if ye think not yourself so satisfied, or that ye might have much more good, as I have understand by you afore, good, true, and loving Valentine, that ye take no such labour upon you as to come more for that matter; but let i(t) pass, and never more to be spoken of, as I may be your true lover and bedewoman during my life.

No more unto you at this time, but Almighty Jesus preserve you both body and soul, &c.

By your Valentine, MARGERY BREWS

123. *John Paston III to Margaret Paston*

1477, 8 March

Right worshipful mother, after all duties of recommendation, in as humble wise as I can I beseech you of your daily blessing. Mother, please it you to wit that the cause that Dame Elizabeth Brews desireth to meet with you at Norwich, and not at Langley¹ as I appointed with you at my last being at Mautby, is by my means; for my brother Thomas Jermyn,² which knoweth naught of the matter, telleth me that the causeway, ere ye can come to Buckenham ferry,³ is so overflown that there is no man that may uneath pass it, though he be right well horsed; which is no meet way for you to pass over, God defend it. But, all things reckoned, it shall be less cost to you to be at Norwich, as for a day or twain, and pass not, than to meet at Langley where everything is dear; and your horse may be sent home again the same Wednesday.

Mother, I beseech you for divers causes that my sister Anne may come with you to Norwich. Mother, the matter is in a reasonable good way, and I trust, with God's mercy and with your good help, that it shall take effect better to mine advantage than I told you of at Mautby; for I trow there is not a kinder woman living than I shall have to my mother-in-law if the matter take, nor yet a kinder father-in-law than I shall have, though he be hard to me as yet. All the circumstances of the matter, which I trust

¹ About 9 miles south-east of Norwich, south of the River Yare.
² He lived at Rushbrooke in Suffolk, 3 miles south-east of Bury St. Edmunds. It is not apparent why John Paston should call him 'my brother'.
³ There was a ferry across the Yare at Buckenham, which is on the north bank, until the Second World War. It would be the normal crossing on a journey from Mautby to Langley, which is a short distance from the river on the south side.

to tell you at your coming to Norwich, could not be written in three leaves of paper, and ye know my lewd head well enough—I may not write long; wherefore I ferry over all things till I may await on you myself.

I shall do tun into your place a dozen ale, and bread according, against Wednesday. If Sim[1] might be forborne, it were well done that he were at Norwich on Wednesday in the morning at market.

Dame Elizabeth Brews shall lie at John Cook's.[2] If it might please you, I would be glad that she might dine in your house on Thursday, for there should ye have most secret talking. And, mother, at the reverence of God, beware that ye be so purveyed for that ye take no cold by the way towards Norwich, for it is the most perilous march that ever was seen by any man's days that now liveth.

And I pray to Jesu preserve you and yours. Written at Topcroft the 8 day of March.

Your son and humble servant, J. P.

124. *Sir Thomas Brews to John Paston II*

1477, 8 March

Right worshipful and my heartily well-beloved cousin, I recommend me unto you, desiring to hear of your welfare, which I pray God may be as continual good as I would have mine own. And, cousin, the cause of my writing unto you at this time is, I feel well by my cousin John, your brother, that ye have understanding of a

[1] See p. 230, n. 1.

[2] John Cook, draper, was sheriff of Norwich in 1473 and mayor in 1484. He lived in St. Andrew's parish, immediately west of St. Peter's Hungate of which John Paston I and Margaret were benefactors.

matter which is in communication touching a marriage with God's grace to be concluded betwixt my said cousin your brother and my daughter Margery, which is far commoned and not yet concluded, nor not shall nor may be till I have answer from you again of your good will and assent to the said matter, and also of the obligation which that I send you herewith; for, cousin, I would be sorry to see either my cousin your brother or my daughter driven to live so mean a life as they should do if the £120 should be paid of their marriage money.

And, cousin, I have taken myself so near in leaving of the said £120 that, whereas I had laid up £100 for the marriage of a younger daughter of mine, I have now lent the said £100, and £20 over that, to my cousin your brother, to be paid again by such easy days as the obligation which I send you herewith specifies. And, cousin, I were right loath to bestow so much upon one daughter that the other her sisters should fare the worse; wherefore, cousin, if ye will that this matter shall take effect under such form as my cousin your brother hath written unto you, I pray you put thereto your good will, and some of your cost as I have done of mine more largely than ever I purpose to do to any twain of her sisters, as God knoweth mine intent, whom I beseech to send you your liefest heart's desire.

Written at Topcroft the 8 day of March, &c.

By your cousin, SIR T. BREWS, Knight

125. *John Paston II to John Paston III*

1477

I recommend me to you, letting you weet that I received a letter of yours by Edward Hensted two days after that Whetley[1] was departed from me which he had forgotten

[1] See p. 232, n. 1.

in his casket, as he said, whereof I should have sent you answer by Whetley if I had had it tofore he went. Notwithstanding I am right loath to write in that matter oft; for for a conclusion I wrote to my mother by Piers Moody[1] all that I might and would do therein. Ye have also now written again. You need not to pray me to do that might be to your profit and worship, that I might do, ofter than once, or to let me weet thereof; for to my power I would do for you, and take as much pain for your weal, and remember it when percase ye should not think on it yourself. I would be as glad that one gave you a manor[2] or £20 by year as if he gave it to myself, by my troth.

Item, where ye think that I may with conscience recompense it again unto our stock of other lands that I have of that value in fee simple, it is so that Snailwell,[3] by my grandfather's will once and by my father's will secondarily, is entailed to the issue of my father's body.

Item, as for Sporle[4] £20 by year, I had thereof but 20 mark by year, which 20 mark by year and the 10 mark over I have endangered, as ye well know of that bargain, which if it be not redeemed I must recompense some other manor of mine to one of my brethren for the said 10 mark over 20 mark that longeth to me; wherefore I keep the manor of Runham. Then have I fee simple land the manor of Winterton, with Bastwick and Billes,[5] which in all is

---

[1] Another of John II's servants, who was at Caister in 1477.

[2] Margaret Paston had promised her manor of Sparham to John III on his marriage; see p. 120, n. 1. John II objected on the ground that it was entailed.

[3] About 2 miles north of Newmarket in Cambridgeshire; it was part of the judge's legacy.

[4] See p. 214, n. 4 and p. 227, n. 1. John II had again pledged the manor of Sporle as security for money borrowed from Townshend.

[5] The manors of Runham, Begviles in Winterton, Repps in Bastwick, and Billes in Stokesby (all within 6 miles of Caister) had belonged to Fastolf.

not 20 mark by year, which is not to the value of the manor of Sparham. And as for Caister, it were no convenient land to exchange for such a thing, nor it were not policy for me to set that manor in such case, for all manner of haps.

I need not to make this excuse to you but that your mind is troubled. I pray you rejoice not yourself too much in hope to obtain thing that all your friends may not ease you of; for if my mother were disposed to give me and any woman in England the best manor that she hath, to have it to me and my wife and to the heirs of our two bodies begotten, I would not take it of her, by God. Stablish yourself upon a good ground, and grace shall follow. Your matter is far spoken of and blown wide, and if it prove no better I would that it had never be spoken of. Also, that matter noiseth me that I am so unkind that I let all together. I think not a matter happy, nor well handled, nor politicly dealt with, when it can never be finished without an inconvenience, and to any such bargain I keep never to be condescending nor of counsel. If I were at the beginning of such a matter, I would have hoped to have made a better conclusion, if they mock you not. This matter is driven thus farforth without my counsel; I pray you make an end without my counsel. If it be well, I would be glad; if it be otherwise, it is pity. I pray you trouble me no more in this matter.[1]

126. *Margaret Paston to Dame Elizabeth Brews*

1477, 11 June

Right worshipful and my chief lady and cousin, as heartly as I can I recommend me to you. Madam, liketh you to

---

[1] The sheet is cut across below the last line, and no subscription or signature remains.

understand that the chief cause of my writing to you at this season is this. I wot well it is not unremembered with you the large communication that divers times hath been had touching the marriage of my cousin Margery your daughter and my son John, of which I have been as glad, and now latewards as sorry, as ever I was for any marriage in mine life. And where or in whom the default of the breach is, I can have no perfect knowledge; but, madam, if it be in me or any of mine, I pray you assign a day when my cousin your husband and ye think to be at Norwich towards Sall,[1] and I will come thither to you, and I think ere ye and I depart that the default shall be know where it is, and also that, with your advice and help and mine togethers, we shall take some way that it shall not break; for if it did it were none honour to neither parties, and in chief to them in whom the default is, considering that it is so far spoken.

And, madam, I pray you that I may have perfect knowledge by my son Yelverton,[2] bearer hereof, when this meeting shall be, if ye think it expedient, and the sooner the better in eschewing of worse; for, madam, I know well if it be not concluded in right short time, that as for my son, he intendeth to do right well by my cousin Margery and not so well by himself, and that should be to me, nor I trust to you, no great pleasure if it so fortuned—as God defend, whom I beseech to send you your liefest desires.

Madam, I beseech you that I may be recommended by this bill to my cousin your husband, and to my cousin Margery, to whom I supposed to have given another name ere this time. Written at Mautby on Saint Barnaby's Day.

By your MARGARET PASTON

---

[1] Stinton in Sall, about 5 miles west of Aylsham, was Sir Thomas Brews's seat before he and his wife acquired Topcroft, which had belonged to Debenham (her father; see p. 232, n. 3) in 1465.

[2] See p. 221, n. 4.

127. *John Paston III to John Paston II*

1478, 21 January

Sir, after all duties of recommendation, liketh you to understand that I have commoned with divers folks of the Duke of Suffolk[1] now this Christmas and sithen, which let me in secret wise have knowledge, like as I wrote unto you, that he must make a shift for money, and that in all haste. Wherefore, sir, at the reverence of God, let it not be lachessed, but with effect applied now while he is in London and my lady his wife also; for I ascertain you that 100 mark will do more now in their need than ye shall peradventure do with 200 marks in time coming an this season be not taken. . . .

And, sir, as for my housewife, I am fain to carry her to see her father and her friends now this winter, for I trow she will be out of fashion in summer; and so in my progress fro my father Brews unto Mautby I took Master Playter[2] in my way, at whose house I wrote this bill the 21 day of January anno E. IV 17. And I beseech God to preserve you and yours.

Your J. PASTON

128. *J. Whetley[3] to John Paston II*

1478, 20 May

Please it your mastership to understand the dealing of everything the which I was charged with at my departing from your mastership. . . .

And as for Hellesdon, my Lord of Suffolk was there on

---

[1] Suffolk still held Hellesdon (cf. no. 71, &c.), but John II hoped to recover it; see no. 128.

[2] See p. 55, n. 1.   [3] See p. 232, n. 1.

Wednesday in Whitsun week,[1] and there dined, and drew
a stew, and took great plenty of fish. Yet hath he left you
a pike or two again ye come, the which would be great
comfort to all your friends and discomfort to your enemies;
for at his being there that day there was never no man that
played Herod in Corpus Christi play[2] better and more
agreeable to his pageant than he did. But ye shall understand that it was after noon, and the weather hot, and he
so feeble for sickness that his legs would not bear him,
but there was two men had great pain to keep him on his
feet. And there ye were judged.[3] Some said, 'Slay'; some
said, 'Put him in prison.' And forth came my lord, and
he would meet you with a spear, and have none other
mends for that trouble at ye have put him to but your
heart blood, and that will he get with his own hands; for
an ye have Hellesdon and Drayton ye shall have his life
with it. . . .

And as for my mistress, your mother hath been greatly
diseased and so sick that she weened to have died, and
hath made her will,[4] the which ye shall understand more
when I come, for there is every man for himself. I know
not the circumstance of everything as yet, and therefore
I write no more to you therein, but I am promised to
know ere I depart from thence. . . .

Written at Norwich on Wednesday, Corpus Christi
Even, anno E. IV 18.

Your servant, J. WHETLEY

[1] 13 May.

[2] Cycles of plays or 'pageants' on Biblical themes were performed
in many cities, including Norwich, on the feast of Corpus Christi (the
second Thursday after Whit Sunday). Herod was conventionally
presented as an embodiment of anger and violence, as for instance in
a stage-direction in the Coventry *Shearmen and Tailors' Pageant*:
'Here Herod rages in the pageant and in the street also.'

[3] Suffolk evidently went through the procedure of a manor court.

[4] This will was superseded by another made in 1482, two almost
contemporary copies of which survive. Margaret did not die until 1484.

129. *William Paston III to John Paston III*

Probably 1478, 7 November[1]

Right reverend and worshipful brother, I recommend me unto you, desiring to hear of your welfare and prosperity, letting you weet that I have received of Alweather a letter, and a noble in gold therein. Furthermore, my creancer, Master Thomas,[2] heartily recommended him to you, and he prayeth you to send him some money for my commons; for he saith ye be 20*s.* in his debt, for a month was to pay for when he had money last.

Also I beseech you to send me a hose cloth, one for the holidays of some colour, and another for the working days, how coarse so ever it be it maketh no matter; and a stomacher, and two shirts, and a pair of slippers. And if it like you that I may come with Alweather by water and sport me with you at London a day or two this term time, then ye may let all this be till the time that I come. And then I will tell you when I shall be ready to come from Eton, by the grace of God, whom have you in his keeping.

Written the Saturday next after All Hallow Day,[3] with the hand of your brother.

WILLIAM PASTON

130. *William Paston III to John Paston III*

1479, 23 February

Right reverend and worshipful brother, after all duties of recommendation I recommend me unto you, desiring to hear of your prosperity and welfare, which I pray God

---

[1] William was at this time at Eton, evidently near the end of his course. This letter is likely to be a few months earlier than no. 130.

[2] See no. 130, first paragraph. Thomas Stevenson became a fellow of Eton on 12 July 1479.   [3] All Saints' Day, 1 November.

long to continue to his pleasure and to your heart's desire; letting you weet that I received a letter from you, in the which letter was 8*d.* with the which I should buy a pair of slippers; furthermore certifying you, as for the 13*s.* 4*d.* which ye sent by a gentleman's man for my board, called Thomas Newton, was delivered to mine hostess, and so to my creancer, Master Thomas Stevenson; and he heartily recommended him to you.

Also, ye sent me word in the letter of 12 lb. figs and 8 lb. raisins. I have them not delivered, but I doubt not I shall have, for Alweather told me of them and he said that they came after in another barge.

And as for the young gentlewoman, I will certify you how I first fell in quaintance with her. Her father is dead. There be two sisters of them, the elder ⟨is just wedded, at⟩[1] the which wedding I was with mine hostess, and also desired by the gentleman himself, called William Swan, whose dwelling is in Eton. So it fortuned that mine hostess reported on me otherwise than I was worthy, so that her mother commanded her to make me good cheer, and so in good faith she did. She is not abiding there she is now, her dwelling is in London; but her mother and she came to a place of hers five mile from Eton, where the wedding was, for because it was nigh to the gentleman which wedded her daughter. And on Monday next coming, that is to say the first Monday of Clean Lent,[2] her mother and she will go to the pardon[3] at Sheen,[4] and

---

[1] The bracketed words have been supplied in a modern hand on a patch over a hole in the paper. They cannot be a true copy of the original, for *just* was not used in this sense until the seventeenth century.

[2] This expression is recorded from about 1400 to the early seventeenth century. Monday, 28 February, was the first Monday of Lent in 1479.

[3] A church festival at which indulgence was granted.

[4] The pardon was not at the famous Charterhouse of Sheen (now

so forth to London, and there to abide in a place of hers in Bow Churchyard.

And if it please you to inquire of her, her mother's name is Mistress Alborow. The name of the daughter is Margaret Alborow, the age of her is by all likelihood 18 or 19 year at the farthest. And as for the money and plate, it is ready whensoever she were wedded; but as for the livelode, I trow not till after her mother's decease, but I cannot tell you for very certain ⟨. . .⟩;[1] but you may know by inquiring. And as for her beauty, judge you that when ye see her, if so be that ye take the labour; and specially behold her hands, for an if it be as it is told me, she is disposed to be thick.

And as for my coming from Eton, I lack nothing but versifying, which I trust to have with a little continuance. . . .

No more to you at this time, but God have you in his keeping. Written at Eton the Even of Saint Matthias the Apostle in haste, with the hand of your brother,

WILLIAM PASTON

131. *Walter Paston to John Paston III*

1479, 30 June

Right worshipful and heartily beloved brother, I recommend me unto you, desiring faithfully to hear of your prosperity, which God preserve, thanking you of divers letters that you sent me. In the last letter that you sent to me ye writ that you should have writ in the letter that

Richmond in Surrey), but at the monastery of Syon on the other side of the Thames. This confusion is commonly found from as early as 1440. Both houses were founded by Henry V.

[1] A hole big enough for about twelve letters.

you sent by Master Brown how that I should send you word what time that I should proceed;[1] but there was none such writing in that letter. The letter is yet to show, and if you come to Oxon. ye shall see the letter, and all the letters that you sent me sithence I came to Oxon.

And also Master Brown had that same time much money in a bag, so that he durst not bring it with him, and that same letter was in that same bag, and he had forgot to take out the letter, and he sent all together by London; so that it was the next day after that I was made bachelor ere than the letter came, and so the fault was not in me.

And if ye will know what day I was made bachelor, I was made on Friday was sevennight,[2] and I made my feast[3] on the Monday after. I was promised venison again my feast of my Lady Harcourt[4] and of another man too, but I was deceived of both; but my guests held them pleased with such meat as they had, blessed be God, who have you in his keeping, Amen.

Written at Oxon. on the Wednesday next after Saint Peter.[5]

                                              W. PASTON

[1] To his degree.

[2] 18 June.

[3] A candidate for a degree who had not fulfilled all the regulations was required to seek a 'grace' from the congregation of regents (masters engaged in teaching); and one of the conditions for their granting it might be that he should provide a feast for them.

[4] The second wife of Sir Richard Harcourt of Wytham, Berkshire. She was Catherine, widow of Sir Miles Stapleton, whom the Pastons had known for many years; see p. 54, n. 5. She married Harcourt by 1468, and died in 1488. Harcourt was M.P. and J.P. for Oxfordshire and Norfolk, King's squire 1460, sheriff of Oxfordshire and Berkshire in 1461 and 1466–7. He died in 1486.

[5] 29 June.

132. *Edmond Paston II to John Paston III*[1]

1479, 21 August

Sure tidings arn come to Norwich that my grandam[2] is deceased, whom God assoil. Mine uncle[3] had a messenger yesterday that she should not escape, and this day came another, at such time as we were at mass for my brother Walter, whom God assoil.[4] Mine uncle was coming to have offered, but the last messenger returned him hastily, so that he took his horse incontinent, to inform more of our heaviness.

My sister[5] is delivered, and the child passed to God, who send us his grace.

Docking told me secretly that for any haste mine uncle should ride by my Lady of Norfolk to have a three score persons. Whether it is to convey my grandam hither or not he could not say; I deem it is rather to put them in possession of some of her lands.

Written the Saturday the 21 day of August anno E. IV 19.

133. *John Paston III to Margaret Paston*

1479, November

Right worshipful mother, after all duties of humble recommendation, as lowly as I can I beseech you of your daily blessing and prayers. And, mother, John Clement, bearer

---

[1] This letter is neither addressed nor signed, but it is in Edmond's hand and is endorsed by John III.

[2] Agnes Paston. [3] William Paston II.

[4] Walter had died at Norwich about 19 August and was buried in St. Peter's Hungate church.

[5] Since no name is given it is likely that only one sister was still alive, namely Anne, wife of William Yelverton; see p. 167, n. 4, and p. 221, n. 4. The other sister, Margery, who had married Richard Calle, may well have died before this. Margaret left nothing to her in her will of 1482, though she did make bequests to three Calle children.

hereof, can tell you, the more pity is, if it pleased God, that my brother[1] is buried in the White Friars[2] at London, which I thought should not have been, for I supposed that he would have been buried at Bromholm.[3] And that caused me so soon to ride to London to have purveyed his bringing home; and if it had been his will to have lain at Bromholm, I had purposed all the way as I have ridden to have brought home my grandam and him togethers, but that purpose is void as now.

But this I think to do when I come to London, to speak with my Lord Chamberlain[4] and to win by his means my Lord of Ely[5] if I can. And if I may by any of their means cause the King to take my service and my quarrel togethers, I will; and I think that Sir George Browne,[6] Sir James Radcliff,[7] and other of mine acquaintance which wait most upon the King and lie nightly in his chamber will put to their good wills. This is my way as yet. And, mother, I beseech you, as ye may get or send any messengers, to send me your advice, and my cousin Lomnor's,[8] to John Lee's house, tailor, within Ludgate. I have much more to write, but mine empty head will not let me remember it.

Also, mother, I pray that my brother Edmond may ride to Marlingford,[9] Oxnead,[10] Paston, Cromer,[11] and Caister,

---

[1] John Paston II.

[2] An important Carmelite priory between Fleet Street and the Thames, commemorated by the present Whitefriars and Carmelite Streets. John II in his will directed that he should be buried there.

[3] See p. 1, n. 2.   [4] See p. 214, n. 2.

[5] John Morton; see p. 224, n. 4.

[6] The second husband of John's aunt Elizabeth; see p. 47, n. 2.

[7] Yeoman of the King's chamber 1477, King's knight and carver 1479, knight of the body 1490.   [8] See p. 26, n. 2.

[9] This manor, 6 miles west of Norwich, was part of Agnes Paston's inheritance. John's title was contested by his uncle William, her son.

[10] See p. 5, n. 3.

[11] The manor of Ropers in Cromer was bequeathed by William I to Agnes for life.

and in all these manors to enter in my name, and to let the tenants of Oxnead and Marlingford know that I sent no word to him to take no money of them but their attornment; wherefore he will not, till he hear fro me again, ask them none, but let him command them to pay to no servant of mine uncle's, nor to himself nor to none other to his use, in pain of payment again to me. I think if there should be any money asked in my name, peradventure it would make my Lady of Norfolk against me and cause her to think I dealt more contrary to her pleasure than did my brother, whom God pardon of his great mercy. I have sent to enter at Stanstead and at Horwellbury,[1] and I have written a bill to Anne Montgomery and Jane Rodon[2] to make my Lady of Norfolk,[3] if it will be.

> Your son and humble servant, J. PASTON

134. *John Paston III to Margaret Paston*

1479, December

Right worshipful mother, after all duties of humble recommendation, as lowly as I can I beseech you of your daily blessing and prayer. Please it you to understand that whereas ye willed me by Poins to haste me out of the air that I am in, it is so that I must put me in God, for here must I be for a season. And in good faith I shall never, while God sendeth me life, dread more death than shame.

[1] The manors of Stanstead in Suffolk and Horwellbury in Hertfordshire were part of Agnes's inheritance; see p. 9, n. 3, and p. 23, n. 1.

[2] These ladies were servants of the Duchess of Norfolk. In 1472 John III wrote to his brother that Jane Rodon 'hath been the most special labourer in your matter and hath promised her good will forth, and she doth all with her mistress'.

[3] Something clearly omitted; perhaps he meant 'make my lady of Norfolk well-willing', or the like; cf. the preceding sentence.

And, thanked be God, the sickness is well ceased here, and also my business putteth away my fear.

I am driven to labour in letting of th'execution of mine unkind uncle's intent, wherein I have as yet none other discourage, but that I trust in God he shall fail of it. I have spoken with my Lord of Ely divers times, which hath put me in certainty by his word that he will be with me against mine uncle in each matter that I can show that he intendeth to wrong me in; and he would fain have a reasonable end betwixt us, whereto he will help, as he saith. And it is certain my brother, God have his soul, had promised to abide the rule of my Lord Chamberlain and of my Lord of Ely, but I am not yet so farforth, nor not will be till I know my Lord Chamberlain's intent; and that I purpose to do tomorrow, for then I think to be with him, with God's leave. And sith it is so that God hath purveyed me to be the solicitor of this matter, I thank him of his grace for the good lords, masters, and friends that he hath sent me, which have perfectly promised me to take my cause as their own; and those friends be not a few. . . .

135. *Margery Paston to John Paston III*

About 1481, 1 November

Right reverend and worshipful sir, in my most humble wise I recommend me unto you as lowly as I can, &c. Please you to weet John Howes, Alexander Wharton, John Fille, with the parson and the new miller of Marlingford, have gotten Tom at Wells'[1] cart of East Tuddenham, farmer to mine uncle William Paston, Harry Harby of Melton Magna, farmer and bailie to my said uncle, Richard

---

[1] For this form of surname see p. 111, n. 6.

Barker's cart of the said town of Melton, late farmer and yet is in danger to my said uncle, and William Smith's cart of Brandon juxta Barnham Broom,[1] late farmer and bailie and also in danger to my said uncle, on Monday and Tuesday last past carried away from Marlingford into the place at Saint Edmund's[2] in Norwich twelve of your great planks, of the which they made six loads, bearing about the said carts bows and glaives for fear of taking away. . . .

My Lady Calthorp[3] hath been at Ipswich on pilgrimage, and came homeward by my Lady of Norfolk. And there was much communication of your matter betwixt you and mine uncle,[4] saying to my Lady Calthorp ye need not a gone to London, ye might have had an end at home; remembering to my said Lady Calthorp of the motion that he made touching the manor of Sporle,[5] promitting to my lady to abide that and to write and seal as largely as any man will desire him. And at his departing from my lady he was not merry; what the cause was I wot not. My Lady Calthorp desireth me to write to you to have end, for he intends largely to have a peace with you, as he saith. But trust him not too much, for he is not good.

My mother-in-law thinketh long she hear no word from you. She is in good heal, blessed be God, and all your

[1] These villages are all near Marlingford (see p. 249, n. 9): East Tuddenham about 3 miles north-west, Brandon Parva and Barnham Broom close together 3 or 4 miles west, and Great Melton 2 miles south. (Latin *juxta* = 'next'.)

[2] The church is in Fishergate, north of the Wensum.

[3] Dame Elizabeth Calthorp, daughter of Sir Miles Stapleton (see p. 54, n. 5) and wife of Sir William Calthorp (see p. 66, n. 8). She died in 1505.

[4] Other letters show that William Paston II was on familiar terms with the Duchess of Norfolk, who was a cousin of his wife Anne Beaufort, third daughter of Edmund, Duke of Somerset (d. 1455; see p. 38, n. 1).

[5] See p. 227, n. 1.

babies also. I marvel I hear no word from you, which grieveth me full evil. I sent you a letter by Brasier son of Norwich, whereof I hear no word.

No more to you at this time, but Almighty Jesu have you in his blessed keeping. Written at Norwich on Hallowmas Day at night.

By your servant and bedewoman, MARGERY PASTON

Sir, I pray you if ye tarry long at London that it will please [you] to send for me, for I think long sin I lay in your arms.

136. *Margery Paston to John Paston III*

About 1481

Mine own sweetheart, in my most humble wise I recommend me unto you, desiring heartly to hear of your welfare, the which I beseech Almighty God preserve and keep to his pleasure and your heart's desire. Sir, the cause of my writing to you at this time: on Friday at night last past came Alexander Wharton, John House, and John Fille, with two good carts well manned and horsed with them, to Marlingford, and there at the manor of Marlingford and at the mill loaden both carts with maslin and wheat, and betimes on Saturday in the morning they departed fro Marlingford towards Bungay, as it is said. . . .

Item, sir, on Saturday last past I spake with my cousin Gurney,[1] and he said if I would to go my Lady of Norfolk, and beseech her good grace to be your good and gracious lady, she would so be; for he said that one word of a

---

1 William Gurney, esq., of Tharston, 5 miles west of Topcroft. He was a retainer of the Duke of Norfolk. He had been escheator of Norfolk and Suffolk 1465–6, served on commissions in 1484 and 1491, and died in 1505.

woman should do more than the words of twenty men,
if I could rule my tongue and speak none harm of mine
uncle. And if ye command me so for to do, I trust I should
say nothing to my lady's displeasure, but to your profit;
for methinketh by the words of them, and of your good
farmer of Oxnead, that they will soon draw to an end. . . .
I understand by my said cousin Gurney that my lady is
near weary of her part, and he saith my lady shall come
on pilgrimage into this town, but he knoweth not whether
afore Christmas or after. And if I would then get my Lady
Calthorp, my mother-in-law, and my mother and myself,
and come before my lady beseeching her to be your good
and gracious lady, he thinketh ye shall have an end, for
fain she would be rid of it, with her honour saved, but
yet money she would have.

No more to you at this time, but I marvel sore that I
have no letter from you. I pray God preserve you and
send me good tidings from you, and speed you well in
your matters. . . . At Norwich the Sunday next after the
feast of All Saints.

By your servant and bedewoman, MARGERY PASTON

137. *John Paston III to Margaret Paston*

Between 1482 and 1484

Right worshipful mother, in my most humble wise I
recommend me to you, beseeching you of your daily
blessing; and when I may, I will with as good will be
ready to recompense you for the cost that my housewife
and I have put you to as I am now bound to thank you
for it, which I do in the best wise I can.

And, mother, it pleased you to have certain words to
my wife at her departing touching your remembrance of

the shortness that ye think your days of, and also of the mind that ye have towards my brethren and sister,[1] your childer, and also of your servants, wherein ye willed her to be a mean to me that I would tender and favour the same. Mother, saving your pleasure, their needeth none ambassadors nor means betwixt you and me; for there is neither wife nor other friend shall make me to do that that your commandment shall make me to do, if I may have knowledge of it. And if I have no knowledge, in good faith I am excusable both to God and you. And well remembered, I wot well ye ought not to have me in jealousy for one thing nor other that ye would have me to accomplish if I overlive you, for I wot well none o man alive hath called so oft upon you as I to make your will and put each thing in certainty that ye would have done for yourself and to your childer and servants. Also, at the making of your will,[2] and at every communication that I have been at with you touching the same, I never contraried thing that ye would have done and performed, but always offered myself to be bound to the same.

But, mother, I am right glad that my wife is anything your favour or trust, but I am right sorry that my wife or any other child or servant of your should be in better favour or trust with you than myself; for I will and must forbear and put fro me that that all your other childer, servants, priests, workmen, and friends of your that ye will aught bequeath to, shall take to them. And this have

---

[1] The use of the singular confirms the deduction at p. 248, n. 5, that Margery Calle had died earlier.

[2] Margaret made her will on 4 February 1482, and died on 4 November 1484. This must be the will meant here, for the earlier one (see p. 243, n. 4) was made in the lifetime of John II, and John III could not have written in these terms about it. John III was his mother's executor, and the copy of her will in the British Museum (Add. Charter 17253) bears the notes he made in his own hand as he dealt with each item.

I and ever will be ready unto while I live, on my faith, and never thought other, so God be my help, whom I beseech to preserve you and send you so good life and long that ye may do for yourself, and me after my decease. And I beshrew their hearts that would other, or shall cause you to mistrust or to be unkind to me or my friends.

At Norwich this Monday, with the hand of your son and truest servant,

JOHN PASTON

138. *The Duke of Norfolk*[1] *to John Paston III*

1485, about 12 August

Well-beloved friend, I commend me to you, letting you to understand that the King's enemies be a land,[2] and that the King would have set forth as upon Monday but only for Our Lady Day;[3] but for certain he goeth forward as upon Tuesday, for a servant of mine brought to me the certainty.

Wherefore I pray you that ye meet with me at Bury,[4] for by the grace of God I purpose to lie at Bury as upon Tuesday night; and that ye bring with you such company of tall men as ye may goodly make at my cost and charge, beside that ye have promised the King. And I pray you ordain them jackets of my livery, and I shall content you at your meeting with me.

Your lover, J. NORFOLK[5]

[1] John Howard; see p. 34, n. 5. He was killed within a fortnight of this letter, at Bosworth on 22 August.

[2] Henry Tudor landed at Milford Haven on 7 August.

[3] The Assumption, 15 August.

[4] Bury St. Edmunds in Suffolk.

[5] This subscription is in Norfolk's own hand.

139. *John Paston III to Margery Paston*

After 1486[1]

Mistress Margery, I recommend me to you. And I pray you in all haste possible to send me by the next sure messenger that ye can get a large plaster of your *flos unguentorum*[2] for the King's Attorney, James Hobart; for all his disease is but an ache in his knee. He is the man that brought you and me togethers, and I had liefer than £40 ye could with your plaster depart him and his pain. But when ye send me the plaster ye must send me writing how it should be laid to and taken fro his knee, and how long it should abide on his knee unremoved, and how long the plaster will last good, and whether he must lap any more cloths about the plaster to keep it warm or not. And God be with you.

Your JOHN PASTON

140. *William Paston III to John Paston III*

1492, 18 February[3]

. . . Sir, the King sendeth ordnance daily to the seaside, and his tents and hales be a-making fast and many of them be made. And there is also great provision made by gentlemen that should go with His Grace for horse, harness, tents, hales, gardevians, carts, and other things that should serve them for this journey that the King intendeth to take on hand, so that by likelihood His Grace will be going soon upon Easter. And so I intend, after that I hear

[1] Hobart did not become King's attorney until 1486; see p. 227, n. 3. Margery Paston seems to have died in 1495.

[2] 'flower of ointments'.

[3] The date appears from the account of Henry VII's preparations to invade France, which he finally did in October 1492.

hereafter, to go to Calais to purvey me of harness and such things as I shall need besides horse, under that form that my costs shall be paid for. Sir, I am as yet no better horsed than I was when I was with you, nor I wot not where to have none, for horse-flesh is of such a price here that my purse is scant able to buy one horse; wherefore I beseech you to hearken for some in your country. . . .

Sir, as towards my journey to Calais, the which I intend[ed] to have tane at my last being with you, it was so I was disappointed of Thomas Day and another man I should have had by his means, as ye have had knowledge of ere now; and also I had weened to have had folks a met with me at Hedingham[1] which did not. My lord,[2] seeing me diseased and also none otherwise purveyed, willed me in any wise to tarry until his coming to London, and sent mine excuse to my Lord Daubeney,[3] under this form, how that I was sore diseased, notwithstanding I was well-willed to have come to fulfil my promise but he could not suffer me, seeing me so diseased. And so my Lord Daubeney was sorry of my disease and content that I tarried.

Sir, I beseech you to hold me excused for keeping of Thomas Linstead your servant, and him both. It is so that he and I both have been in hand with my uncle for his matter, and yet we have him at no good point, but I trust we shall have. Sir, if I take this journey to Calais I must beseech you to forbear him lenger, and if I go not to Calais, though I be loath to forbear him, yet I shall bring

---

[1] Hedingham Castle in Essex, 9 miles north of Braintree, was the seat of the Earl of Oxford (see p. 185, n. 3), in whose service William Paston III now was.   [2] Oxford.

[3] Giles, created first Baron Daubeney in 1486. He was one of Henry VII's commanders in his war against France. In June of 1492 he was sent as ambassador to negotiate a treaty of peace, and when this came to nothing the invasion of October was ordered. This led to an early treaty, which Daubeney arranged.

him with me shortly into Norfolk, ye to have him if ye list, with the grace of God, who have you in keeping.

Written at London the 18 day of February, with the hand of your poor brother,

WILLIAM PASTON

141. *The Earl of Oxford to John Paston III*

After 1495

Right worshipful and right entirely beloved, I commend me heartily to you. And whereas your brother William, my servant, is so troubled with sickness and crazed in his minds that I may not keep him about me, wherefore I am right sorry, and at this time send him to you; praying especially that he may be kept surely and tenderly with you to such time as God fortune him to be better assured of himself and his minds more sadly disposed, which I pray God may be in short time, and preserve you long in good prosperity.

Written at my place in London the 26 day of June.

OXFORD

142. *William Warham[1] to William Paston IV*

1503, 6 September

Cousin Paston, I recommend me unto you, and have received your letter by the which I have understand of the

---

[1] Warham was elected Bishop of London in October 1501, though not consecrated until 25 September 1502. He was translated to Canterbury by a papal bull of 29 November 1503, but must have been elected earlier. His concern with the administration of the estate, which was in the province of the Archbishop, shows that it is to this

death of my cousin your father, whose soul Jesu assoil. I will counsel and exhort you to take it as well and as patiently as ye can, seeing that we all be mortal and born to die.

And whereas ye desire to have a letter *ad colligendum*,[1] after mine advice ye shall do well to be here with me at Michaelmas next coming, and at your then coming I shall be glad to do you the best comfort and help that I can; counselling that ye in the meantime do not entermeddle in any wise with th'administering of any part of your father's goods nor with the receiving of his debts, for divers causes, as at your coming hither ye shall know more.

The mean season, look that ye be of as comfortable cheer as ye can, exhorting my lady your mother-in-law[2] to be in like wise; to whom I pray you to have me recommended. Thus fare ye heartily well.

From London the 6th day of September.

> Your WILLIAM elect
> of London

latter election that the subscription refers; and other documents also prove that John Paston III lived until 1503.

[1] A commission to *collect* the goods of a deceased person, issued normally in cases of intestacy. The first duty of the administrator of an estate after probate was to draw up an inventory of the property (cf. no. 29, first paragraph); but probate was often granted to executors who swore that they would later draw one up.

[2] This must mean 'stepmother', a sense found occasionally up to the nineteenth century. John III's second wife was Agnes, daughter of Nicholas Morley, esq., of Glynde, Sussex, who had been married twice before. She died in 1510.

GLOSSARY

THE glossary sets out to explain words, forms, and meanings that are unfamiliar or not self-evident to a modern reader. Many of the meanings given occur rarely, and the same word will often have its modern sense in other places. Grammatical descriptions are given only when distinctions are necessary. The swung dash ~ represents either the headword or the part of it to which endings are added.

A, (*prep.*) of; on.

A, (*pron.*) he.

A(N), (*vb., auxil. of perf. infin.*) have.

ABIDE, observe; endure, face. ~EN, (*past pl. and part.*) stayed, waited.

ABIDING, constant.

ABUY, pay for, atone (for).

ACCOMPLISH UP, complete.

ACOLD, cold.

ACQUIT (OF), repay (for).

ACUMBER, encumber.

ADO, activity; *have* ~, have to do.

ADOUBTED, afraid.

ADVERTISED, informed.

ADVISE (*reflex.*) reflect, take heed; *is* ~*ed*, intends; *well-*~*ed*, judicious.

AFEARED, afraid.

AFFRAY, attack.

AFTER, (*prep.*) according to; at (the rate or price of); (*conj.*) ~ (*that*) according as, considering how.

AFTERCLAPS, unfortunate consequences.

AGAIN, (*prep.*) against; towards; for. (*adv.*) back. ~WARD, in return.

AGAINST, by the time that; opposite; off (shore).

A LIERRE, a kind of cloth; see p. 4, n. 3.

ALLIES, relatives.

ALMIGHT, almighty.

ALMS, charity.

ALSO, as.

AMEND, mend one's ways, reform.

AMONG, at the same time.

AN (IF), if.

ANEMPS, in respect of, in the sight of.

ANNUITY, an annual payment differing from rent in being charged to persons rather than land.

ANON, immediately.

APAID, pleased.

APAIR, deteriorate; make worse.

APEACH, accuse. ∼MENT, charge.

APPEALED, accused.

APPOINT, agree; decide. ∼MENT, agreement; terms, capitulation.

APPURTENANTS, appurtenances, rights appertaining.

ARRAYED, in a (specified) state.

ARTICULARLY, point by point.

AS, as if.

ASCERTAIN, inform; report.

ASKERS, plaintiffs, creditors.

ASSIEGE, siege.

ASSIGNED, signed.

ASSIZE, in take ∼, begin legal proceedings.

ASSOIL, absolve, pardon.

AT, that.

ATTORNMENT, transfer to a new lord of the manor.

ATWEEN, ATWIXT, between.

AULA, hall.

AVAIL, (*n.*) benefit, advantage. (*vb.*) profit.

AVAUNT, boast.

AVOID, remove, take away; go away.

AVOW, vow.

AWARD, custody, keeping.

BAILIE, bailiff.

BANNERET, a rank of knighthood conferred for bravery in battle in the King's presence.

BAR, band.

BARE, threadbare.

BEAR, in ∼ on hand, deceive; accuse falsely; ∼ it out, keep up appearances; ∼ out, carry through.

BEDEMAN, ∼WOMAN, one who prays for another, 'humble servant'.

BEHALF, in on that ∼, on that account.

BEHEST, (*n. and vb.*) promise.

BEHIND, still to come.

BEHOLD, ∼EN, ∼ING, obliged.

BELONG, be a duty.

BEND, draw (a crossbow).

BENEFITED IN, endowed with.

BESEEN, appointed, dressed.

BESET, (*reflex.*) bestow oneself (in marriage).

BESHIT, fouled.

BESHREW, curse.

BEWARE[1] (OF), take care (about), pay attention (to).

BEWARE[2], lay out (money), spend.

BILL, letter; petition; list; record; ∼ copy, official copy.

BLAVER, talk foolishly.

BOGEY, sheepskin.

BOLD, (*reflex.*) make bold, venture.

BOMBARDS, kind of large-bored cannon.

BONDLY, in return for customary services rather than rent.

BOROUGH TOWNS, towns having charters of incorporation.

BOTH(EN), too, also.

BRAZIER, brass-worker.

BREAK, break into; (of a letter, &c.) open; (of cloth) tear; reveal, declare.

BREDE, breadth.

BRETHEL, good-for-nothing, wretch.

BREVE, make up accounts.

BRIBERS, thieves.

BRIGANDINES, body armour of metal rings or plates on a cloth or leather base, originally made in two parts.

BROTHEL, (*collect.*) ruffians.

BURGOYNE, Burgundy.

BUT (IF), unless.

BY, from the behaviour of; ∼ *his life*, in his lifetime.

CAN, in ∼ *skill*, has knowledge. Cf. CON.

CANNEL, gutter.

CASE, event, incident; position, state.

CAST, intend to; in ∼ *jeopardy*, run a risk.

CERTAIN, in *a* ∼, a certain number or amount.

CERTAINTY, true account.

CHAMLET, camlet, a kind of fabric.

CHARGE, (*n.*) responsibility; *take* ∼, assume responsibility (for administration); expense; importance. (*vb.*) order, proclaim.

CHASSEVILAINS, some kind of ordnance.

CHEAP, value; *best* ∼, cheapest.

CHEER, (*n.*) demeanour; reception, entertainment; *make (someone)* ∼, behave (in a specified way) towards, welcome. (*vb.*) enjoy oneself.

CHEVISANCE, arrangement (for raising money).

CHEVISH, raise (money), borrow; get on, succeed.

CHILD, servant.

CIRCUMSTANCE, ceremony; subordinate detail.

CLEANLIER, more handsomely.

CLEPE, call.

CLERK, scholar.

CLOG, block attached to leg to prevent escape.

CLOSE, (*n.*) enclosed field. (*adj.*) confidential.

CLOSET, enclosed pew.

CLOUT, patch.

COLOUR, (*n.*) in *by, under* ∼ *of*, under pretext of (being). (*vb.*) ∼ *under*, blame falsely on.

COMB, measure of 4 bushels.

COMFORT, (*n.*) encouragement; *put in* ∼, encourage. (*vb.*) encourage. ∼ABLE, encouraging, reassuring; agreeable.

COMMON, confer, discuss.

COMMONS, common people; provisions, board.

COMMUNICATION, conference, discussion.

COMPANABLE, friendly.

CON, be able to, know how to; ~ *good will*, be well disposed (to). Cf. CAN.

CONCEIT, opinion, understanding.

CONCEIVE, understand.

CONDESCENDING, acquiescent.

CONDITE, conducted, brought.

CONDITION, disposition, temper; (*pl.*) social position; *fair* ~*ed*, well-disposed.

CONSTABLE, local officer of the peace.

CONSTRUE, deduce, infer.

CONTENT, pay back.

CONTINUE, adjourn (a court). ~ANCE, adjournment.

CONVENTICLES, assemblies (esp. for an illegal purpose).

CORRECT, punish.

COST(S), in *do* ~, incur expense, spend money.

COUNSEL, secrecy, secret; *a, of* ~, a party.

COUNTENANCE, show.

COUNTERVAIL, be equal in value to, cancel out.

COUNTRY, district, region.

COUPLED, associated.

COVERT, cover.

CRAFT, skill; dissimulation. ~Y, skilful, able.

CRAZED, broken in health, ill; insane.

CREANCER, tutor.

CREDENCE, confidence; *of* ~ confidential.

CREMIL, a kind of fabric, perhaps lace.

CROD, (*past part. of* CROWD) pushed (in a wheelbarrow).

CRY, in ~ *mercy*, beg mercy.

CUNNING, learned; skilful. ~LY, skilfully.

CUPSHOTTEN, given to drink.

CURSE, excommunicate. ~ING, excommunication.

CURSED-HEARTED, vicious, malignant.

CUSTOMS, duties, on exports as well as imports.

DAINTY, regard, esteem.

DANGER, liability, debt; power. ~OUS, difficult to deal with.

DAY, an appointed day, as for a settlement, judgement, or inquest; respite.

DEATH, plague.

DEBATE, fight, quarrel.

DECEIVED, disappointed.

DEEM, attribute. ~ING, inkling, suspicion.

DEFAULT, lack; negligence; fault.

DEFENSIBLE, protective. ~LY, for defence.

DEFERRED, delayed.

DELIVER, (*vb.*) hand over; give up, release.

DELIVEREST, most agile.

DEMEAN, (*reflex. and pass.*) conduct oneself, behave, act. ∼ING, conduct.

DEPART, part, separate; divide, share; bestow.

DESIRED, invited.

DESPITOUS, spiteful, malicious.

DESPOIL, strip, plunder.

DETERMINED, concluded.

DEVOIR, duty; *do his* ∼, apply himself.

DIRECTION, (course of) action, arrangement, disposition.

DISAVAIL, do harm to.

DISCOMFORT, annoyance.

DISCOURAGE, (*n.*) grounds for confidence in ability to obstruct.

DISCOVER, reveal; betray; find out.

DISCURE, reveal.

DISDAIN, think unfitting.

DISEASE, inconvenience, trouble; illness.

DISGUISINGS, masquerades.

DISOBEISANCE, disobedience.

DISPLEASANCE, displeasure.

DISPORT, game, amusement.

DISSEISED, dispossessed.

DISSOLUTE, negligent.

DISTRESS, (*n.*) distraint; property distrained. (*vb.*) distrain.

DISWORSHIP, dishonour, discredit.

DO, cause, have (with *infin.*,

as ∼ *buyen*, have bought); *done me to weet*, made known to me; do a service; (*for*) *to do*, to be done; ∼ *on*, put on, wear.

DOGBOLTS, tools, catspaws.

DOLES, boundary marks.

DREW, dragged, fished (a pond) with a net.

DUTY, payment due, charge, debt.

EARTHLY, on earth.

EASE, (*n.*) in *at* ∼, in good health; *do* ∼, give assistance. (*vb.*) assist.

EASY, light; insignificant.

EFTSOONS, again.

ELL, else.

ELLEN, ELN, ell (45 in.).

EME, uncle.

END, in *make an* ∼ *with*, pay off.

ENDANGERED, mortgaged.

ENFEOFFED, invested with an estate held in fee.

ENFORCING, reinforcement.

ENOW, enough.

ENSURE, assure. ∼ED, engaged, betrothed. ∼ANCE, engagement.

ENTERMEDDLE, interfere.

ENTITLE, provide with a legal title (to property).

ENTREAT, deal with, treat.

ENTREN UPON, take possession by force against.

ENTRESS, entry.

ERE, before, earlier.

ERST, before.

ESCUTE, crown (a silver coin).

ESSAY, try, test the opinion of.

ESTATE, in *take ~ in*, draw up an account or statement of.

EVEN, eve; evening.

EVIDENCE, (*often treated as pl.*) title-deeds.

FACE, (*n.*) in *make a ~*, put on an outward show. (*vb.*) defy.

FAIL (OF), lack, be without.

FAIN, glad(ly); obliged.

FAIR, fittingly; carefully.

FALL (OF), happen (to); *~ in with*, come to terms with.

FANTASY, fancy; *have a ~ in*, be well-disposed to.

FARE, deal, behave.

FARFORTH, far.

FARM, fixed yearly payment for the occupation of land. ~ER, occupier of land who pays a fixed sum to the owner.

FARSIN, a tumour arising from a disease of horses allied to glanders.

FASTINGONG, Shrovetide.

FEE, land held in fee (by heritable right subject to feudal obligations); estate; *~ simple*, held without restriction to any special class of heirs. FEED MEN, men holding land in fee, vassals.

FEEBLE, poor in quality.

FEEL, understand, judge, have an impression (of); test.

FELLOW, equal, match. ~SHIP, company, body of men.

FEOFFEES, trustees.

FERD WITH, dealt with, treated.

FERRY, pass.

FETIS, neat, elegant; well-made.

FIND, pay for (subsistence). ~ING, keep.

FLICKERING, wavering, shifty.

FOR, (*prep.*) because of; in exchange for; to prevent. (*conj.*) because.

FORBEAR, spare, do without; lose. ~ABLE, patient.

FORBY, past.

FORCE, in *no ~ therefor*, that does not matter; *give no ~*, do not care.

FOREIGN, not domestic.

FORSAKE, neglect.

FORSWEAR, deny (on oath).

FORTH, forward. ~WARD, forward, on.

FORTUNE, allot, grant.

FORWARD, in future.

FOT, fetched.

FRAID, afraid.

FRAY UPON, attack.

FREEST, noblest.

FRIEND, relative. ~LIHOOD, friendliness.

FRIEZE, a coarse woollen cloth.

FRO, from.

GARDEVIANS, travelling trunks.

GARNISON, garrison.

GENTLE, well-bred, courteous; kind.

GILL, lass.

GIPSER, purse.

GIVE OVER, postpone.

GLAIVES, spears, or perhaps bills.

GOOD, goods, property, money; *for no* ~, on no account.

GOODLY, conveniently.

GOODMAN, ~WIFE, master, mistress of the house.

GOSSIP, familiar acquaintance, crony.

GOSSOON, lad (see p. 43, n. 7).

GOVERNANCE, keeping; management; behaviour; wise conduct, self-discipline.

GRACE, favour; mercy, clemency.

GRACIOUS, well-disposed.

GRAINS, a West African spice called in full 'grains of Paradise'.

GROUND, in *on* ~, on earth, alive.

GUIDE, manage, dispose of; (*reflex. and pass.*) conduct oneself, behave. ~ING, conduct; management; protection.

GUISE, habit, way.

HAIN, raise.

HALES, pavilions.

HAN, (*pres. pl.*) have.

HAND, in *in* ~ *with*, engaged in negotiation with.

HAP, (*n.*) chance; *in* ~, perhaps. (*vb.*[1]) happen, come about.

HAP, (*vb.*[2]) wrap.

HARM, trouble. ~LESS, see SAVE.

HARNESS, armour.

HEADED, beheaded.

HEAL, health.

HEARTLY, earnestly.

HEAVY, sad, sorrowful, grave; ill-disposed. ~NESS, sadness, grief.

HEREAFTER, about this.

HERETO, in addition.

HIGHT, called.

HIGHT YOU, hasten.

HITHERWARD, on this account.

HOLP(EN), helped.

HOMELY, familiarly.

HONE, in *set upon the* ~, made to feel anxious.

HOPE, think, believe.

HOUSELLED, administered the Eucharist to.

HOUSING, buildings.

HUDDER-MUDDER, secrecy.

HUMS, in *by* ~ *and by hays*, with meaningless mumbling.

HURLING, disturbance.

HUSBAND, manager of a household.

IMMORTIZING, alienation of lands 'in mortmain', i.e. to a corporate body.

INBILLED, listed.

INCONTINENT, at once.

INCONVENIENT, difficulty.

INDIFFERENT, impartial.

INDUCED, persuaded, led to believe.

INQUIRANCE, inquiry.

INQUISITION, inquest, public inquiry by a jury.

INTENT, purport.

INTO, up to, as much as; until.

IWIS, certainly.

JACK, padded or plated leather jacket.

JAPE, (*n.*) deception. (*vb.*) deceive.

JOURNEY, day's work, esp. battle; particular task.

JUNKERIES, feasts.

JUSTLY, exactly; properly.

KEEP, guard, protect; hold (a court); care.

KERCH, ∼IE, kerchief.

KIRTLE, gown, dress.

LABOUR, (*n.*) effort, initiative. (*vb.*) work for, try to achieve; seek to persuade, canvass. ∼ERS, agents.

LACHESSED, neglected.

LANCEGAYS, lances.

LANGUAGE, words; conversation, talk; *hath such* ∼, speaks in such a way.

LARGE, liberal; (of conscience) lax; (of language) gross, offensive. ∼LY, generously; in broad terms.

LATEWARD(S), recently.

LAY TO, allege.

LEAD, carry.

LEARN, teach.

LEAST, smallest.

LEAVE, leave off, desist.

LEECHCRAFT, treatment.

LEET, court.

LEISURE, time.

LENGER, longer.

LESS THAN, unless.

LET[1], cause, in ∼ *send*, have sent.

LET[2], hinder, prevent; omit. ∼ING, hindrance, obstacle, obstruction.

LEVATION, elevation (of the Host).

LEVE, believe.

LEWD, ignorant, foolish; vulgar, low. ∼LY, ignorantly, foolishly. ∼NESS, low behaviour, coarseness.

LIE, sleep, stay the night; ∼ *upon*, be incumbent upon.

LIEFER, rather. ∼EST, dearest.

LIKE, (*adj.*) likely.

LIKE, (*vb.*) please.

LIKELY, promising. ∼NESS, probability.

LIST, it pleases; likes.

LIVELODE, property yielding income; estate; rents.

LIVERY, delivery, release.

LOLLARDY, heretical be-
haviour.

LONG, (*adj.*), in *think* ∼, grow
weary of waiting, find the
time long; ∼ *to*, long.

LONG, (*vb.*) belong.

LORDSHIP, manor, estate;
good ∼, patronage, favour.

LOVER, friend.

LUMISH, malicious.

LUSTETH, pleases.

MAIL, bag.

MAILED, covered with metal
rings or plates.

MAKE, mate.

MANSLAUGHT, killing.

MARK, the sum of 13*s.* 4*d.*

MASLIN, mixed grain, esp. rye
and wheat.

MASTER, general title of
courtesy, used specifically of
a man who has taken a
degree. ∼FAST, bound to a
master. ∼SHIP, in *good* ∼,
favour.

MATTERS, affairs, business.

MAUGRE, in spite; see p. 71,
n. 2.

MEAN, (*n.*) means; inter-
mediary. ∼S, efforts, in
great ∼; *made their* ∼, strove.

MEAN, (*vb.*) speak.

MEAT, food.

MEDDLED, mixed up.

MEETLY, fitting, suitable.

MEINIE, household.

MENDS, compensation.

MESEEMETH, it seems to me.

METHINK, ∼ETH, ∼S, it seems
to me.

MIND, intention.

MINISHED, reduced.

MINISTER, administer (an
estate). ∼TRATION, administration.

MISCHIEF, (*n.*) injury, harm.
(*vb.*) come to grief; injure.

MISTER, need.

MO, more (usually of number).

MOANED, mourned, lamented.

MORN, morrow, day after.

MORWEN, morning.

MOST, greatest.

MOTE, may.

MOVE, urge; prompt, apply
to, try to influence.

MOW, be able; may.

MUCH, large.

MURREY, a purple-red cloth.

MUSTERDEVILLERS, a grey
woollen cloth; see p. 4, n. 1.

NAIL, a sixteenth of a yard,
2¼ in.

NE, nor; not.

NEARHAND, almost.

NEAT, cattle.

NECKERCHES, neckerchiefs.

NEXT, nearest.

NILL, will not.

NOBLE, a gold coin worth
6*s.* 8*d.*

NOISE, (*n.*) rumour, scandal.
(*vb.*) rumour; accuse; report
of.

NOY, trouble.

O, one.

OBLIGATION, bond.

OFFEND, break.

ORDAIN, order (to be made).

ORDINANCE, warlike preparations; equipment.

OUGHT, owed; owned; (*impers.*) me ~, it is my duty.

OVERLIVE, survive.

OVERMORE, moreover.

OWE, have; (of feelings) bear; ought.

OWL, ? collect.

PAGEANT, play, part.

PAID, pleased.

PARCELS, instalments.

PARCLOSE, partition.

PARTY, part, side; behalf.

PASSING, exceedingly.

PEACED, calmed down.

PEACHED, accused.

PEASE, calm.

PENSILY, sadly.

PEOPLE, company, force.

PERCASE, perhaps.

PERSE, grey-blue.

PICK, rifle, rob.

PILL, pillage, plunder.

PINE, pain, sorrow.

PINFOLD, pound.

PIPES, rolls (of gold thread).

PITOUS, pitiful.

PLAINNESS, plain truth.

PLAINT, complaint, charge.

PLANCHER, floor.

PLAY, (*reflex.*) play, amuse oneself.

PLEASANCE, pleasure.

PLEDGED OUT, redeemed.

PLOUGH-WARE, plough horses, team.

PLUNKET, grey blue.

POINT, in *at a* ~, agreed. ~S, tagged laces for attaching hose.

POINTMENT, see APPOINTMENT.

POLICY, prudence, discretion.

PRATS, tricks.

PRECEDENTS, earlier records.

PREMISSES, matters above-mentioned, things said.

PREVAIL, avail, benefit.

PREVISION, foresight.

PROCESS, action at law.

PROCTOR, attorney.

PROFITABLE, serviceable.

PROMIT, promise.

PROVE, experience; come about, succeed.

PROVISION, foresight, prudence.

PURCHASE, acquisition.

PURPOSE, intend, propose.

PURVEY, provide, arrange (for). ~ANCE, provision, measures; management.

PUT, in ~ *me in God*, commit myself to God; ~ *up*, keep in custody.

QUAINTANCE, acquaintance.

QUARREL, bolt (for cross-bows); (*also collective*).

QUEASY, unsettled.

QUIT, recompense.

RAISED, brushed (with teasels) to bring up nap.

RAISINS OF CURRANTS, (= Corinth) currants.

RANSOMED, exacted ransom for.

RAPE, haste.

REAR, raise, levy.

RECEIVER, treasurer, collector of money due.

RECOMMEND, commend.

REHEARSE, mention; recount; state (a claim). ~AL, recounting, description.

REHETED, rebuked, scolded.

RELEASE, legal conveyance of an estate.

REMEMBER, remind.

RENTS, property let at rent, houses.

REPARATION, repairs, maintenance.

REPLEVIN, writ of restitution.

REQUIRE, ask, request.

RESCUE, (*n.*) forcible release of a person or goods rom custody. (*vb.*) release by force.

REST, peace.

REVEL, riot, disturbance.

REVERENCE, honour; *at the* ~

of God, for God's sake; see SAVING.

RIDE, leave, go.

RIPPLED, grazed, scratched.

ROAD, riding.

ROME-RUNNER, one constantly travelling to Rome.

RUELY, deplorable.

RUETH, causes regret.

RULE, (*n.*) conduct, habits, behaviour; régime; (civil) order; authority; guardianship; *have the* ~, be in power; *take a* ~, impose order. (*vb.*) ~ *oneself to*, submit to; (*pass.*) conduct oneself, behave. ~ER, commander.

RUNLET, cask.

SACRING, consecration of the Eucharistic elements; the Host.

SAD, sound, wise, sensible; serious. ~LY, solemnly; ~NESS, soberness, gravity.

SAFEGUARD, guarantee of safety, safe-conduct.

SANGUINE, blood-red.

SAVATION, preservation, protection.

SAVE, in ~ *harmless*, guarantee against loss or injury.

SAVING, without offence to, subject to; ~ *your reverence*, with respect.

SCARLET, a kind of cloth.

SCROW, roll, document.

SCUSATION, excuse.

SEEM, think.

SELD, seldom.

SEMBLABLE, similar, like.

SERJEANT, a member of a superior class of barristers.

SERVANT, a person employed on another's business (in a much wider field than in modern use).

SET BY, value, esteem.

SEVENNIGHT, week.

SEWER, server; see p. 78, n. 3.

SHAMEFULLY, as a shame.

SHENT, put to shame.

SHIFT, in *make* ~, make an effort; manage, contrive.

SHOOT, firearms.

SHREW, villain.

SHREWD, hurtful, malicious, bad; dangerous. ~LY, badly.

SICKLOW, ill, infirm.

SIDE, long; see p. 46, n. 1.

SILVER, money.

SIMPLE, plain, mean; foolish. ~LY poorly; foolishly.

SIN, SITH, SITHEN, SITHENCE, since; later.

SKILL, knowledge.

SMOCK, woman's undergarment, shift.

SO (THAT), provided that.

SOLEMNITY, ceremony.

SOLICIT, conduct, deal with. ~OR, petitioner, negotiator.

SORE, (*n.*) illness. (*adv.*) bitterly, painfully, gravely.

SPARE, save.

SPEED, (*n.*) success. (*vb.*) further, assist, advance; discharge; prosper, succeed; ~ me, hasten.

SPEER, ask.

SPINNER, pinnace.

SPLAYED, injured in the shoulder muscles.

SPORT, (*reflex.*) amuse oneself.

START, spring, make a sudden attack.

STATELY, arrogant(ly).

STEW, fish-pond.

STICKED, pierced.

STILL, all the time.

STILLED, became quiet.

STOMACH, appetite.

STOMACHER, a kind of waistcoat.

STORED, restored; supplied.

STRANGE, reluctant; difficult. ~LY, in a hostile way.

STRENGTH, (*n.*) force. (*vb.*) reinforce.

STRONG, flagrant, arrant.

SUBTLETY, strategem, trick.

SUPPLICATION, petition.

SUPPOSE, think, believe; expect.

SWEAMFUL, grievous, distressing.

SYED, sank, fell.

TABLES, backgammon.

TACKLING, gear; *abide by their* ~, stand their ground.

TAIL, limitation of an inheritance to a particular person and his heirs.

TAKE, give, hand over (to).

TALL, brave.

TANE, taken.

TARRY, (*trans.*) delay.

TENANTRY, property held by a tenant.

TENDER, have regard for, esteem; receive favourably.

TERCEL, male hawk.

THAT, that which, what.

THEE, thrive, prosper, in the common asseveration *so mote I ~.*

THERE (AS), where.

THEREAFTER, accordingly.

THEREFOR, for that.

THEREUP, accordingly.

THEREWHILE, meanwhile.

THO, those.

THOUGHT, anxiety.

THRIFTY, worthy, respectable.

THROUGH, concluded, agreed.

TIPPET, a kind of scarf.

TISSUE, a rich kind of cloth often interwoven with gold.

TONE, in the ~, the one.

TOTHER, in the ~, the other, the next.

TOUCH, quality (as tested by a touchstone).

TOUCHANT, ~ING, concerning.

TO . . . WARD(S), towards; favourable to.

TOWARD(S), (*prep.*) close to, in attendance on. (*adv.*) in prospect, imminent; forward. ~NESS, progress.

TOWN, ~SHIP, manor.

TREATY, negotiation.

TRIED, sifted; *clean* ~, pure.

TROTH, truth, word of honour.

TROUBLE, (*n.*) dispute. (*adj.*) disturbed, anxious. (*vb.*) contend.

TROW, believe.

TRUSSING, in ~ *doublet*, padded jacket.

TUN, put into a tun or cask.

UNDERSTAND, understood.

UNEATH(S), scarcely, with difficulty.

UNLIKELY, unpromising.

UNSITTING, unsuitable, unbecoming.

UNSPED, not discharged.

UNTHRIVE, fare badly.

UNWARES, in *his* ~, unknown to him.

UNWIST, unknown.

UNWITTING, in *mine* ~, without my knowledge.

UP, (*prep.*) upon, in consideration of; after. (*adv.*) open.

UPHOLD, maintained.

UPON, taking after, resembling; after.

USE, (*n.*) practice. (*vb.*) accustom; be accustomed.

UTTER, outer.

VERY, true.

VICARY, vicar.

VISAGE, in *bear great* ∼, put on a bold front.

VISIT, chastise.

VITALY, food.

WAGE, engage for wages, hire.

WAGES, soldier's pay; in *take* ∼, enlist.

WAIT, expect.

WARD, custody.

WARD(S), associated with *to* in such phrases as *to him ward*, 'towards him'.

WARE, careful, ∼LY, carefully.

WARN, give notice (of).

WASTE, destruction, damage.

WATCHED, stayed up late.

WEAL, well-being, good.

WEEN, think.

WEET, WIT, know, find out. *Past* WIST, WOST.

WEETING, knowledge.

WELK, walked.

WELL-ASSURED, trustworthy.

WESH, washed.

WHERE AS, where.

WHETHER, which of the two.

WHOLE, (*adj.*) well, in good health; cured. (*adv.*) entirely.

WICKETS, loop-holes.

WIFLES, battle-axes.

WILLY, favourably disposed.

WINDASES, winding devices for drawing crossbows.

WINTER, year.

WISE, way; in *do his* ∼, done what he could; *manner* ∼, kind of way.

WIST, WIT. See WEET.

WITE, (*n.*) blame. (*vb.*) blame (on), impute (to).

WITHHOLDEN, retained.

WITHSET, seized in compensation.

WITH THAT THAT, provided that.

WITTILY, wisely, intelligently.

WORLD, state of affairs.

WORSHIP, honour, respect; *of* ∼, of good standing. ∼FUL, honourable. ∼FULLY, with honour, respectfully. ∼LY, with due honour.

WOST, see WEET.

WOT, know.

YEDE, went.

INDEX

Figures in roman type are numbers of pages; those in italic are numbers of letters

PRINTED IN GREAT BRITAIN
AT THE UNIVERSITY PRESS, OXFORD
BY VIVIAN RIDLER
PRINTER TO THE UNIVERSITY